North Cyprus

the Bradt Travel Guide

Diana Darke
updated by
Nick Redmayne

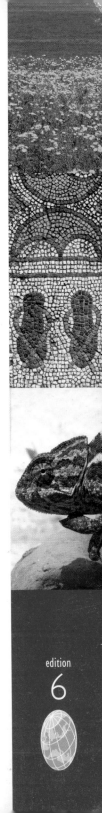

edition
6

www.bradtguides.com

Bradt Travel Guides Ltd, UK
The Globe Pequot Press Inc, USA

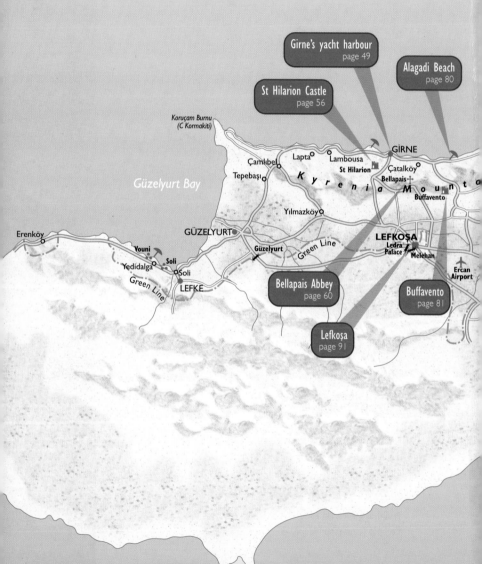

KEY
Capital ■
Town ●
Village ○
Main road
Other road
International boundary
Airport ✈
Beach
Castle 🏰
Major historical site
Turtle conservation area

AKDENİZ
(MEDITERRANEAN SEA)

Girne's yacht harbour
page 49

Alagadi Beach
page 80

St Hilarion Castle
page 56

Koruçam Burnu
(C Kormakiti)

Çamlıbel   Lapta   Lambousa   GİRNE
Tepebaşı   St Hilarion   Çatalköy
                              Bellapais
Güzelyurt Bay   K y r e n i a   M o u n t a
                                   Buffavento
        Yılmazköy

Erenköy   GÜZELYURT   LEFKOŞA
    Vouni   Green Line   Ledra
Yedidalga Soli   Palace   Melehan
        Soli   Ercan
Green Line   LEFKE   Airport
    Güzelyurt

Bellapais Abbey
page 60

Buffavento
page 81

Lefkoşa
page 91

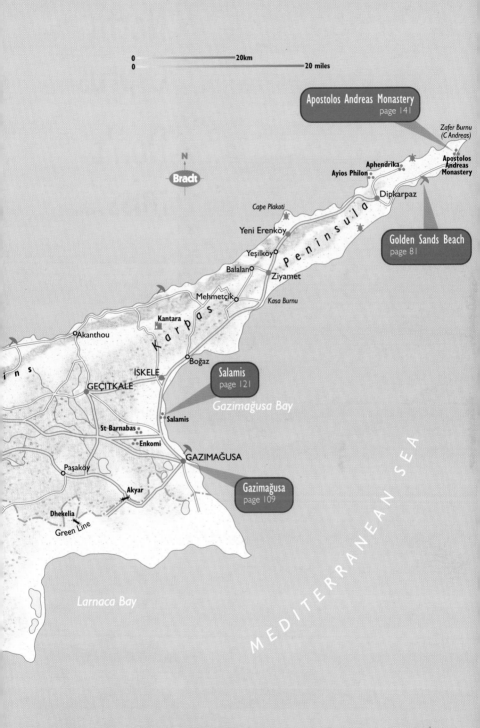

0 | 20km
0 | 20 miles

Bradt

N

Apostolos Andreas Monastery
page 141

Zafer Burnu
(C Andreas)

Aphendrika
Ayios Philon

**Apostolos
Andreas
Monastery**

Cape Plakoti

Dipkarpaz

Yeni Erenköy

Golden Sands Beach
page 81

Yeşilköy

Peninsula

Balalan
Ziyamet

Mehmetçik

Kasa Burnu

Karpas

Kantara

Akanthou

Boğaz

İSKELE

Salamis
page 121

ins

GEÇİTKALE

Gazimağusa Bay

Salamis

St Barnabas

Enkomi

GAZIMAĞUSA

Paşaköy

Gazimağusa
page 109

Akyar

Dhekelia

Green Line

Larnaca Bay

MEDITERRANEAN SEA

North Cyprus
Don't miss...

Girne Harbour
One of the most
picturesque in the
Mediterranean
(NW) page 49

Golden Sands Beach
A magnificent stretch of coastline,
Karpas Peninsula (RC) page 81

Lala Mustafa Paşa Mosque (St Nicholas Cathedral)
With its imposing façade, Gazimağusa
(JC) page 115

Crusader castles
St Hilarion —
a 'picture book castle for elf kings'
(JC) page 56

Lefkoşa
Home to Crusader Gothic and Turkish Ottoman monuments. The Büyük Han (Great Inn) was build by the Ottomans.
(NR) page 98

above left A sculpture near Karaoğlanoğlu commemorates the Peace Operation (NW) page 78

above right Children from the north and south of the island helped paint the *Ode to Aphrodite and Hala Sultan*, Lefkoşa (NW) page 104

below left Lapta is one of the most picturesque towns in the north of the island (JC) page 76

below right The Lala Mustafa Paşa Mosque is visible from most parts of the old town, Gazimağusa (NW) page 109

above **Bellapais village and its enchanting abbey** (NW) page 60

below left **The village of Karaman has been entirely renovated by foreigners** (NW) page 78

below right **Quiet back street, Girne** (JC) page 41

above **Ayias Mamas Church, Güzelyurt** (NR) page 73

left **The keeper of the key maintains high-level security at Apostolos Andreas, Karpas Peninsula** (NR) page 141

below **Church painting, St Barnabas Monastery** (ZY) page 128

bottom **Kanakari Byzantine Monastery with Boltaşli's new mosque in the background** (NR) page 137

ORIGINAL AUTHOR

Diana Darke first became interested in the Near East when she read Arabic at Oxford. For the last 26 years she has lived, worked and travelled extensively in Turkey and the Arab world, initially with the Foreign Office, then as an Arabic consultant. Work and pleasure have taken her to both sides of Cyprus on many occasions.

Most recently, Diana has written *Syria: The Bradt Travel Guide* and co-authored *Oman*. She has recently purchased an old merchant's house in Damascus and is devoting much of her time to its restoration.

UPDATER OF THE SIXTH EDITION

Nick Redmayne's first forays outside the UK were tempered by paranoid xenophobia, a hangover from a particularly infamous French master. Despite consciously eschewing the garlic and onions, there was to be no escape and he eventually ended up in francophone Chad, amongst a unit of the French Foreign Legion, attempting to hitchhike a military aircraft from Abéché to N'Djamena. After a decade-long stint in London as a travel consultant, his love of getting off-the-beaten track finally led to the wilds of Northumberland where he now runs a travel press liaison business and freelances for several UK and international publications specialising in emerging destinations.

The first Bradt travel guide was written in 1974 by George and Hilary Bradt on a river barge floating down a tributary of the Amazon. It was followed by *Backpacker's Africa*, published in 1979. In the 1980s and '90s the focus shifted away from hiking to broader-based guides to new destinations – usually the first to be published on those places. In the 21st century Bradt continues to publish these ground-breaking guides, along with guides to established holiday destinations, incorporating in-depth information on culture and natural history alongside the nuts and bolts of where to stay and what to see.

Bradt authors support responsible travel, with advice not only on minimum impact but also on how to give something back through local charities. Thus a true synergy is achieved between the traveller and local communities.

* * *

There has been a recent, welcome thawing of relations between North and South Cyprus – epitomised by the opening of a pedestrian crossing at Ledra Street, a further chink in the Green Line of the world's last divided capital. Of course, as access becomes easier, there's a danger that the north will lose some of its charm; a rash of villas built as holiday homes over the last few years has in part changed its face already. However, earlier this year I joined Nick Redmayne on a press trip to the island, and he showed me that away from the main resorts lie some of the most unspoilt corners of the Mediterranean. We spent a day hiking in the Kyrenia Mountains and didn't meet a soul (unless you count a harmless whipsnake); we visited one of the world's best beaches on the Karpas Peninsula; and we enjoyed several beers overlooking the harbour at Girne. For the moment at least, North Cyprus still has charm aplenty.

Sixth edition November 2008   First published 1993
Bradt Travel Guides Ltd, 23 High Street, Chalfont St Peter, Bucks SL9 9QE, England
www.bradtguides.com
Published in the USA by The Globe Pequot Press Inc, 246 Goose Lane,
PO Box 480, Guilford, Connecticut 06475-0480

Text copyright © 2008 Bradt Travel Guides Ltd
Maps copyright © 2008 Bradt Travel Guides Ltd
Illustrations © 2008 Individual photographers and artists
Editorial Project Manager: Anna Moores

British Library Cataloguing in Publication Data
A catalogue record for this book is available from the British Library
ISBN-13: 978 1 84162 244 6

Photographs Peter Baker (PB), Jean Clark (JC), Ruth Croome (RC), Sonya Jeffs (SJ), Nick Redmayne (NR), Hannah Thompson (HT), Nigel Wallis (NW), Zeynel Yesilay (ZY)
Front cover Bellapais Abbey (PB)
Back cover Girne Harbour (NW), Salamis (ZY)
Title page Tatlısu, Mosaic at Ayia Trias (both ZY), European chameleon (JC)
Illustrations Carole Vincer   **Maps** Dave Priestley and Maria Randell

Typeset from the author's disk by Wakewing   Printed and bound in India by Nutech Photolithographers

Acknowledgements

Nick Redmayne would like to thank Kadir Doruhan and the staff of the North Cyprus Tourism Centre in London for their support and assistance with numerous seemingly esoteric queries. A special mention for Özbek Dederkorkut and Ute Rodriguez at Örnek Holdays for their enthusiastic insights and professional guidance on the ground in KKTC. To Adrian and Anna at Bradt – thanks for entrusting me with the project and dealing with the fallout, respectively. And finally to my wife Wendy, for keeping the family on track during my absences abroad and far away in the office.

FEEDBACK REQUEST

Every effort has been made to ensure that the details contained within this book are as accurate and up to date as possible. Inevitably, however, things move on. Any information regarding such changes, or relating to your experiences in North Cyprus – good or bad – would be very gratefully received. Such feedback is priceless when compiling further editions, and in ensuring a pleasant stay for future visitors, so please contact us at Bradt Travel Guides Ltd, 23 High St, Chalfont St Peter, Bucks SL9 9QE, England; ✆ 01753 893444; f 01753 892333; e info@bradtguides.com; www.bradtguides.com.

Contents

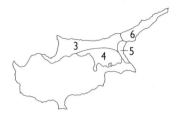

Introduction

The northern, Turkish-speaking part of Cyprus – 37% of the island – still remains less visited than the Greek south. No-one denies that when the island was divided in 1974, the Turks took the more beautiful and fertile region, but while holidaymakers jostle for beach space at Paphos and Limassol, for many years it was a case of spot the tourist at Girne (Kyrenia) and Gazimağusa (Famagusta). The Greek Cypriots are skilful political lobbyists and have since 1974 conducted an effective boycott of the north, presenting it as 'occupied and inaccessible'. They have done an excellent job, as both the economy and tourist industry in the north have stagnated. Only an initiated few saw through the propaganda and went to find out for themselves, and many became loyal devotees who returned each year to enjoy the wealth of cultural sites and the relaxing atmosphere.

The Greek Cypriots have also done a good job of rebuilding the tourist industry in the south, but in doing so have disfigured the landscape with concrete high-rise buildings, fast-food restaurants and associated ill-considered tourist tat shops. Less commercially minded than their southern counterparts, the Turkish Cypriots have until recently hatched few ambitious development projects of their own, and were in any event starved of the international finance needed to carry them out. For better and for worse, times are changing. With the establishment of six border crossing points to date (Ledra Street being a recent addition), more flights into Ercan, EU money starting to filter through, and a strengthening economy, the north is no longer an isolated backwater. Property investment is big business and indeed recent out-of-control levels of construction represent an unlearned lesson. However, at the time of writing, as up to 2,000 new holiday villas lie empty and a new road ends in the dust, this seems to have reached a contemplative hiatus. Furthermore, leave these main population areas behind and the rural, tranquil charm of North Cyprus remains most definitely in place. Family-owned chalets and restaurants are still the norm and with a good *meze* and glass of wine, the north can still offer some of the most unspoilt corners of the Mediterranean.

Prices in North Cyprus remain relatively low and although inflation and growing tourism nudged costs up, there has been a recent fall in the prices compared with 2005 levels, making the north even better value for travellers. A meal for two plus wine costs around £15–23 and car hire £16–38 a day. Turkish Cypriots are very friendly and hospitable and do not as a rule hassle or pester visitors. Petty crime rates are very low and the environment is safe and, outside population centres, pollution-free. There are daily flights from the UK to Ercan encompassing a politically expedient touchdown in Turkey and, with the advent of cross-border travel, both Greek Cypriots and foreigners are exploring the entirety of the island again.

The political status of the north is an emotive subject for both Greek and Turkish Cypriots, and no guidebook would presume to try to analyse the rights and wrongs of the question. The historical summary in *Background information* (pages 5–10) attempts to summarise what happened when and interested readers will no doubt pursue their enquiries and make up their own minds. Ironically, the political situation has worked in the tourist's favour, secreting North Cyprus beyond the range of the worst excesses of mass tourism; it is here that the Mediterranean of 20 years ago can still be recaptured in places.

Ensuring that its natural environment is maintained and the genuine welcome of its people is not abused is increasingly the responsibility of visitors – we can all do our part.

Since 1974, descriptions of the north have been inevitably relegated to the back few pages of travel guides covering the whole island. Here it is given the comprehensive coverage it deserves. Right now North Cyprus lies at a crossroads: it is still 'another country' and for the inhabitants of a divided island, identity is understandably an emotive issue. Turkish-speaking Cypriots possess a distinct ethnicity together with their own cultural and religious traditions. Waves of immigration from Turkey and emigration by Turkish-speaking Cypriots to the UK and elsewhere have seen Turkish-speaking Cypriots reduced to a minority in their own land. However, though the Turkish Republic of North Cyprus is only recognised by Turkey and the economic and cultural links are plain for all to see, it is most definitely not the same country. In this guide, references to Turkish in the context of North Cyprus should be read simply as a method of differentiating between the subject and the Greek-speaking Republic of Cyprus.

Loggerhead turtles

Part One

GENERAL INFORMATION

NORTH CYPRUS AT A GLANCE

Location Island in the Mediterranean Sea, south of Turkey

Neighbouring countries Turkey, 65km to the north; Syria, 100km to the east; and Egypt, 400km to the south (approx)

Size 224km long x 96km wide

Climate Mediterranean with hot, dry summers and cool winters

Population 264,000 (2006 census)

Capital Lefkoşa (Nicosia)

Main towns Girne (Kyrenia), Gazimağusa (Famagusta)

Languages Turkish (English widely spoken)

Religion No official religion; 98% of the population is Muslim

Currency New Turkish lira (YTL)

Exchange rate £1 = 2.2YTL, US$1 = 1.2YTL, €1 = 1.8YTL (Aug 2008)

International telephone code +90 392

Time End of March to mid-September, GMT+3; winter, GMT+2

Electrical voltage 220–240 volts AC, UK-style 3-pin plug in general use

Flag The Turkish Cypriot flag has a horizontal red stripe at the top and bottom between which is a red crescent and red star on a white field

Public holidays 1 January, 23 April, 1 May, 19 May, 20 July, 1 August, 30 August, 29 October, 15 November. See pages 29–30 for further details.

Background Information

GEOGRAPHY

Within its tiny boundaries, Cyprus offers a microcosm of history. Just as Constantinople was always a bridge, so Cyprus was always a stepping stone, where culture after culture left their footprints. Scarcely 224km long and 96km wide, the island has an unrivalled mix and concentration of landscape, history and culture, and, with 768km of coastline, the sea and a beach are always close by. Turkey is its nearest neighbour, just 65km away, followed by Syria approximately 100km distant. It is roughly 400km to Egypt and 480km to the nearest Greek island.

In the current division, the Turkish sector is undoubtedly the more beautiful. The fact that, pre-1974, 80% of Cyprus's hotels were in the Girne (Kyrenia) and Gazimağusa (Famagusta) areas, shows only too clearly where the tourist potential of the island always lay. The Greek Cypriots energetically set about rebuilding the south, and with the help of foreign aid and investment have now succeeded in developing Paphos, Limassol and Larnaca to be their new resort centres.

Dominating much of the northern part of the island, and rising dramatically from the coast to heights in excess of 1,000m, the Kyrenia Mountains (also known as the Beşparmak Range) lend North Cyprus much of the striking scenery that forms the background to any number of postcards and holiday snaps. With such spectacular scenery, and a cooling breeze blowing off the Mediterranean, it's no surprise to find most of the holiday options clustered along this northern shore.

On the southern side of the Kyrenia Mountains, and comprising most of North Cyprus, the central Mesaoria Plain is notable more for its contribution to the country's economy than its attraction for visitors. From Güzelyurt in the west, the most fertile region and thronged with citrus groves, all the way to Gazimağusa in the east, the terrain is flat, dusty and uninspiring, with a mean altitude of just 70m above sea level. It is perhaps fitting that Lefkoşa, despite its enviable collection of Crusader Gothic and Turkish Ottoman monuments, should be found here. The drab, featureless suburbs of the modern town seem to blend perfectly with such an unremarkable backdrop.

Moving east, Gazimağusa continues to draw its fair share of tourists away from Girne. North Cyprus has 396km of the island's total coastline, and some of the finest beaches are to be found here along Gazimağusa Bay, sweeping north from the town towards Salamis and Boğaz.

North Cyprus's final region, and surely its most treasured, is the Karpas Peninsula, a rugged finger tapering away from İskele and out towards the İskenderun Bay of Turkey. With development rampant seemingly everywhere else, the Karpas is the place where you can still find small, traditional villages and the old way of life. Unspoilt golden sands, turtle beaches and wild flowers continue to draw those in search of nature. You might only be a hundred kilometres or so from major civilisation but, under the stars on a clear summer's night, it could well be thousands.

3

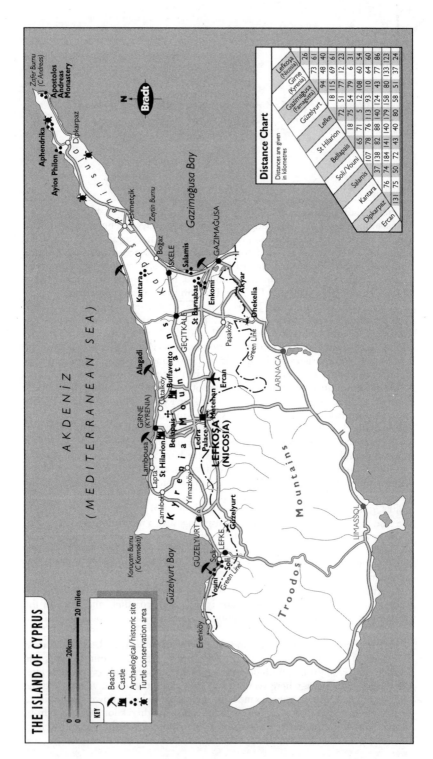

THE ISLAND OF CYPRUS

KEY

- ⚓ Beach
- 🏰 Castle
- ⚹ Archaeological/historic site
- ✹ Turtle conservation area

0 ————— 20km
0 ————— 20 miles

A K D E N İ Z

(M E D I T E R R A N E A N   S E A)

Konuçam Burnu
(C Karmaktı)

Güzelyurt Bay

Erenköy

Zafer Burnu
(C Andreas)

Apostolos Andreas Monastery

Aphendrika

Ayios Philon

Dipkarpaz

K a r p a s   P e n i n s u l a

Mehmetçik

Zeytin Burnu

Boğaz

İSKELE

Salamis

GAZİMAĞUSA

Gazimağusa Bay

Kantara

St Barnabas

GEÇİTKALE

Enkomi

Akyar

Dhekelia

Paşaköy

Green Line

LARNACA

Alagadi

Çatalköy

Buffavento

GİRNE (KYRENIA)

Ercan

Metehan

Ledra Palace

LEFKOŞA (NICOSIA)

Lambousa

St Hilarion

Bellapais

Lapta

Yılmazköy

Çamlıbel

GÜZELYURT

Yeşilırmak

LEFKE

Soli

Vouni

Green Line

Güzelyurt

T r o o d o s

M o u n t a i n s

K y r e n i a   M o u n t a i n s

LIMASSOL

N ⊕ Bradt

Distance Chart

Distances are given in kilometres

	Lefkoşa (Nicosia)	Girne (Kyrenia)	Gazimağusa (Famagusta)	Güzelyurt	Lefke	St Hilarion	Bellapais	Soli/Vouni	Salamis	Kantara	Dipkarpaz	Ercan
		26	61	40	23	31	60	54	60	86	123	24
			73	48	12	6	64	10	77	133	37	
				94	61	79	93	108		43	80	51
					18	51	54	113	124	140	158	58
						69	77	72	75	5	12	40
							18	76	88	140	179	80
								65	71	82	138	43
									107	138	184	74
										37	141	50
											76	72
												131

HISTORICAL SUMMARY

There is no specific historical section in this guide, since historical background is woven into the text as and when appropriate. For an overview therefore, the following detailed chronology is provided as a handy reference and summary.

6000–2500BC Neolithic settlements. Earliest yet found is Khirokitia near Larnaca.

5800BC Beehive huts of stone.

2500–2300BC Chalcolithic period. Discovery of copper on island led to growth in trade.

1st Bronze Age (2300–1900BC) Contemporary with early Egyptian dynasties and Minoan civilisations of Crete. Cyprus inhabited by people identical to those found in central Europe, Asia Minor and Syria.

2000BC Enkomi, near Gazimağusa, major trading centre in copper, becomes capital of Alassia (as Cyprus was then called).

2nd Bronze Age (1900–1500BC) Contemporary with middle Egyptian dynasties, Mycenaeans and Phoenicians colonising the Mediterranean. Cyprus paid tribute to them, but only the Phoenicians and Greeks colonised and left settlements. The Egyptians never occupied. Greek city states of Salamis, Soli, Marion, Curium and Paphos. Cult of Aphrodite introduced. No political link with Greece, as settlers were always breakaways from the mainland, exiles or entrepreneurs wishing to set up a new life in a different land.

1200BC Phoenician King Hiram of Tyre invades and gathers tribute. Phoenicians rule Cyprus. Main Phoenician settlement at Kition near Larnaca.

725–575BC Assyrian rulers, Sargon to Nebuchadnezzar. Cyprus joins with them in wars against Egyptians.

525–425BC Persian rulers including Darius and Xerxes. Cypriots join them in campaigns against Egyptians and Greeks.

411–374BC Evagorus, King of Salamis, first native ruler. Cyprus independent after Persia and Greece sign truce. Evagorus introduces monarchy, Greek coinage and alphabet; Greek culture favoured.

350–325BC Persia regains the island after long siege of Salamis.

335–263BC Zeno, founder of Stoic philosophy, born at Kition. Only really great name to come out of Cyprus.

325BC Alexander the Great. Cypriots were to send ships to Tyre to help lift siege, but sent them to Alexander instead, thus ensuring overthrow of Persians. Cyprus becomes part of Alexander's empire.

300–50BC Hellenistic period. From Alexander's death until arrival of Romans, Cyprus ruled from Alexandria, Egypt, first by Ptolemy, Alexander's general, finally by Cleopatra. Arsinoe (Gazimağusa) built. Fragments of Egyptian granite and statues found at Salamis. Island, united as four districts for first time, flourishes under relatively peaceful conditions.

58BC–AD330 Almost 390 years of Roman rule. Romans make Cyprus part of the province of Cilicia (southern Turkey), capital Tarsus, ruled by military governor. Roman engineers build roads, harbours, bridges and aqueducts. Prosperity enjoyed.

AD45 St Paul and St Barnabas arrive at Salamis on first missionary journey. Roman proconsul converted to Christianity.

AD100 Under Roman emperor Trajan, Jews on island (who had fled here to escape Roman persecution in Palestine) massacre 240,000 Cypriots, including St Barnabas, native of Salamis. As a result, Romans expel all Jews from Cyprus.

AD125	Under Hadrian, climax of Roman monumental art.
AD313	Emperor Constantine officially recognises Christianity. Most of Cyprus is already Christian by this time.
AD325–1191	Rule of Byzantium.
AD325–350	Empress Helena, mother of Constantine, visits on return from trip to Jerusalem. Salamis rebuilt as Constantia after severe earthquakes of 4th century.
AD395	Division of Byzantine empire into east and west; Cyprus comes under eastern half, with capital at Constantinople, but is ruled from Antioch in Syria.
AD477	Under Emperor Zeno, autocephalous Church of Cyprus is recognised, with independent Cypriot archbishop. Monastery of St Barnabas built.
AD525	Climax of Byzantine art; period of peace and unity.
AD650–965	Series of Arab raids at intervals over next 300 years. Salamis destroyed, never rebuilt; many churches pillaged and torn down. Byzantine art stagnates.
1184	Isaac Comnenus, rebel Byzantine prince from Trabzon, arrives on island and proclaims himself Emperor of Cyprus. Rules for seven years in style of despot, but this is only the second time in Cyprus's history when it is independent of a foreign power.
1191	Richard the Lionheart captures Cyprus on way to Third Crusade.
1192	Richard sells Cyprus to Knights Templar to raise money for his army. Then sells it to Guy de Lusignan, last king of Jerusalem before Saladin's conquest, as a consolation for Guy's loss of Jerusalem.
1192–1489	Norman French occupation under the Lusignan dynasty. Castle and town of Nicosia built under Amaury, Guy's brother. Feudal system created, as in Kingdom of Jerusalem. Rulers take titles of King of Cyprus and King of Jerusalem (in absentia).
1225	Byzantine castles of Hilarion, Buffavento and Kantara refortified and elaborated by the Lusignan Crusaders.
1250	Cathedral of Nicosia built.
1300	Cathedral of Famagusta built after fall of Acre, last Christian toehold in Holy Land.
1325	Bellapais Abbey built. Native islanders isolated from new wealth by ruling Catholic French-speakers and treated as serfs. Orthodox Church persecuted, humiliated and made subject to Rome and the Pope.
1375–1464	Cyprus partly ruled by Genoa. Island at war and Famagusta is ceded to Genoese as settlement. Rest of the island stays under Lusignans.
1425	Egyptian Mamelukes pillage towns and weaken Lusignan dynasty.
1464	Genoese expelled. Last Lusignan king takes Venetian bride, Catherine Cornaro, but both he and his newborn son are murdered, leaving Catherine nominally in control, while Venetian nobles arrange her retirement to Italy.
1481	Leonardo da Vinci visits, possibly advising on fortification design.
1489–1571	Venetian Republic occupation. Fortification of castles at Kyrenia, Famagusta and Nicosia. Dismantling of mountain castles of Hilarion, Buffavento and Kantara to discourage internal uprising.
1571–1878	Three centuries of Turkish rule under the Ottomans. Only resistance offered by Venetian strongholds of Nicosia and Famagusta. Islanders themselves glad to see end of oppressive Venetian rule. Orthodox Church recognised again and

archbishopric restored. Feudal system abolished, but heavy imposed, using Church as tax collectors.

1625–1700 Great depopulation of Cyprus. Plagues wipe out over half ...c population.

1821 Greek Cypriots side with Greece in revolt against Turkish rule. Island's leading churchmen are executed in punishment.

1869 Suez Canal opens.

1878–1960 British occupation. British take on administration of the island, ceded from the Ottomans, for its strategic value, to protect their sea route to India via the Suez Canal. In exchange, Britain agrees to help Turkey should Russia attack.

1914 Cyprus annexed by Britain when Turkey joins with Germany and Austro-Hungary in World War I.

1925 Cyprus becomes British Crown Colony.

1931 First serious riots of Greek Cypriots demanding Enosis, union with Greece.

1939 Greek Cypriots fight with British in World War II, but remain set on Enosis after war is over. Turkish Cypriots, however, want British rule to continue.

1950 Archbishop Makarios III elected political and spiritual leader. Heads the campaign for Enosis with the support of Greece.

1955 Series of bomb attacks, start of violent campaign for Enosis by EOKA (National Organisation of Cypriot Fighters) led by George Grivas, ex-colonel in Greek army, born in Cyprus. Grivas takes name of Dighenis, legendary Cypriot hero, and conducts guerrilla warfare from secret hideout in Troodos Mountains. Estimated to have 300 men maximum, yet successfully plagues 20,000 British troops and 4,500 police.

1956 Britain deports Makarios to Seychelles in attempt to quell revolt. Turkish Cypriots used as auxiliaries of British Security Forces, allegedly torturing EOKA captives during British cross-examinations.

1957 Field Marshal Sir John Harding replaced by civilian governor Sir Hugh Foot in conciliatory move.

1958 Turkish Cypriots alarmed by British conciliation and begin demands for partition. Inter-communal clashes and attacks on British.

1960 British, Greek and Turkish governments sign Treaty of Guarantee to provide for independent Cypriot state within the Commonwealth and allowing for retention of two Sovereign Base Areas of Dhekelia and Akrotiri. Under the treaty, each power has the right to take military action in the face of any threat to the constitution. Cyprus truly independent for first time. Archbishop Makarios is first president, Dr Fazıl Küçük vice-president. Both have right of veto. Turkish Cypriots, who form 18% of population, given 30% of places in government and administration, 40% in army, and separate municipal services in the five major towns.

1963–73 Greek Cypriots view constitution as unworkable and propose changes which are rejected by Turkish Cypriots and Turkish government. Inter-communal fighting escalates and UN Peace Keeping Force sent in, but powerless to prevent incidents.

1974–76 Military government (junta) in Greece supports coup by Greek National Guard to overthrow Makarios. Makarios forced to flee. Puppet regime imposed under Nicos Sampson, former EOKA

7

fighter. Rauf Denktash, Turkish Cypriot leader, calls for joint military action by the UK and Turkey, as guarantors of Cypriot independence, to prevent Greece imposing Enosis. The Turkish prime minister travels to London to persuade the UK to intervene jointly with Turkey, but fails, so Turkey exercises its right under the 1960 Treaty of Guarantee and lands 40,000 troops on the north coast of Cyprus. Turkey describes this invasion as 'a peace operation to restore constitutional order and protect the Turkish Cypriot community'. UN talks break down and Turkish forces are left in control of 37% of the island. Refugees from both communities cross to respective sides of the de facto border. Turks announce Federated State in the north with Denktash as leader. UN forces stay as buffer between the two zones. Some 20,000 mainland Turks, mainly subsistence farmers, are brought in to settle and work the underpopulated land. Those that stay more than five years are given citizenship of North Cyprus.

1977   Makarios dies, having been restored as President of Greek Cyprus after 1974. Succeeded by Spyros Kyprianou.

1983   Turkish Federated State declares itself independent, as Turkish Republic of North Cyprus (TRNC), still with Denktash as president. New state is not recognised by any country except Turkey.

1992–95 UN-sponsored talks between the two sides run into the sand, but with a commitment to resume.

2002–03 Concerns in Europe that a divided nation could join the European Union in 2004 prompted further UN-brokered peace talks. The plans, authored by UN Secretary-General Kofi Annan, envisioned the establishment of a Swiss-style confederation made up jointly of the two sides. Proposals included the formation of a common state with one single Cypriot citizenship and a reduction in Turkish

THE DAWNING OF A NEW ERA

Nigel Wallis

After years of failed negotiations and with the situation beginning to look hopeless, an announcement in early 2003 made everyone sit up and take notice. Out of the blue, on 23 April, Turkish Cypriot president Rauf Denktash declared a relaxing of the border controls between Greek and Turkish sectors. For the first time in almost 30 years, people from both sides were allowed to cross the Green Line at the Ledra Palace checkpoint and visit the other half of the island on a day trip.

For some the experience proved an emotional one as they returned to communities and met former neighbours and friends that they hadn't seen for the past three decades. For many from the north it was a chance to gaze at the comparatively lavish lifestyle of the wealthier south. For others, particularly Greeks returning to the north, it was a bewildering day as they found that their homes, for which they still had the title deeds, were now being lived in by former neighbours or, in many instances, British expats, who also held title deeds issued by the Turkish authorities. For almost everybody who made the trip, however – and in the first week of regulations over 50,000 people did – the experience was tinged with sadness as they realised that, while the move was certainly a positive step towards peace, the same intractable obstacles to a united Cyprus remained.

Quite why Denktash decided upon such a huge shift in policy – one that seemed to go against all his policies of the previous 30 years – was unclear. The official line was that border restrictions were being eased to build confidence between the two communities,

Cypriot land from 36% to 28.5%; while the Greek Cypriots, for their part, would have to formally acknowledge that not all their refugees could return to their houses in the north. A three-year interim government was also mooted, with Turkish and Greek Cypriot representatives as co-leaders.

Despite a willingness by many Turkish Cypriots to seek a solution, the talks break down; Denktash rejects revised proposals within hours of having received them. In the south public opinion holds that too many concessions have been offered and perhaps as a result, February sees the election of Tassos Papadopoulos, a leader at odds with many pro-unification forces. In the north, Denktash loses much public support, many citing him as intransigent and an obstacle to successful negotiations. Perhaps to boost his popularity, Denktash makes the momentous decision to unilaterally open the border with the south as the latter moves closer to EU membership. The Greek Cypriot government reciprocates and soon thousands from the north and south are queuing to cross over to the other side.

2004 Years of political word games and cajoling from the UN came to a head on 24 April, when Cyprus went to the polls to vote on the reunification proposals laid down by the Annan Plan. The turnout on both sides of the divide was high (84% in the north and 89% in the south), reflecting the depth of feeling that exists amongst both communities. Alas this was the only commonality to be found – the respective votes could not have been more disparate. In the clearest sign yet that the Turkish Cypriots favour a resolution, 65% voted 'Yes' to reunification, whilst the Greek ballots yielded a depressing and overwhelming 86% 'No' vote, with the Greek Cypriot government citing 'unacceptable' restrictions on property rights as an insurmountable hurdle. As a result, on 1 May the southern

though few believe that this was the only reason. One theory is that the move was designed to counter accusations abroad that the failure of the peace process was largely Denktash's fault and to repair his image on the international stage. Another suggestion is that the new relaxed border policy was implemented to mollify the northern Cypriots who, opposed to his hardline stance, had taken to protesting on the streets of Girne and Lefkoşa. A third theory suggests that Denktash's motive was largely an economic one, a chance for North Cyprus to gain financially from closer contact with its richer neighbours, a premise which seems all the more plausible with the Republic of Cyprus now a fully fledged member of the EU.

Some of those fiscal benefits came immediately, with an announcement by the Greek Cypriot foreign minister of proposals to allow trade between the two sides, and to enable Turkish Cypriots to work in the south.

Five years on from this historic development and feelings are mixed. Denktash has been replaced by the younger, more moderate and media-friendly Mehmet Ali Talat, the north is seeing its strongest economic growth for decades, European Union grants continue to fund a range of regenerative projects and the new border crossings have proved a resounding success. Despite the Greeks' rejection of the Annan plan in 2004, the recent election of pro-unification Demetris Christofias has seen rapid tangible rapprochement. Lefkoşa's Ledra Street has been reopened, making six north/south crossing points, and in September 2008, talks aimed at unifying the island will recommence.

	Republic of Cyprus ascended to full member status of the EU (with all the associated benefits) whilst the north continues to remain in political isolation.
2005	17 April becomes a watershed in the history of North Cyprus as Denktash stands down from the presidency he has held since independence was declared in 1983. His successor, Mehmet Ali Talat, is a radically different character. Reserved, softly spoken and, by eastern Mediterranean standards, still young, Talat cuts the image of a more moderate politician and carries the north's hopes for a unified and peaceful future. A fierce supporter of the UN's reunification plan, Talat's centre-left Republican Turkish Party has been gaining momentum for some time and, with anti-Denktash feeling escalating amongst the population, most agree that the time for change had arrived.
2006–08	In a surprise result, the incumbent Greek Cypriot President, Tassos Papadopoulos, was knocked out of February 2008's election race and was replaced by Communist Demetris Christofias who rode to victory on a pro-unification platform. By early April, amidst tumultuous scenes, Lefkoşa's Ledra Street, once the capital's main shopping street, reopened to cross-border pedestrian traffic. July saw the joint announcement by Mehmet Ali Talat and Demetris Christofias that formal direct talks towards reunification will begin again in September 2008.

POPULATION

In 1980 the population of the whole island was 625,000, of which 77% were Greek Cypriots, 18% Turkish Cypriots and 5% minorities (Armenians, Maronites and British). The Greek Cypriots consider themselves ethnically Greek, tracing their ancestry back to the Mycenaean settlements of the 14th century BC. In its early history, the island allied itself with Greece against Persia and against the Arabs, and under the 800-year rule of Byzantium the independent Orthodox Church was established on the island.

The Turkish Cypriots are the descendants of the mainland Turks who stayed behind after the Ottoman conquest, or of settlers who came across from the mainland at that time. They are Muslim, though generally not especially devout. Since the breakdown of the 1960 Constitution they have been self-administered.

Post-1974, immigrants were brought in from mainland Turkey, often rural subsistence farmers from eastern Anatolia, to settle in the underpopulated north and work the land. They are thought to number about 50,000 today. Figures published in 2006 suggest that the entire population of North Cyprus is now in excess of 264,000. The permanent populations of the main towns, to the nearest thousand, are as follows – Lefkoşa, 39,000; Gazimağusa, 28,000; Girne, 14,000; Güzelyurt, 13,000; Lefke, 6,000; İskele, 3,000.

RELIGION

Turkish Cypriots are Sunni (ie: Orthodox) Muslims, but research studies have consistently shown them to be far less practising than their mainland counterparts. Islam is not a dominant force on the island. The call to prayer is rarely heard although you will find a gleaming white mosque in even the smallest of villages. As in Turkey, the secular weekend of Saturday/Sunday is followed, rather than the Muslim Friday. Shops and restaurants function as normal during the fasting month of Ramadan. See also *Public and religious holidays*, pages 29–30.

The Turkish north, which proclaimed itself the independent Turkish Republic of North Cyprus (TRNC) in 1983, is still not recognised by any country other than Turkey. Recent years, however, have witnessed a new air of confidence. Turkish Cypriots who left in the 1970s have been returning, mainly from Britain and Australia and, increasingly confident in the status quo of partition, are investing their savings in small but well-planned tourist developments. As attempts continue to reunite the island EU funding has begun to find its way to the north, with several large-scale regeneration programmes currently under way. The property market has undergone a virulent boom and this combined with tourism earnings has transformed the local economy.

EDUCATION

Even before partition, schools were separate for Greek and Turkish Cypriots, though there was a bi-communal school in Lefkoşa established by the British. In 1971, there were 542 Greek primary and 42 secondary schools, and 166 Turkish primary and 19 secondary schools. Schooling has been much expanded in the north since partition, with a growing number of colleges and technical schools. Universities are expanding across the island, all teaching in the English language, and now offering a wide range of courses, diplomas and degrees. Indeed, the fees these courses attract have now become a significant source of foreign income for the island.

The Eastern Mediterranean University (EMU) has established itself in Gazimağusa as an international university catering now for 11,000 students from over 30 different countries around the world. Science, engineering and management are the largest faculties but it also offers courses in law, international relations and both Turkish and English literature. The newly developed European University of Lefke offers courses in architecture, business administration and English language and literature. Proficiency in the English language is a requirement for enrolment, although a one-year foundation course is offered to improve students' English ability. Girne American University (GAU), previously called the University College of North Cyprus, now offers a range of courses, extending dramatically from its original position as a liberal arts college. Its main faculties cover architecture, engineering and economics as well as tourism and hospitality.

ECONOMY

Partition in 1974 resulted in dramatic changes. Some 180,000 Greek Cypriots were rehoused in the south. With aid and investment from abroad, especially in agriculture, construction and tourism, Greek Cyprus made a remarkable recovery from the Turkish invasion and was able to provide near full employment. About 45,000 Turkish Cypriots were rehoused in the north. Some 80% of the tourist infrastructure lay in the northern zone but a huge lack of skilled workers prevented the developments of which the south proved capable. Even now, when major investment is in hand, the majority of tourists to the north come from Turkish mainlanders. With them comes no hard currency, only the volatile Turkish lira, which has suffered from rampant inflation (53.2% in 2001) since the 1994 devaluations. On 1 January 2005 the Turkish lira was re-indexed to correct for inflation and six zeros were dropped from the currency. The result was the new Turkish lira (YTL).

Thus, while nowhere near a third world country, North Cyprus has struggled economically. GDP per capita is around one-third of that in the south (US$7,000 as opposed to US$20,000). Unemployment hovers at around the 5% mark, while the industrial production growth rate has been negative for the past few years. That said, the overall economy grew by a respectable 7% in 2007, fuelled by growth in the construction and education sectors as well as increased employment of Turkish Cypriots in the Republic of Cyprus.

Agriculture makes up about 10% of the economy. Güzelyurt, the market garden of Cyprus, now lies in the north and provides some employment and income. Citrus fruits are exported from here, along with tobacco, vegetables and carob nuts from other areas of Turkish Cyprus, to Turkey, Britain and Germany. Just 13% of produce is exported to the Arab world. Along with industrial and agricultural activities, the Güzelyurt region supplies approximately 50 million tonnes of the estimated 65 million tonnes of water available annually in the north.

For many years negotiations were ongoing to consider Cyprus as a candidate for EU membership. The Treaty of Guarantee of 1960 (to which Britain was party) bars the island from membership of any union unless both Greece and Turkey are also members. With Greece already a member, the spotlight was shining firmly in the direction of Turkey, whose aspirations of joining the club had always foundered on its weak economy and, following years of fighting the Kurds in the east of the country, poor human rights record.

The 2004 reunification referendum provided the opportunity for real progress to be made, but alas the chance was missed. With the Greek Cypriots voting 'No' to the UN resettlement plan, the south joined the EU as the independent Republic of Cyprus whilst the north remains in political exile. While money is coming to the north as a result of the relaxing of border controls, this is nothing in comparison with the benefits that fully fledged EU membership would provide. And so the ball seems set to land back in Turkey's court – with their accession to the EU set to be a major issue over coming years. The Cyprus debate will be a significant factor in the equation.

NATURAL HISTORY AND CONSERVATION

Despite recent development, North Cyprus maintains a wide range of natural habitats and is home to several endemic species of wildlife. For the budding botanist or birdwatcher, it is a treasure trove of rarities while for others the north boasts a fabulous array of scents, sights and sounds. The vibrancy of springtime poppies, the constant chatter of cicadas, the predatory swoop of a red kite – North Cyprus has it all.

FLORA Plant species across the north of the island number about 1,600, of which 22 are endemic to Cypriot soil including the golden drop (*Onosma fruticosa*). Each season brings with it a new selection of buds, fruits and flowers.

Springtime is probably the best season for flowers when the fields are covered with anemones, cyclamens, narcissi and wild tulips. North Cyprus plays host to over 30 species of wild orchids, some clinging to tree roots and rocks, showing off their unique flowers and rainbow varieties. The yellow Cyprus sun rose (*Helianthemum obtusifolum*) crawls lazily over dry, rocky hillsides, transforming from small, hairy purple buds into pale yellow flowers. In a completely different habitat, hidden amongst the early cereal crops around Çamlibel, the black tulip (*Tulipa cypria*) thrives in great numbers; it looks much as its name suggests. Up in the mountains, the scenery is transformed by a sweeping blanket of poppies, dressing the pine-covered slopes in scarlet.

As summer draws closer, the air is filled with the scent of citrus blossoms. Orange, lemon and lime groves around the Güzelyurt region are covered with white flowers, a precursor to the fruit harvest to come. Pomegranate trees

(Punicaceae) blaze with their red blossoms and, as the summer draws on, tiny, fragrant, white flowers appear on the silver-leafed olive trees (*Olea europaea*). Legend dictates that olive trees are the safest trees to sit, relax and sleep under as, according to island superstition, evil spirits are afraid of them. The heat of the summer sun means that fruits ripen early. By August, the citrus groves are ready to harvest, the pomegranate blossoms have given way to orange fruits, olives are well on their way and the vines are heavy with grapes.

Autumn brings with it rain and colour. In shady woodland areas, look out for the Cyprus cyclamen (*Cyclamen cyprium*), with its white or pale pink, magenta-tipped petals. They grow only in Cyprus but are common throughout the island. Around Girne and along the Karpas Peninsula, the late narcissus (*Narcissus serotinus*) begins to flower in October. Its fragrant white flowers grow close to the ground on elegant green stalks, coiling and curling around the rocks. Towards the end of autumn, the Cyprus autumn crocus (*Crocus veneris*) appears on the northern slopes of the Girne mountain range. It has narrow, white petals and bright green leaves often laced with violet and silver stripes.

The winter months are not devoid of life either, as the yellow oleander *(Thevitia pruviana)* flowers break up its evergreen leaves with splashes of funnel-shaped yellow and orange blooms. Many of the autumn flowers persist throughout the winter, and on into spring. The crown anemone (*Anemone coronaria*) flowers late for its species but graces the foothills of the mountains south of Girne and the agricultural land around Güzelyurt from December through to April. The large petals vary in colour, appearing most commonly in red or purple shades, sometimes two-coloured and more rarely in a paler apricot pink.

FAUNA

Birds Cyprus is home to 347 different species of bird, with seven species endemic to the island. Added to these species, many others use Cyprus as a resting point during migration to other countries in the Middle East and Africa.

Resident breeders include the griffon vulture (*Gyps fulvus*) with its wingspan well in excess of 2m. It can be spotted high above the mountains between Kantara and St Hilarion. Kestrels, buzzards and falcons are fairly commonly seen and pairs of red kite nest in the pine-covered mountains around Lapta. The population of birds of prey has, inevitably, been somewhat diminished over the years by the Turks' enthusiastic commitment to the hunting season. Over-hunting is a present-day problem throughout the island.

Kantara Castle is a mini paradise for springtime birdwatchers with a whole host of resident and visiting species. The blue rock thrush (*Monticola solitarius*), black-headed bunting (*Emberiza melanocephala*) and spectacled warbler (*Sylvia conspicillata*) may all pay you a visit. You may even spot Alpine swift (*Apus melba*) hiding in the cliffs and crags to lay their eggs or the endemic Cyprus warbler (*Sylvia meleonothorax*) flitting around the more scrub-covered areas of the island.

Reptiles and amphibians Although Cyprus is home to a number of varieties of snake. All of them hibernate during the winter and tend to be rather sluggish during the hot summer months. Of the harmless species, the pink worm snake (*Typhlos vermicularis*) looks exactly as its name suggests, the whip snake (*Coluber jugularis*) has a dark grey/black back and its close cousin, the Cyprus whip snake (*Coluber cypriensis*), is dark green. The only species to be aware of for safety reasons is the blunt-nosed viper (*Viper lebetina lebetina*). It varies in colour but has a distinctive yellow, horny tail. It will not bite other than in defence and is extremely rare.

Throughout North Cyprus you will see lizards everywhere. They scuttle around the ruins, bobbing their heads then disappearing into thin air before your

Nick Redmayne

Despite coastal development and increased visitor numbers, North Cyprus's beaches continue to be favoured nesting grounds for around 2,000 endangered loggerhead (*Caretta caretta*) and up to 400 green (*Chelonia mydas*) sea turtles. It is estimated that this equates to 30% and 10% of the Mediterranean's green and loggerhead populations respectively.

The Society for the Protection of Turtles in Northern Cyprus (SPOT) was founded by the late Ian Bell, a former major in the British army and a committed conservationist. Through a mixture of Bell's ex-army rigour and tireless enthusiasm, SPOT has highlighted the importance of the island's beaches to the Mediterranean's sea turtle population. Since 1992 volunteers from a number of UK and European universities have joined in SPOT's efforts from a base at the island's best-known turtle rookery on Alagadi Beach. Currently SPOT works with the UK's Exeter University-based Marine Turtle Research Group to promote turtle conservation across North Cyprus.

At Alagadi, volunteers from the project are involved in clearing the beach of potentially harmful rubbish, marking and protecting nesting sites, occasionally relocating eggs, collecting data identifying individual turtles and, most recently, electronically tagging turtles so that their movements may be monitored via the internet.

Between 20.00 and 08.00 from May to October, Alagadi Beach is closed overnight, thus minimising disturbance to nesting females. During the nesting season, SPOT guides take one group of up to ten individuals per night to observe nesting turtles. To book a place you need to visit the SPOT HQ at Alagadi (there is no phone); there is no guarantee of sightings, but if you're lucky the experience is worth much more than the suggested £10 donation.

Other turtle conservation activities sponsored by the local Department of the Environment take place on the Karpas Peninsula (in particular Golden Sands Beach,

---

eyes. They vary considerably in size, and some have a clear black stripe down their back. The largest species of lizard on the island is the starred agama (*Agama stelio*) which has a strangely proportioned body; its large head may be seen peeping out from cracks in stone walls or tree trunks.

The European chameleon (*Chamaeleo chamaeleon*) also inhabits parts of the north although you would be very fortunate to see one. Our wildlife questions were met with great excitement by one resident in Lapta who had seen his first chameleon in the ten years that he had lived there.

Sea turtles are a species which has attracted considerable attention recently. Projects are now well under way to help protect both the loggerhead turtles (*Caretta caretta*) and the green turtles (*Chelonia mydas*) which nest on north Cypriot shores.

On bright, moonlit nights throughout June, turtles make the tiring journey up the beach to lay their eggs, and then return to the sea having buried them safely in the sand. It is important that the temperature of the eggs stays relatively constant during their incubation period of about eight weeks. Eggs buried deeper in the sand will be cooler and the incubation period may therefore be longer. The tiny turtles have a tough start to their life, emerging from the sand during the cooler hours of the day, and heading straight for the huge expanse of Mediterranean Sea which awaits them. Human intervention can be a positive force, but care must be taken by visitors to the island to help guarantee the species' future (see box above).

Mammals The Cyprus moufflon (*Ovis musimon*) is the largest mammal on the island and is now a protected species to save it from hunters. Vegetation is perfect

Ronnas Bay and Ayios Philon) where until recently the beaches have remained relatively untouched by development. However, future battles are afoot between those who want the entire Karpas declared a conservation area and those espousing the 'benefits' of a 25,000-bed tourist capacity.

Outside Alagadi the Marine Turtle Research Group has published a set of guidelines for interaction with turtles:

- Always use minimal torchlight – turtle watching is best on a moonlit night
- Avoid approaching turtles until they are well under way with egg laying. The earlier in the nesting process the easier the turtle is disturbed. When the turtle is laying (sitting still after a long period of throwing sand), you can approach her quietly using minimal torchlight.
- Never touch a turtle and certainly never ride on a turtle's back
- Bright lights will attract hatchlings away from the sea and therefore reduce the chance of survival. If you are on a beach at night please avoid using bright lights.
- Do not light bonfires or barbecues on the beach during the main nesting or hatching season (May–Oct)
- Remember to take litter home
- Do not drive on the beaches. This may not only destroy incubating eggs but also creates ruts that make passage to the sea difficult for hatchlings, leaving them susceptible to depredation and dehydration.

More information about the projects in North Cyprus, including how to sponsor a turtle or to make a donation towards the project work can be obtained on www.seaturtle.org/mtrg/projects/cyprus/.

for herds of sheep and goats and, as you head out along the Karpas Peninsula, they may become your sole companions.

Other mammals which you may see on your travels include foxes, hedgehogs and bats. Cyprian hares (*Lepus cyprius*) keep themselves scarce, darting for cover to protect themselves from predators and thus sustain the species. Cypriot donkeys roam freely on the Karpas Peninsula. They are a breed unique to the island and should be approached with caution.

Insects Butterflies are in abundance in North Cyprus, and many of the species are unique to the island. Spring and summer bring out the Cyprus festoon butterfly (*Zerynthia cerisyi cypria*) with its strangely shaped wings, and the bright, sunny-coloured Cleopatras (*Gonepteryx cleopatra*) which decorate mountain glades. There are other, numerous species and the overall effect of colourful wings can be fantastic as they criss-cross your path or play around hotel gardens.

On any night-time stroll you cannot fail to notice the hum of cicadas (Cicadidae) by the roadside. They are large, winged insects, with one species (*Tibicen plebejus*) growing up to 15mm in length. They lead a strange existence, developing for years beneath the earth from grub to adult, then emerging into daylight for a 24-hour life of laying new eggs and making a lot of noise. Their method of sound production is unique as cavities either side of the abdomen resonate to produce a long droning whistle. If you do happen to see one, let it be; they are harmless and have waited seven long years for a few hours of daylight!

2

Practical Information

WHEN TO VISIT

North Cyprus is a year-round holiday destination but spring and autumn are the best times to visit. From late February until late April the island comes alive with thousands of colourful flowers, and in March and April the air is infused with the scent of citrus blossom. Rain is virtually unheard of between June and mid-September, with the midsummer months of July and August sending the mercury soaring.

The rainy season generally lasts from November until February, although occasional showery days do occur in October and even more so in March. December and January are the wettest months, while January and February are the coldest. April and May can yield terrific rainstorms, but you never have to wait for more than a day or two before brilliant sunshine breaks out again. If you are considering a winter visit, bear in mind that some hotels may be closed from October to March.

SUGGESTED ITINERARIES Recent years have seen a boom in package holidays and property development, and North Cyprus now gives other Mediterranean resorts a run for their money when it comes to choosing a week away in the sun. Nonetheless, for those willing to circumvent an occasionally gaudy tourist veneer the heart of what makes North Cyprus special remains the same.

In such a small country, and with most people choosing to base themselves in and around Girne, all the major sights can comfortably be visited as day trips – the one exception being the Karpas Peninsula, where at least one night should be spent to experience the unique tranquillity of this still unspoilt wilderness.

The following suggestions listed overleaf summarise the most popular options:

CLIMATE FACTS

AVERAGE TEMPERATURES IN °C

Jan	Feb	Mar	Apr	May	Jun	Jul	Aug	Sep	Oct	Nov	Dec
14	14	15	18	21	24	29	29	25	23	18	13

AVERAGE MAXIMUM TEMPERATURES IN °C

Jan	Feb	Mar	Apr	May	Jun	Jul	Aug	Sep	Oct	Nov	Dec
18	19	21	23	27	30	36	36	32	28	24	17

AVERAGE SEA TEMPERATURES IN °C

Jan	Feb	Mar	Apr	May	Jun	Jul	Aug	Sep	Oct	Nov	Dec
11	12	14	19	21	24	26	27	26	23	14	11

Half-day trips
St Hilarion
Bellapais
Buffavento (by car)
Lefkoşa (Nicosia)
Mountain monasteries
Beaches to east and west

Day trips
Vouni, Soli and Güzelyurt
Buffavento (on foot)
Kantara Castle
Gazimağusa (Famagusta)
Salamis

Overnight trips
Karpas Peninsula

TOUR OPERATORS

GENERAL
Alternative Cyprus 146 Kingsland High St, London E8 2NS; ℡ 020 72499800; f 020 923 3508; e info@alternativeturkey.com; www.alternativecyprus.com

Anatolian Sky Holidays Anatolian Hse, 81 Warwick Rd, Solihull B92 7HP; ℡ 0800 247 1011; f 0121 764 3559; e info@anatolian-sky.co.uk; www.anatolian-sky.co.uk

C&A Travel 247 Lewisham Way, Lewisham SE4 1XS; ℡ 020 8694 2814

CTA Holidays Ltd 11–12 Pall Mall, London SW1Y 5LU; ℡ 0870 600 1123; f 020 7839 4004; e cta@ctaholidays.com; www.ctaholidays.com

Cox & Kings Travel 4th Floor, Gordon Hse, 10 Greencoat Pl, London SW1P 1PH; ℡ 020 7873 5000; e sales@coxandkings.co.uk; www.coxandkings.co.uk

Cyprus Direct 22 Picton Hse, Hussar Court, Westside View, Waterlooville PO7 7SQ; ℡ 0870 460 1234; f 0870 027 2461; e info@cyprusdirectholidays.com; www.cyprusdirectholidays.com

Cyprus Paradise 638–640 High Rd, London N12 0NL; ℡ 020 8343 8888; f 020 8343 8800; e info@cyprusparadise.com; www.cyprusparadise.com

Direct Traveller 40–42 Hawks Rd, Kingston upon Thames KT1 3EG; ℡ 0845 123 5383; f 0845 123 5384; e reservations@directtraveller.com; www.directtraveller.com

Diplomat Travel 12 Eccleston St; London SW1W 9LT; ℡ 020 7730 2201; f 020 7730 9754; e sales@diplomat-travel.com; www.diplomattravel.co.uk

The Discovery Collection 35a High St, Dunmow, Essex CM6 1AB; ℡ 0845 456 4500; f 0845 456 4600; e sales@thediscoverycollection.com; www.thediscoverycollection.com

Globalbright 19 Albermarle St, London W1S 4HS; ℡ 020 7499 6963; f 020 7499 6964; e info@globalbright.co.uk; www.globalbright.co.uk

Green Island Holidays 114 Great Portland St, London W1W 5PF; ℡ 020 7637 7338; f 020 7637 7296; e sales@greenislandholidays.com; www.greenislandholidays.com

Havana Travel 261 Green Lanes, London N13 4XE; ℡ 020 8447 9833; f 020 8447 9830; e info@villahavana.co.uk; www.villahavana.co.uk

Happy Days Holidays & Tours 341 Green Lanes, London N4 1DZ; ℡ 020 8800 3836; f 020 8800 9659

Indigo Tours 435 Green Lanes, London N4 1HA; ℡ 020 8348 8355; f 020 8348 3455; e business@indigotours.co.uk; www.indigotours.co.uk

Jet Tourism & Travel 449 West Green Rd, London N15 3PL; ℡ 020 8888 3831; f 020 8365 8003; e info@jtta.co.uk; www.jtta.co.uk

Metak Holidays Compass Hse, 30–36 East St, Bromley BRI 1QU; ℡ 020 8290 9292; f 020 8290 9234; e info@metakholidays.co.uk; www.metakholidays.co.uk

Mosaic Holidays 26 Windmill Pl, Windmill Lane, Hanwell UB2 4NJ; ℡ 020 8574 4000; f 020 8574 4999; e sales@mosaicholidays.co.uk; www.mosaicholidays.co.uk

New President Holidays 25 Cheston Av, Shirley CR0 8DE; ℡ 020 8406 4440; f 020 8406 4441; e sales@newpresidentholidays.com; www.newpresidentholidays.com

Noble Caledonia Ltd 2 Chester Close, London SW1X 7BE; ℡ 020 7752 000; f 020 7245 0388; e info@noble-caledonia.co.uk; www.noble-caledonia.co.uk

Page & Moy Compass Hse, Rockingham Rd, Market Harborough LE16 7QD; ℡ 0116 217 8005; www.pageandmoy.com (email via website)

Sunel Travel 434 St Ann's Rd, London N15 3HJ; ℡ 020 8800 3399; f 020 8802 9437; e sanel_sanli@hotmail.co.uk

Transit Tours 252 High St, Orpington BR6 0LZ; ℡ 01689 832 532; f 01689 837 160; e r.hatherly@transit-travel.com

Travelsphere Compass Hse, Rockingham Rd, Market Harborough LE16 7QD; ℡ 0870 240 2426; www.travelsphere.co.uk (email via website)

Tulip Holidays 9 Grand Parade, Green Lanes, London N4 1JX; ✆ 020 8211 0001; f 020 8211 8308; e info@tulipholidays.com; www.tulipholidays.com

SPECIALIST

The Adventure Company Cross & Pillory Hse, Cross & Pillory Lane, Alton GU34 1HL; ✆ 0845 450 5316; f 0845 450 5317; e sales@adventurecompany.co.uk; www.adventurecompany.co.uk

Cricketer Holidays Beacon Hse, Croft Rd, Crowborough TN6 1DL; ✆ 01892 664 242; f 01892 662 355; e info@cricketerholidays.co.uk; www.cricketerholidays.co.uk

Explore Nelson Hse, 55 Victoria Rd, Farnborough GU14 7PA; ✆ 0870 333 4001; f 01252 391 110; e info@explore.co.uk; www.explore.co.uk

Interest & Activity Holidays PO Box 59, Ruardean GL17 9WX; ✆ 0871 855 2925; f 0871 855 2929; e reservations@iah-holidays.co.uk; www.iah-holidays.co.uk

Island Holidays PO Box 26317, Comrie PH6 2YL; ✆ 01764 670 107; f 01764 670 958; e info@islandholidays.co.uk; www.islandholidays.co.uk

Kudu Travel Teffont Manor, Teffont Ewyas, Salisbury SP3 5RJ; ✆ 01722 716167; f 01722 716167; e kuduinfo@kudutravel.com; www.kudutravel.com

Voyages Jules Verne 21 Dorset Sq, London NW1 6QG; ✆ 0845 166 7003; f 020 7723 8629; e sales@vjv.co.uk; www.vjv.co.uk

Maranatha Tours Trafalgar Hse, Horton SL3 9NU; ✆ 01753 689 568; f 01753 689 768; e michael@maranatha.co.uk; www.maranatha.co.uk

Naturetrek Cheriton Mill, Cheriton, Alresford SO24 0NG; ✆ 01962 733 051; f 01962 736 426; e info@naturetrek.co.uk; www.naturetrek.co.uk

Ramblers Holidays PO Box 43, Welwyn Garden City AL8 6PQ; ✆ 01707 331133; f 01707 333276; e info@ramblersholidays.co.uk; www.ramblersholidays.co.uk

Solo's Holidays 54–58 High St, Edgeware HA8 7EJ; ✆ 0870 499 2233; f 020 8951 1051; e travelsolos@solosholidays.co.uk; www.solosholidays.co.uk

Travelone 17 Blossom St, London E1 6PL; ✆ 0870 757 2488; f 0870 757 2486; e holidays@travelone.co.uk; www.travelone.co.uk

Walks Worldwide 12 The Square, Ingleton, Carnforth LA6 3EB; ✆ 01524 242 000; f 01524 242 627; e info@walksworldwide.com; www.walksworldwide.com

IN NORTH CYPRUS Despite growing opportunities for independent travel, most visitors to North Cyprus still go on package holidays. Operators and hotels offer a range of tours and activities, but seek advice locally to find some of the more interesting ecotourist options that aren't part of the usual range of offerings. KITSAB, the Cyprus Turkish Tourism & Travel Agents Association (*www.kitsab.org*) currently has around 140 local members across North Cyprus. Their website is a good starting place if you're looking for an accredited local travel agent. Examples include **Dreams Tour** (✆ *228 40 44;* e *dreamstour@superonlone.com; www.bookindreams.com*), **Green Man Ltd** (✆ *815 85 82;* e *info@green-manltd.com; www.green-manltd.com*), **Holication Travel** (✆ *816 05 16;* e *info@holicationtravel.com; www.holicationtravel.com*), **Ideal Tour** (✆ *366 50 32;* e *info@idealtourcyprus.com; www.idealtourcyprus.com*) and **Örnek Holidays** (✆ *815 89 69;* e *info@ornekholidays.com; www.ornekholidays.com*).

For local tour operators dealing with sports and recreation, see page 31.

ℹ️ TOURIST INFORMATION

In London, the North Cyprus Tourism Centre (*29 Bedford Sq, London WC1B 3EB;* ✆ *020 7631 1930;* f *020 7631 1873;* e *info@northcyprus.cc; www.northcyprus.cc*) produces a monthly magazine and will send free maps and colour pamphlets, and provides a wealth of other assistance.

On the island, there are also tourist offices distributing maps and pamphlets in Girne, Gazimağusa, Lefkoşa, Yeni Erenköy and Ercan Airport, together with a small concession at the Ledra Palace checkpoint. Opening hours are given in the respective sections of the book, although in traditional Turkish Cypriot style these hours are somewhat flexible and visitors should prepare for the fact that offices seemingly open and close on the whim of the staff.

PASSPORTS AND VISAS British and US passport holders do not need visas for TRNC and a three-month stay is permitted to all visitors. If your flight is simply transiting Turkey *en route* to Ercan and you do not leave the transit lounge, you do not require a visa. If, however, you want to leave the airport and visit Istanbul for a few hours or a few days, you will have to buy a visa, currently £10, as you go out through passport control. These regulations were introduced in November 1989, and the visa must be bought in foreign cash, preferably sterling. The procedure is very quick and simple.

For those who wish to avoid a North Cyprus stamp in their passports, there is a special form which can be requested from the cabin crew before landing, and this can then be stamped in place of the passport. Contrary to what most people believe, a TRNC stamp in your passport does not in fact prevent a future visit to Greece or its islands. The TRNC stamp is simply cancelled with your permission on arrival in Greece.

Ⓔ FOREIGN MISSIONS Turkey is the only country to have a full embassy in North Cyprus. Britain, the USA, Germany and Australia have liaison offices in Lefkoşa for consular services and for cultural and social relations with TRNC.

Association Culturelle Française Chypriote-Turque 1 Hasene Ilgaz Sokak, Lefkoşa; ✆ 228 33 28; www.ambafrancechypre.org (email via website). Established in 1985 to help promote cultural relations with France.

'Australia Place' – Australian Information Bureau 20 Güner Türkmen Sokak, Lefkoşa; ✆ 227 73 32; f 228 54 58; e nicosia.ahc@dfat.gov.au; www.embassy.gov.au/cyprus; ✇ 09.00–12.30 Tue & Thu only

British Council 28 Kasim Sokak No 1, Lefkoşa; ✆ 227 49 38; f 228 58 09; e enquiries@ cy.britishcouncil.org; ✇ 09.00–13.00 Mon/Wed/Thu, 09.00–12.30 & 13.30–17.30 Tue, 09.00–12.30 Fri. The British Council organises some cultural events in North Cyprus, like films & exhibitions. The All-Party British Parliamentary Group of the 'Friends of Turkish Cyprus', established at the House of

Commons, London, in 1985, promotes the Turkish Cypriot viewpoint & aims to help find a solution to the Cyprus problem that treats both communities fairly.

British High Commission Shakespeare Av, 23 Mehmet Akif Caddesi, Lefkoşa; ✆ 227 49 38; e nicosia.consular@fco.gov.uk; www.britain.org.cy; ✇ 08.00–12.00 Mon–Fri. This office can also relay any calls through to the High Commission in the Greek sector.

German Embassy Liaison Office 15, 28 Kasim Sokak, Lefkoşa; ✆ 227 51 61

Turkish Embassy Bedreddin Demirel Caddesi, Lefkoşa; ✆ 227 23 14; f 228 22 09

United States Embassy North Cyprus Office 6 Şerif Arzic Sokak, Lefkoşa; ✆ 227 39 30; ✇ 08.00–17.00 Mon–Fri

GETTING THERE AND AWAY

✈ BY AIR TRNC's airport for tourist traffic is Ercan (formerly called Tymbou). Small, but newly equipped and expanded, it is situated some 12km east of Lefkoşa.

Flights from London to Ercan take a maximum of six hours, but don't expect much in the way of in-flight entertainment. Bring your own books, music and stimulating conversation to pass the time!

Flights direct to Ercan, on a range of different aircraft, run up to twice daily from Heathrow, Gatwick, Stansted and Manchester by Cyprus Turkish Airlines (*www.kthy.net*), Pegasus (*www.pegasusairlines.com* or *www.flypgs.com*) or Turkish Airlines (*www.thy.com*). Fares vary from £180 to £400 according to season and availability. All flights to Ercan have to touch down on the Turkish mainland, since TRNC is not recognised by anyone except Turkey. From Europe, the touchdown points are usually Istanbul or Izmir, or occasionally Antalya or

Dalaman. When touching down in Turkey, passengers for Ercan do not leave the plane, but simply wait a while on the tarmac for upwards of 45 minutes. During peak season, these flights fill up surprisingly quickly, so you need to book well in advance if you have specific time constraints on your travel dates.

In the past another method for those who do not mind the hassle was to get the cheapest available flight to Istanbul, then buy a return ticket to Ercan from the Turkish Airlines (THY) or Cyprus Turkish Airlines (CTY, a subsidiary of THY) office at Istanbul. However, unless you actually want to include mainland Turkey in your travels, the advent of Pegasus flights to Ercan negates any saving by utilising the route except in the most exceptional circumstances. Scheduled flights by THY and CTY run at least twice daily from Istanbul. The return fare Istanbul–Ercan ranges from about £100 to £180 and is classed as an internal domestic flight. Despite this, all flights to Ercan use Atatürk International Airport, rather than the scruffy domestic terminal used for other internal flights. This is a great bonus as any time spent waiting for connections is far more pleasant, Atatürk International Airport being very modern and efficient, with an extensive range of shops. Its restaurant on the upper floor serves good, wholesome food at reasonable prices. Flights to Ercan get fairly full, so it is advisable to have reserved in advance, then pay and collect the tickets at Istanbul. Payment is in Turkish lira, and the airport banks are always open if you need to change money. Check-in time at Istanbul is two hours ahead of flight time. It may also be useful to note that, from the Turkish mainland itself, there are additional direct flights to Ercan from Ankara, Antalya, Adana, Dalaman and Izmir.

Of course it is now possible to move freely between the Turkish and Greek Cypriot sectors, and the alternative of flying in to the south shouldn't be overlooked. With healthy competition between scheduled and charter operators, it can be an attractive proposition to enter North Cyprus by this method. British Airways offers direct flights from Heathrow to Larnaca, and flies to Paphos from Gatwick and Manchester. Cyprus Airways (*www.cyprusairways.com*) operates to Larnaca and Paphos from Heathrow, Gatwick (Larnaca only) and Stansted, and also serves Paphos from Birmingham and Manchester. Fares on these routes can be as low as £140 if you book far enough in advance, but rise to a totally ridiculous £550 for short-notice reservations in peak season. It's worth shopping around though because a tenacious independent travel agent can often come up with return charter seats for around £100, and in some cases as little as £79, from a whole host of regional airports including Bristol, Exeter, Doncaster, Newcastle, Glasgow, East Midlands, Birmingham, Cardiff, Norwich, Teesside, Bournemouth and Belfast.

Some Turkish and Greek Cypriot taxi drivers now hold special licences that allow them to cross the border either at Lefkoşa or Gazimağusa. From Larnaca, expect to pay in the region of £50 for the 90-minute journey to Girne.

Should you want to travel on a tailored package then it's worth knowing that Direct Traveller will fly you to Larnaca and then whisk you across the border to your chosen destination in the north (see *Tour operators*, page 17).

Airline companies

Cyprus Airways 5 The Exchange, Brent Cross Gdns, London NW4 3RJ; ✆ 020 8353 1333; www.cyprusairways.com
Cyprus Turkish Airlines 11–12 Pall Mall, London SW1Y 5LU; ✆ 020 7930 4851; f 020 7839 4004; e info@kthylondon.com; www.kthy.net.

Pegasus Airlines ✆ 0845 0848980; www.pegasusairlines.com or www.flypgs.com. No UK-based office so phone enquiries are re-directed to Turkey where there are a limited number of English speakers to take your calls.
Turkish Airlines 125 Pall Mall, London SW1Y 5EA; ✆ 0844 800 6666; f 020 7976 1738; e info@ turkish-airlines.co.uk; www.turkishairlines.com

BY BOAT The Cyprus Turkish Shipping Company operates a car ferry round from Mersin in southern Turkey to Gazimağusa. Currently they ru weekly in each direction, departing Gazimağusa 20.30 Monday, Wednese Friday and departing Mersin 20.30 Tuesday, Thursday and Sunday. The boat carries up to 350 passengers and the journey takes approximately ten hours. Foot passenger fares are currently £30 one-way and £54 return. Cars must be booked in advance and a standard saloon car costs £54 one-way and £104 return, with tickets for passengers on top of this.

Cheaper and quicker routes are operated by Akfer Shipping, an imaginatively named amalgamation of former rivals, Akgunler Shipping and Fergün Shipping. Three scheduled routes serve Girne's ferry port. From Taşucu in southern Turkey, the fastest is for passengers only and carries 250 people, departing daily at 11.30 or 09.30 from Girne, and making the crossing in two and a half hours or less. The fares are currently £20–40 for a single or return ticket. A car ferry runs five times a week, departing Taşucu every day, except Friday and Saturday, at 24.00 and leaving Girne Monday to Friday at 12.00, with an extra, late Friday sailing at 22.30. The voyage takes up to six hours and carries 120 cars and 800 passengers. Passenger fares are £22 one-way and £36 return, standard saloon cars cost £48 one-way and £100 return.

During the summer there is also a twice-weekly passenger service from Alanya to Girne, departing Monday and Thursday at 12.00 and returning Sunday and Wednesday at 11.00. This route costs £26 one-way and £46 return, taking around four hours.

In addition to ticket prices, ferry travellers are liable for port fees and taxes, currently £6 one-way and £14 return.

Cars can be imported into TRNC without customs duty for up to three months, a permit being issued at the port of entry. The permit can be renewed for up to a year. Vehicles must be accompanied by an insurance certificate valid for TRNC, which can be bought at the port.

Ferry companies The first two companies are both part of Akfer Shipping and jointly market the same boats.

Akgunler Shipping Ramadan Cemil Meydani No 1, Girne; ℡ 815 35 10; f 815 38 70; e denizcilik@akgunler.com.tr; www.akgunler.com.tr
Fergün Shipping Girne Yeni Liman Yolu, Fergün Apt No 1, Girne; ℡ 815 17 70; f 815 19 89; www.fergun.net (email via website)

Cyprus Turkish Shipping (KTD) 3 Bülent Ecevit Bulvari, Gazimağusa; ℡ 366 59 95; f 366 78 40; e sales@kibrisdeniz.net; www.kibrisdeniz.net

ACCESS TO AND FROM GREEK CYPRUS The stringent border regulations that for so long prevented free movement between the north and south sectors of Cyprus are slowly eroding. Since 2003 both Cypriot locals and EU tourists have been able to cross at one of five designated checkpoints, open 24 hours. A further crossing at Locmacı Street/Ledra Street in Lefkoşa was opened to pedestrians in April 2008. The formalities are straightforward – simply present yourself with your passport and complete the appropriate visa application. The current crossings are:

Metehan (aka Agios Dometios or Kermia) (Lefkoşa) This crossing handles the most traffic of the five and may be utilised by vehicles and pedestrians alike. If you have any queries the crossing's TRNC office may be contacted on ℡ 223 63 18.

Akyar (aka Black Knight or Agios Nikolaos) (Gazimağusa) Within the British Eastern Sovereign Base Area and open to all traffic.

Ledra Palace (aka Ledra Gate) (Lefkoşa) Right by the Green Line in Lefkoşa. Open to pedestrians, cyclists and diplomatic vehicles only.

Locmacı Street (aka Ledra Street) (Lefkoşa) A result of recent north/south rapprochement, this is the newest of the pedestrian-only crossings and perhaps the most interesting. The familiar repository of global high-street names that is Nicosia's Ledra Street contrasts starkly with Lefkoşa's Locmacı Street. The distance walked is insignificant, but the gulf of culture and affluence is huge – truly 'east meets west.'

Dhekelia (aka Pergamos or Beyarmudu) (Gazimağusa) The other gate in the British Eastern Sovereign Base Area, again open to all traffic.

Güzelyurt (aka Zohdia, Bostanci, Morpho, Astromeritis, Morfu, Omorfo) (Güzelyurt) The most recent crossing point to be instituted and the one with the most names. Open to all traffic.

Privately owned cars can be driven from north to south, and vice versa, so long as the driver purchases the requisite third-party insurance at the crossing point. For vehicles entering from the south this costs from £5 for three days, though a month's cover is not much more. Travelling in the opposite direction, insurance costs around £12 for one month.

Some Greek Cypriot hire companies now allow rental cars to cross to the north, although the increased insurance premiums need careful scrutiny – some will cover up to a maximum of only £2,000–3,000 worth of damage in case of an accident, irrespective of the total repair bill. Currently no North Cypriot hire cars are able to cross to the south.

The relaxation of the border policy has led to an increase in traffic, both local and tourist, between the sectors. The scheme so far can be considered to be a success, and further crossing points are being planned in order to reduce congestion and expedite the rate of reform.

However, despite recent developments to ease border regulations and make North Cyprus an altogether more visitor-friendly country, travellers should still remain vigilant against seemingly irrational and vindictive actions from police and checkpoint guards. Those visiting the south after arriving directly in the north are still deemed to have arrived illegally though as passports are generally not stamped either side of the Green Line, it's difficult to know how this would be determined and, in practice, this illegality is overlooked. However, when crossing the border bear in mind that import limits on various goods do apply. Shopfront signs in Lefkoşa indicate goods to the value of 135 euros or 80 Cypriot pounds may be taken across the border before duty is payable. One Bradt reader contacted us in a state of some shock having been threatened with arrest for alleged tobacco smuggling when crossing from north to south. He eventually escaped with a fine but nonetheless such encounters can spoil any holiday. Just try and remember the politics of Cyprus – feelings still run deep and irrational behaviour on either side of the border is more likely to be the result of such ingrained disagreements than it is to be a personal vendetta against the tourist.

Those purchasing property in North Cyprus are strongly advised not to carry any deeds or documentation relating to their purchase across the land border. If these papers are discovered by Greek Cypriot authorities, at best they'll be confiscated, at worst the holders will be arrested and under certain circumstances charged with the illegal purchase of Greek-owned property – an offence that can attract a substantial fine or even imprisonment. You have been warned.

✚ HEALTH

All visitors are entitled to free emergency medical treatment at state hospitals, and all blood banks have been AIDS screened. Chemist shops (Turkish *eczane*) are also well capable of recommending medicines for common holiday illnesses, and many drugs such as antibiotics are available over the counter, with no need for prescriptions.

WATER Water is safe to drink in Turkish Cyprus but taste varies throughout the region, so most people prefer bottled mineral water which is cheap and widely available. The natural springs in Lapta provide some of the purest water in the north.

VACCINATIONS No vaccinations are required or advised. However, as with any trip abroad, it is recommended that your tetanus, diphtheria and polio vaccinations are up to date. Hepatitis A vaccination may be recommended for longer trips where good food and water hygiene cannot be guaranteed. The vaccine (eg: Harvirx Monodose, Avaxim) can be given even up to the day before travel and lasts for one year. A booster dose given at least six months after the first dose will extend cover for approximately 25 years. Foreign nationals intending either to work or study in Cyprus are required to undergo an HIV test. There is no reciprocal health care with Britain and therefore adequate medical insurance is strongly recommended.

DIARRHOEA Diarrhoea is a common cause of illness in travellers. The most important treatment is to replace fluid loss and to prevent dehydration. Continue to eat plain foods and avoid alcohol, dairy products and anti-diarrhoea drugs unless absolutely necessary. Seek medical advice for the very young and elderly as soon as possible or if there is blood and/or slime in the stool and if you have a fever or if the diarrhoea persists for more than two days.

SKIN IN THE SUN Heightened awareness of safety in the sun can only help towards a more enjoyable holiday for everyone. It is advisable to protect your skin from the sun's rays at all times, especially over the midday period.

TRAVEL ADVICE For journey preparation information, consult www.fitfortravel.scot.nhs.uk. Information about various medications may be found on www.emedicine.com.

SAFETY

The atmosphere in the north is relaxed and friendly. The Turkish Cypriot people are by nature easy-going, and violent crime is virtually nil. The aggravating hassling of foreigners by street sellers and shop owners, rampant in other parts of the Mediterranean, is blissfully absent here. If you ask for help, it will be offered willingly, but if you are just strolling and looking, you will be left to yourself. Women alone are not propositioned and it is quite safe to walk around after dark. Your privacy is respected and people keep their distance.

However, an explosion in North Cyprus's construction industry saw tens of thousands of workers arrive from mainland Turkey, many without permits, to fuel the demand for labour. Without legal status this workforce was open to exploitation and endured meagre wages and miserable living conditions. An inevitable rise in crime led to some headline cases in 2005, shaking the confidence of the local and expat population. In response, legislation was enacted in November 2006 making it considerably more difficult for unscrupulous employers to operate with illegal workers. In any case, the republic's labour market reached saturation point with 60,000 mainland Turks currently working legally across all areas of the economy. A rise in crime statistics must be viewed in this context and statistically North Cyprus remains one of the safest holiday destinations, especially for those who take the usual common-sense precautions. Although there are some 26,000 troops from the Turkish army stationed in camps here, they are highly disciplined and under strict instructions to be courteous to foreigners. Should you inadvertently stray into a military area, you will be politely escorted out and redirected; notices saying 'No Photography' should always be taken seriously. The following **inaccessible military zones** should be noted by tourists:

• Lambousa, on the coast west of Girne
• Paleokastro, on Güzelyurt Bay
• Ayios Panteleimon Monastery at Çamlibel
• Ayios Chrysostomos Monastery below Buffavento Castle
• Ayios Spiridon, southeast of Ercan Airport
• Varosha, south of Gazimağusa
• Chrysokava quarries, east of Girne

In general, you will find that the local people will bend over backwards to make you feel welcome. They make a hospitable nation, keen to please and eager to ensure that visitors are happy.

SEASIDE SAFETY Although the Mediterranean is free from tidal activity, this does not mean that the beaches are free from currents, although in most situations they only run parallel to the shore, thus posing little risk.

Some of the hotel beaches have lifeguards present, but the same is not the case on public beaches. Care should be taken on any of the beaches; awareness of the potential dangers of currents, rocks and waves may prevent any trouble. Weak or non-swimmers should be properly supervised, and care should be exercised if using any inflatable swimming aids, particularly rubber rings.

WHAT TO TAKE

There's very little you need to take to North Cyprus that can't be sourced when you arrive, especially in the shops around Girne. Cosmetics, sun protection and photographic accessories (including film and digital media) are readily available. In all but rare circumstances an adaptor plug will be unnecessary. The electricity supply is 220–240 volts AC, and three-pin UK-style plugs are the norm.

Don't forget that North Cyprus still suffers from the misfortune of non-recognition by the international community. Whilst you're unlikely so suffer any problems, should the unthinkable happen and difficulties arise, it could be worth the effort to travel with duplicates of all important documents or forms of identification – passport, airline tickets, hotel reservation, insurance documents, credit cards and the like. Leave a copy with somebody at home so the information's always available.

CLOTHING North Cyprus is not a dressy place and comfortable informal clothing is best. Although nominally Muslim, Turkish Cypriots are very relaxed, and you can dress as you would when holidaying in Italy or Spain. Comfortable shoes are essential for climbs up to the mountain castles. Bikinis are fine and toplessness is increasing, especially among Germans on the private fee-paying beaches.

From the end of October until mid-April it is usually still chilly, especially in the evenings. Take a light raincoat in the winter months, or an umbrella, as rainstorms are very heavy.

Women may also wish to take a light scarf with them when visiting the mosques. It is not always required but it shows respect for the local culture and will make you feel more comfortable. Sometimes the mosques will provide appropriate clothing where the rules are enforced.

$ MONEY

In an attempt to adjust the effect of years of rampant inflation, on 1 January 2005 the Turkish lira was revalued and never were so many people demoted from the ranks of the millionaires' club in such a short space of time. Overnight, six zeros were wiped from bank accounts throughout the nation. 'Old' Turkish lira has now disappeared from circulation, and though some pricings still reflect the prior preponderance of zeros, YTL (Yeni (new) Türk Lirasi) is the order of the day. Whatever the situation, it remains fairly easy to use sterling, euros or even US dollars.

CHANGING MONEY The exchange rate is better in the country and in Turkey than it is abroad, and the rate offered for cash is slightly better than for travellers' cheques. Indeed, due to the lack of crime in North Cyprus and the fact that almost everywhere, including hotels, restaurants and petrol stations, accepts sterling (and other 'hard' currencies such as euros and US dollars), many tourists choose to bring just cash, with a credit card or two as back-up. When paying in a foreign currency, you'll find that the locals will almost always know the correct exchange rate, and will be scrupulously fair in handing you the correct amount of change (invariably in Turkish lira).

As such, there's no real need to visit a bank or moneychanger throughout your time in North Cyprus. However, should you find you have to, you won't find it difficult to find a place to change your money: hotels, car-hire firms, shops and agencies will all provide this service. The banks offer the best rate of exchange, although they are open only in the mornings. All exchange bureaux will accept cash and travellers' cheques, and a few (notably Sergeant Mustafa in Girne will even take personal cheques when supported by a cheque card.

PLASTIC MONEY Credit cards such as Visa, MasterCard, and to a lesser extent American Express and Diners Club, are accepted by most – if not all – hotels and major restaurants, together with petrol stations and larger shops. Turkish lira can be drawn directly from cashpoints with an international debit or credit card. Furthermore, there is now a branch of HSBC in Girne, with its own cash machine. Other cash machines belonging to local banks can readily be found in most towns.

COSTS AND BUDGETING In the past costs in Turkish Cyprus have gone only one way. However, 2007 has seen a reverse in this upward movement, particularly in and around Girne. A reasonable budget is still £35–45 per day for two people, to cover all food, drink, petrol and entry fees. Car hire costs £16–38 per day and a meal out for two in a reasonable restaurant with wine will cost £15–23. During the off-season, this allowance may be significantly reduced. For information on tipping, see page 29.

Prices in this guide Sterling is a readily quoted currency in North Cyprus and is usually accepted by hotels, larger shops, restaurants and airport/transfer taxis in the main towns. The prices in this guide are therefore quoted in pounds sterling.

GETTING AROUND

BY PUBLIC TRANSPORT Public transport in North Cyprus is limited and you are far better advised to hire a car. For those who do not want this extra cost, there are buses, but they are infrequent and do not run to a timetable. Lefkoşa is the main transport hub, and you'll find buses and *dolmuş* (shared taxis) run to all of the major towns from the bus station in the south of the town. Fares are very reasonable (£2.40 return by *dolmuş* between Lefkoşa and Girne, for example). The only problem is, many of North Cyprus's main attractions are in isolated and remote locations far from any town or village.

Private taxis (with yellow TAKSI signs on the roof) are also reasonably priced, charging fixed official tariffs, but they do not cruise and can only be found at taxi-stands, which close at night. There are no functioning railways. Sightseeing tours are widely available from numerous tour operators and these are perhaps the best options for non-drivers. Your hotel will generally have noticeboards or folders maintained by tour operators alerting you to their services.

BY CAR As in Greek Cyprus, by far the best way for the visitor to travel is self-drive hire car. All you need is a UK/international driving licence, and vehicles can be picked up and returned at Ercan Airport to avoid taxi transfer costs, which amount to about £25 one-way to Girne. The road network is very good and is being regularly improved, with an increasing number of dual carriageways between the main towns. Car-hire rates are cheap. Most traffic still drives on the left – a hangover from British administration – though it's worth keeping watch for the occasional rebellious exception. Fuel prices have increased dramatically of late, though are still cheaper than in the UK. Petrol currently costs £1.02 per litre, whilst diesel is cheaper still at around £0.94 per litre. When buying petrol, it is often easier to hand over the amount of money you would like to spend, or just to say, *doldur* ('fill it up'), than it is to start explaining quantities. There are no self-service petrol stations. Front passengers must wear seatbelts whilst rear seatbelts are little used.

In some areas at peak times driving in North Cyprus can be a considerable chore compared with the idyllic traffic-free days of yesteryear. So rapid has been the pace of development that the road system in some places is horrendously overstretched and congestion is commonplace. Around major towns queues of traffic are to be expected during the day and though various works are in progress to alleviate delays there's currently nothing for it but to just be patient. Even outside working hours traffic in towns can still back up. For a few hours Girne's evening restaurant rush, during the holiday season, turns the roads around the harbour and old town into one big pulsating mass of idling engines – my advice is to walk if possible.

Lefkoşa to Girne is a prime commuter route and, if you can, it's wise to avoid the morning and afternoon rush hours as your journey time can be more than doubled. However, elsewhere the lure of the open road can still reveal a side of North Cyprus otherwise hidden from the casual visitor. East from Girne, there's no denying that the new north coast road has opened up remote areas of the island to tourism and associated property development, although debate still rages about the environmental impact of the project. At present the new stretch leads as far as Tatlısu, with a mixture of unmetalled new roadbed and old road continuing to the Mersinlik, where progress seems to have stalled. If the shiny new tarmac is completed it should more than halve the journey time to the Karpas.

Wherever travel times are noted in the guide, these do not allow for any congestion which may be met, especially in crossing from one side of Girne to the other. The best advice is to set off early, otherwise excursions could be lengthened considerably.

Car hire There are plenty of car-hire agencies in North Cyprus. In summer, even they can be fully stretched meeting demand and it is definitely best to book in advance, before you reach the country. The minimum age for rental is 21, although some companies have a higher minimum age, and the only document required is a valid UK driving licence, national or international. Third-party insurance is compulsory, but fully comprehensive is recommended at just a few extra pounds a day. Insurance is invalid if you are found to be drunk at the time of an accident. All hire cars have red registration plates which are prefixed by 'Z', so have the advantage of being immediately recognisable by police and military, should you go astray.

Speed-limit signs are in kilometres, while distance markers are in a random mixture of miles and kilometres. The hire cars, too, are a mixture of right-hand and left-hand drive, and if you have a preference, it is best to state it at the time of booking. Because traffic drives on the left, left-hand-drive cars are sometimes cheaper. The cheapest cars to hire are usually Renault 9s or Opel Corsas, at about £12 per day (inclusive of unlimited mileage and collision damage waiver insurance) while a 4x4 'Suzuki Jeep' costs slightly more at about £14. Lower rates are often available for longer rentals and during the off-season.

Something to look out for is any company's promise of '24-hour guaranteed services'. One couple wrote to Bradt after their hired Jeep broke down on the Karpas Peninsula and they were left waiting for help overnight, without any financial compensation. It is worth checking just how far the company will go to help you out in case of a problem.

Petrol is cheaper than in Europe, and there are just two grades, unleaded and 'super'. Petrol stations are not hard to come by; they are dotted frequently along the main roads, both in towns, where prices are minimally higher, and between main destinations.

Below are a selected number of car-hire agencies in the TRNC, although the tourism centre in London will be happy to provide a comprehensive list.

Girne

Abant Rent-A-Car 12 Iskenderun Caddesi; ☏ 815 45 24; f 815 72 09; e info@abantrentacar.com; www.abantrentacar.com

Atlantik Car Rental Dome Hotel; ☏ 815 30 53; f 815 56 73; e atlanticcarrentals@yahoo.com

Bellapais Rent-A-Car Bellapais; ☏ 815 75 10; e info@bellapaisrentacar.com; www.bellapaisrental.com

Gunray Rent-A-Car Dursun Ozsarac Sok, No 23; ☏ 815 42 55; f 815 28 49; e info@gunrayrentacar.com; www.gunrayrentacar.com

Green Rent-A-Car 20 Karaoğlanoğlu Cad. Alsancak; ☏ 821 88 37; f 821 89 78; e info@greenrentacar.com; www.greenrentacar.com

Inter Rent Car Rentals Altinkaya 2, Ozankoy; ☏ 815 50 01; f 815 50 03; e altinkaya@altinkaya-cyprus.com; www.altinkaya-cyprus.com

Oscar Rent-A-Car Kordon Boyu; ☏ 815 22 72; f 815 38 58; e reservation@oscar-rental.com; www.oscar-rental.com

Sun Rent-A-Car Zafer apt, 20 Temmuz Kordonboyu Av, Girne; ☏ 815 23 02; f 228 37 00; e info@sunrentacar.com; www.sunrentacar.com

Gazimağusa

Benzincioglu Ltd Yeni Lefkoşa Magusa Yolu; ☏ 366 54 79; f 366 13 76; e benzincioglultd@yahoo.com

Sur Rent-A-Car ☏ 366 47 96; e surcarhire@hotmail.com; www.surcarhire.com

Trip Rent-A-Car Esref Bitlis Caddesi, Limasol Bankasi Yani, Sakarya; ☏/f 365 15 75; e triprentacar@mail.com; www.triprentacar.com

Lefkoşa

Akdenız Rent-A-Car Ataturk Caddesi, Yenisehir; ☏ 227 06 88; e akdenizrentacar@hotmail.com; www.akdenizrentacar.net

Sun Rent-A-Car Abdi Ipekci Caddesi; ☏ 227 87 87; f 228 37 00; e info@sunrentacar.com; www.sunrentacar.com

Sur Rent-A-Car Mehmet Akif Caddesi, 111/D, Mustafa Dervis Apt, Kumsal; ☏ 228 26 36; e surcarhire@hotmail.com; www.surcarhire.com

Maps The map provided free by the tourist offices is adequate, but a better one, prepared by Oxford Cartographers in 1989, can now be bought from Rüstem's Bookshop near the Saray Hotel in Lefkoşa (see page 98).

ACCOMMODATION

Accommodation options are expanding rapidly in North Cyprus; the range covers everything from five-star hotels to seaside camping facilities. Accommodation is listed under the respective area of the country.

Costs do vary throughout the year, with anything up to a 50% discount during the off-season (November to March), a lower 10–20% discount during the 'shoulder' season (April and October) and a substantial discount for children. In the listings, hotel rates are based on high-season costs for a double room for two people including breakfast; see box below for details.

Note that these rates are merely a guide. The chances are that when you arrive at the hotel, the rates quoted to you will not tally exactly with the ones given in this book, though hopefully the difference should be minimal. The rate you will actually pay for your hotel will depend on whether you booked your accommodation at home or have just walked in without pre-booking (the latter is usually more expensive), whether your accommodation is part of a package deal, how long you are staying and in what season.

Don't take ratings at face value. The comparative systems used in official accommodation guides seem to reflect the attitude that 'the bigger the casino, the better the hotel'. Such establishments are liberally awarded multiple stars, whilst many more attractive options are rated as if they were the local drop-in centre.

HOTEL PRICE CODES	
Double room per night including breakfast:	
$$$$	£100+
$$$$	£75–100
$$$	£50–75
$$	£25–50
$	up to £25

✗ EATING AND DRINKING

The range of food and restaurants on offer in North Cyprus, especially in and around Girne, is enormous, from local cuisine to Chinese, Italian and French. You can snack on a doner kebab from a street stall or savour dinner at a chic restaurant which can hold its own with top restaurants in Europe.

Most local specialities will be familiar to visitors to Turkey – various *meze* (selection of hot and cold appetisers), *börek* (hot pastries stuffed with spinach, cheese or meat), kebab, *kofte* (spiced meatballs), *dolma* (stuffed vine leaves) and salads which feature aubergines, tomatoes, onions, cucumbers, peppers, watercress, parsley, radishes and olives. Freshly caught sea creatures are widely offered, and include red and grey mullet, lobster, crab, mussels, rock bream, squid and sea bass. Fish is usually simply cooked, grilled or fried, though a few more sophisticated places offer it prepared in special sauces. Specifically Cypriot is the *halloumi* cheese, with that wonderful rubbery texture, often served grilled as a very tasty *meze*. There is also the crumbly white goat's cheese, and thick creamy yoghurt (excellent on meat, mixed with herbs, or as a sweet, drizzled with local mountain honey). Good-quality fresh fruit according to season includes melons, cherries, apples, strawberries, bananas, figs, grapes, oranges, grapefruits and pears. Turkish delight is available in a variety of flavours, and that with walnuts or pistachios inside is especially delicious.

To wash it all down, there is the cheap and widely available mineral water and the usual range of fizzy drinks, while on the alcoholic front the Turkish Efes beer is very good. The local beer is Goldfassl, produced in Gazimağusa, though not so widely available or popular. The North Cyprus wines (Aphrodite, Kantara and Monarch) are, by their own admission, inferior to those from the Turkish mainland, as wine-making is still a newly developing skill in the north. Of the Turkish wines, those that are consistently the best are those by Kavaklidere and by Doluca. Kavaklidere produce the red Yakut, the white Çankaya, the rosé Lâl and the primeur Nevsehir. Doluca produce the red and white Doluca and the more upmarket red Villa Doluca. Also recommended is the Special Reserve Karmen, and the semi-sweet Valdı. Raki is the local spirit, clear and aniseed flavoured, drunk either neat with ice or mixed with water, when it turns cloudy, thus explaining its description as 'lion's milk'. It goes well with *meze*, fish and lamb. The Turkish Yeni Raki is better than the local Has Raki, for the same reasons as the wine. Then there's the Turkish version of grappa, Zivania. Turkish coffee is widely drunk, introduced here, as elsewhere in the eastern Mediterranean, by the Ottomans in the 15th century. It is drunk *sade* (without sugar), *orta* (medium sugar) or *şekerli* (heavily sugared).

WHERE TO EAT As on the Turkish mainland, restaurant hours are very flexible and there is generally no problem about eating lunch at 16.00 and dinner at 20.00 if that is what happens to suit you. Turkish Cypriots eat out a lot themselves, especially at weekends, and the whole family partakes, from grandparents to babies. Should you need any help choosing a place to eat, *The Yellow Guide to Eating Out*, rating over 150 establishments, is available for £5 from the Green Jacket Bookshop and the Round Tower Gallery in Girne (see pages 50 and 48 respectively). Though the cost of eating out will depend to a large extent on personal taste and appetite, listings here include a price guide based on the average cost of a main course.

Tipping Tipping is not expected when a service charge is added to the bill, though a small extra amount will indicate gratitude for especially attentive service.

PUBLIC AND RELIGIOUS HOLIDAYS

1 January	New Year's Day
23 April	National Sovereignty and Children's Day
1 May	Labour Day
19 May	Youth and Sports Day
20 July	Peace and Freedom Day
1 August	TMT Day (birth of Turkish Cypriot Resistance Movement)
30 August	Victory Day
29 October	Turkish National Day
15 November	Independence Day (proclamation of TRNC)
25 December	Christmas Day

Turkey and North Cyprus follow the Gregorian calendar like the rest of Europe but, being predominantly Muslim, the major Islamic festivals are celebrated. The dates of these religious holidays change each year as they are calculated by the lunar system, and so move forward by about 11 days in the Gregorian calendar each year. There are two major Islamic holidays, the equivalents, if you like, of our Christmas and Easter. The first is Kurban Bayramı, the Feast of the Sacrifice, which commemorates Abraham's willingness to sacrifice his son Isaac. Each family traditionally sacrifices an animal (a sheep or a chicken, according to means), which is then cooked and eaten in large family gatherings. In 2008 Kurban Bayramı will fall in the second week of December and in late November 2009. It is a four-day national holiday, the longest of the year. The second festival celebrates the end of fasting during the 30-day month of Ramadan and is called Şeker Bayramı, the Sugar Festival, because much sweet food is eaten. It is a three-day national holiday and in 2008 fell from the end of September to the beginning of October, and slightly earlier in 2009. Ramadan itself is not strictly observed as a fasting month, and restaurants stay open as usual during the day.

SHOPPING AND ENTERTAINMENT

SHOPPING Shopping can be a perfect way to spend a few hours, milling around the markets and variety of local shops which can range from higgledy-piggledy little stores to very chic, upmarket boutiques. The best shopping is to be found in Girne, along the main street and in the side roads off it. Lefkoşa also has good shops but they are scattered and therefore more difficult for the visitor to find and use. Shops are generally open from 08.00 to 13.00 and 14.00 to 17.30 in winter, while in summer the hours shift to 07.30–13.00 and 16.00–18.00. Most shops shut on Sundays, though a few grocery stores remain open.

Traditional crafts to look out for are pottery, ceramics, leather shoes and bags, rugs and kilims, canvas suitcases and bags (very cheap and handy when your new purchases threaten to burst your existing suitcase), basketwork, dolls, jewellery, copper, brass and Lefkara lacework. These types of traditional purchases are not difficult to come by. The large souvenir shop, **Hello Basket**, in Edremit (see page 63) has some excellent basketware. The **Cyprus Pottery Shop** opposite The Ship Inn, on the main road west out of Girne; **Dükkan**, a little nearer the centre of Girne on the same road; and the shop next to and part of **Petek Pastanesi** (see page 110) in Gazimağusa are other suggestions. Don't forget, too, when visiting Lefkoşa, to call in at the **Folk Arts Institute**, opposite the Municipalities Union just north of the Aya Sofya Mosque (look for the house with Halk Sanatları Enstitüsü above the door), which produces, exhibits and sells traditional handicrafts. There is also a new initiative, **Delcraft**, set up on the Karpas in the small village of Büyükkonuk, where traditional objects such as wooden dolls and village costumes are made and sold alongside more modern souvenirs such as shell-framed mirrors. Büyükkonuk sits in the mountains at the western edge of the Karpas. To get there, head along the coast road east of Girne, and follow it as it heads inland. The road passes through the village.

Usually, items are priced in Turkish lira and prices are frequently lower than in the UK. Prices tend to be fixed and not subject to haggling. Purchases will often be patiently wrapped, tied up with ribbon and accompanied by the traditional Turkish talisman – the evil eye (see box, page 32).

For something other than souvenirs, check out Ronnie's Auctions on the coast road west out of Girne, near Karaoğlanoğlu. Finally, the Pegasos Bar, also on the coast road to Karaoğlanoğlu, holds a flea market every Friday, and there's an occasional car boot sale just outside Lapta.

SIGHTSEEING North Cyprus, with its rich and far-reaching history, has no shortage of monuments and museums. Most charge an entrance fee of about £1–4, although almost all offer a significant discount to students, children and indeed war veterans – just make sure you were on the appropriate side. Many of the larger sites offer a typed sheet of A4 explaining the site in some detail. Try and avoid the summer midday heat when looking around ruined sites, as they offer very little shade and can be scorchingly hot. Many of the sites are fascinating and, in parts, wonderfully well preserved and restored. Tour companies offer trips to most of the popular sites although, with a car, they are just as easy to visit independently.

The widely available North Cyprus guide, published by the North Cyprus Hoteliers Association and distributed through tourist offices and holiday operators, lists the opening times and entrance fees for all major attractions. It has to be said though that practical experience reveals a big chunk of this information to be inaccurate, and it definitely shouldn't be relied upon as being definitive.

BEACHES The whole of Gazimağusa Bay is one long sandy beach, and any hotel built along it will have excellent bathing.

The northern coast is much more mixed, with sandy bays interspersed with rocky coves, cliffs and headlands. On many beaches, especially the sandy ones, you will notice clumps of eel grass, a kind of seaweed, which accumulates and needs to be removed regularly. Local environmentalists, frequently expatriate residents, are active in beach clear-up days. North Cyprus does not escape the general pollution of the Mediterranean, and tar, along with plastic bottles, etc, often mars virgin beaches. Clean sand is the main advantage of using one of the private fee-paying beaches. Prevailing winds are from the west, so a bay tucked into the eastern side of a promontory generally offers wind protection, the calmest water and the least tar and eel grass.

Individual beaches are detailed here with their appropriate areas. For information on beach safety, see page 24.

EVENING ENTERTAINMENT North Cyprus is not an all-night party zone. The evenings are blissfully peaceful, filled with social gatherings in restaurants and bars, which seem happy to accommodate you for hours. Live music is an added bonus and time passes with ease. Very occasionally, there are also musical performances held in Kyrenia Castle or at Bellapais Abbey. However, as package tourism increases so do the options, and there's now a fairly active bar scene around Kyrenia. Ayia Napa it may not yet be (thankfully) but any visit in summer is likely to find a young crowd in town who'll give anyone a run for their money.

There are options for those seeking the delights of discotheques and casinos. Many of the big hotels offer these facilities, particularly those in and around Girne. Generally speaking, the discos are very much filled with locals and are far from being overtaken by tourists. Be warned, however, that a lot of establishments that advertise themselves as 'nightclubs' are very different from clubs back at home, being filled with 'Natashas' (prostitutes from eastern Europe) and very seedy. Some of the more reputable clubs are mentioned in this guide.

SPORT AND RECREATION

Please note that many of the following activities are summer-only (usually around April–September).

▲ BOAT TRIPS For information on boat trips around the coast, see page 50.

CYCLING In former years, North Cyprus was an idyllic a place as any cyclist could ever hope to find. Today, with significantly busier roads, cycling along any of the major routes is likely to be a chore rather than a pleasure. Bicycles can be rented locally at a number of hotels across the island, and areas such as the Karpas in the east and Cape Kormakiti in the west still make pleasurable destinations.

FISHING Fishing North Cyprus (m *0533 839 25 12*) is a new venture run by a couple of English chaps, Paul and Ian. They promise big 'carp, cats and more' and will tailor a trip to suit, including Girne hotel pick-up and drop-off. Prices start from £25 for four hours' fishing time including some refreshments.

✓ GOLF Located near Esentepe and opened very recently, **Korineum Golf and Country Club** (✆ 600 15 00; f 600 15 15; e info@korineumgolf.com; www.korineumgolf.com) is North Cyprus's first 18-hole international standard course. Though profligate water usage goes hand in hand with beautiful greens and fairways, here the club has invested in its own desalination plant thus avoiding impact on local supplies. First reports on the course are very favourable and although currently course-side accommodation is not available, it is planned for the future. Green fees for non-members are £52 per round though various special packages are available and it's always possible that a resident may sign you in. A host of other facilities is available at the clubhouse including restaurant and bar, sauna, massage and, in case your last double bogey caused you to pull it out, a unisex hair stylist.

The **CMC Club**, formerly Cengiz Topel Golf Club(✆ 0533 840 17 98; e info@ cmcgolfnorthcyprus.com; www.cmcgolfnorthcyprus.com), is an 11-hole course just past Güzelyurt near Yeşilyurt. It is the island's oldest club, founded in 1926, and probably the best of the sub 18-holers. Though its facilities are not in the same league as the Korineum – greens are 'browns' made of sand and oil – upgraded irrigation, new holes and a new clubhouse were added in 2006. What it lacks in glitz it makes up for in friendliness. Play all day for £10.

ⴽⵓ GO-KARTING The go-karting track, **Tazkarts** (✆ 815 04 39), in Çatalköy is open for most of the year. There is a second track, **Zet Karting** (✆866 61 73), 7km east of Lefkoşa.

🐴 HORSERIDING At **Çatalköy Riding Club** (m 0533 845 47 41; f 824 40 30; e info@catalkoyridingclub.com; www.catalcoyridingclub.com; ☉ Tue–Sun from 08.00, but often much earlier in summer – call to check) horses are trained and managed to a high standard by former Merseyside police instructor, Beverley Jones. There's learn-to-ride group or private lessons, or trail riding in the Kyrenia Mountains for experienced horseriders. Maximum weight is 90kg, minimum age is seven years and prices range from £10 for an introductory lesson to £675 for fully accommodated seven-night trails.

PARAGLIDING At **Highline Tandem Paragliding** (m *0542 855 56 72;* f *223 61 73;* e *highlineinfo@yahoo.com; www.highlineparagliding.com*) no experience is necessary as your English-speaking pilot takes the strain; enjoy the view and collect the T-shirt. Daily two-hour adventures take off from 750m above sea level in the Kyrenia Mountains. Expect to pay from £55, including a pick-up from Girne.

SCUBA DIVING Diving courses are growing in popularity in North Cyprus, and costs are similar between schools. A three-day PADI scuba course will set you back around £185; this will allow you to dive to a depth of around 10–12m. The full PADI open-water course (allowing you to dive up to 18m) costs around £225. If you're unsure whether diving is for you, the schools also run trial dives for around £20.

North Cyprus offers some of the best scuba-diving sites in the Mediterranean, including the underwater formations at Mansinis Reef and the ancient shipwreck at Girne, as well as providing the opportunity to photograph and feed the wildlife at Fred's Reef. Fish abound, including among their number stingray, amberjack, cuckoo wrasse, scorpionfish, bream and grouper. Bear in mind though that North Cyprus has no decompression chamber – the nearest is across the border in the south of the island.

Some of the more popular schools are:

Amphora Scuba Diving Centre m 0542 851 4924; f 228 28 41; e Easimuygur@superonline.com; www.amphoradiving.com. Based at Escape Beach, this friendly company offers PADI, BSAC & CMAS courses for beginners & experts alike. They have daily trips & dive around some of the local reefs, sometimes allowing diving on preserved shipwrecks just outside the harbour.

Blue Dolphin Scuba Diving m 0542 851 5113; f 223 43 60; e bluedolphinscubadiving@hotmail.com; www.bluedolphin.4mg.com. Operating from Jasmine Court Hotel (see page 43) & offering some of the most comprehensive programmes, all with a top-notch PADI rating. If you're around the harbour in Girne you won't fail to notice their pushy sales reps, so if that's not your style you'd be best advised to give them a wide berth.

Scuba Cyprus m 533 865 23 17; e info@scubacyprus.com; www.scubacyprus.com. Situated at Santoria Holiday Village off the road towards Lapta, Scuba Cyprus offers PADI & BSAC courses in scuba diving, plus try-dives, jet-skiing & boat trips. It will cost you approximately £14 for an all-inclusive try-dive day.

Turtle Bay Dive Centre m 0533 849 62 66; e turtlebaydivers@hotmail.co.uk; www.turtlebaydivecentre.com. Based at the Sempati Hotel, 10 miles west of Girne, this operation is run by Scottish couple, Drew & Caroline. PADI-certified boat dives are offered for all levels of experience from Bubblemaker to Dive Instructor. Specialities include wreck dives on the Zenobia car ferry (£70).

WALKING In general the Kyrenia mountain range offers the best walking, with many quiet forest tracks well maintained by the Forestry Department. Some of the loveliest include the 1.5km walk from Malatya to İlgaz, passing a waterfall on the way; from İlgaz to Karaman, a 4km walk taking one and a half hours; along the ridge from the Five Finger Mountain pass towards the Armenian monastery; and along the ridge from St Hilarion towards Lapta. The last track is also driveable in a saloon car. It passes a fountain at about 8km, then at 10km reaches Sisklip, the point above Malatya where there is a junction with three tracks. The middle track continues 9.2km past Mt Selvili at 1,024m to reach the tarmac road down to Karşiyaka, while the right fork leads 6.3km to Lapta; the left fork leads down to the tarmac at Akçiçek and is of less interest to walkers.

The village of Ozanköy has many lovely walks through ancient olive groves in all directions and specifically up towards Bellapais and its abbey. Lapta is another village particularly well placed for walks into the olive and citrus groves and up into the mountains.

One further walk that used to be very popular was the hike from the village of Karaman (Karmi) to St Hilarion. The walk starts by the rough road leading away from the village in front of the Treasure Restaurant, from where a right fork takes you climbing up the mountain. The total time is about two hours, but the path is steep and unforgiving. Appropriate footwear and plenty of water are recommended, particularly in the summer. Occasional military activity has led to closure of this path in the past. Check with villagers in Karmi before setting out.

Walks and Wild Orchids (\ *721 30 13;* m *0542 854 4329;* e *thutchinson@ iecnc.org; www.walksnorchidsnorthcyprus.com*) is run by two expats, Tony and Maureen Hutchinson, who arrange orchid and wild-flower walks around Hisarköy. Maureen is the botanist expert, while Tony is a keen birdwatcher. The walks operate during the peak wild-flower season, February to May, and those who've taken part can't praise them too highly. The cost of £15 includes lunch.

Yucel Asan has set up his own walking company based at his Follow Me Restaurant (\ *815 38 03*) above Edremit. With seven years' experience of guiding walks (not to mention 23 years in the Forestry Department before that), Yucel knows the best places to hike and the names of all the plants, birds and animals you're likely to encounter on the way. Highly recommended by readers, cost for a half-day walk is £10, or it's £20 for a full day (including lunch and transport).

Kyrenia Range Walks (\ *815 72 97;* m *0542 857 81 12;* e *info@kyrenia-range-walks.com; www.kyrenia-range-walks.com*) organise guided walks, from short rambles to the full 220km cape-to-cape trek. Prices start at £15 and rise to £350 for the epic 10-day yomp.

The **National Trust of the Turkish Republic of North Cyprus** (*PO Box 582, Girne, Mersin 10, Turkey*) produces maps for walkers. Maps published so far cover a tour of Girne's old harbour, a long mountain walk between St Hilarion Castle and Lapta, a tour of Gazimağusa and an uphill trek eastwards from Bellapais towards Buffavento Castle. They are usually available from local hotels or at Girne's excellent Green Jacket Bookshop (see page 50).

Finally, there is a book, *Walks in North Cyprus*, which covers 30 walks of varying difficulty, and which was produced locally in 2001. It is available in Girne at the Green Jacket Bookshop (see page 50) and Cypriot Handicrafts Art Gallery at the Round Tower (see page 48), price £7.

WATERSPORTS Watersports are widely practised and most hotel beaches offer windsurfing, sea-kayaking, waterskiing and pedalos. The British company **Dolphin Cyprus** (*www.dolphin-cyprus.com*) offers tuition in all the usual watersports including dinghy sailing, waterskiing, windsurfing and canoeing.

Swimming is an easy activity to come by in North Cyprus – there are plenty of beaches and most hotels have swimming pools. Specifically with children in mind, the **Octopus Aqua Park**, east of Girne, and **Exotic Hotel** (see page 134), near Gazimağusa, both have waterslides.

WEIGHTS AND MEASURES

North Cyprus is a total jumble of measuring systems, with all sorts of Ottoman relics which are still used, curiously, in the Greek sector as well. The *oke*, for example, is the standard weight measure, and remember when buying fruit, meat and vegetables that, at 2.8lb, it is rather more than a kilo – which is only 2.2lb. There are 400 drams to the *oke*, and 800 *okes* = a ton. The other Ottoman measure still in use is the *donum*, the land measure, which is a little under a third of an acre. The British administration left its heritage of driving on the left, and any distance signposts which remain from that time are in miles. More recent ones are usually, though not always, in kilometres and hire cars may be either right- or left-hand drive and should be calibrated in kilometres or miles accordingly.

TIME

From the end of March until mid-September, North Cyprus is on GMT+3; in winter GMT+2. The usual time difference with the UK is therefore two hours.

MEDIA AND COMMUNICATIONS

✆ **TELEPHONE** To telephone North Cyprus from the UK, dial 00 (international), then 90 (Turkey country code), then 392 (North Cyprus code), before dialling the relevant town code, and finally the actual number itself. To dial the UK from North Cyprus it is 00 (international), then 44 (UK country code), then the town code minus the initial 0, then the number itself. For a considerable period after 1974 it was not possible to call Greek Cyprus from the north. These days as long as you use the international codes, 357 for Greek Cyprus and 90 for Turkey and North Cyprus, and appreciate the international call charges, there's no problem contacting the south.

Public telephone booths are not that common and are generally associated with main post offices in major towns. They only accept telephone cards which can be purchased from post offices and some kiosks. A 300-unit card (around £4.40) gives you almost 25 minutes off-peak to the UK.

Mobile phone networks provide good coverage using the GSM 900 and GSM 1800 standards, and pre-pay SIM cards and top-up cards for the local networks are readily available, packaged with varying amounts of calling credit. To utilise a local SIM, Turkcell or Telsim, your mobile phone needs to be 'unlocked' from its home network. If this is not already the case more specialised phone shops in Girne and Lefkoşa will be able to set you free for a small charge. If you plan on using a mobile phone, even if you're just visiting for a week, a local SIM card makes immediate sense in order to avoid hefty international roaming charges when making and receiving calls. Remember to dial 392 in front of all local numbers from your mobile. Remember that there's no roaming agreement between Greek Cypriot and Turkish Cypriot mobile networks. So if you're planning a trip south, or vice versa, you'll need another SIM card. UK and many other international mobile phones will roam in a reassuringly expensive manner from network to network, both north and south.

North Cyprus telephone codes

Gazimağusa	✆ 366
Girne	✆ 815
Lefkoşa	✆ 227 or ✆ 228

Emergency telephone numbers

Fire	✆ 199
Police	✆ 155
First aid	✆ 112

e **INTERNET CAFÉS** Access to the internet has taken off in North Cyprus with broadband access readily available in all larger towns either via net cafés or through hotel facilities. Most dedicated internet cafés charge around £0.80 per hour whilst some cafés, such as Gazimağusa's D&B Café, and many hotels have free wireless access for their patrons. Here are a few better known internet cafés:

2

A&A Net Café University of Eastern Mediterranean, Gazimağusa; ☎ 365 4444 (university switchboard)
Café Net Efeler Sokak, Girne; ☎ 815 92 59
Easy Net İskenderun Caddesi, Nergiz Apt No 2/F, Girne; ☎ 815 58 99; m 0533 869 14 02

Fistik Net Café Sht Salih Cibir Sokak No 15 Kermiya, Lefkoşa; ☎ 227 37 27
M@avinet Mustafa Çağatay Caddesi 4 Mevsim Apt No 5, Girne; ☎ 815 33 25; m 0533 866 72 46
Nethouse Başbuğ Sok, Karasal apt, Zeminkat, Karakol, Gazimağusa; ☎ 365 4765

✉ **POST** Postal rates are very reasonable with one rate for Europe and the Middle East. Postcards take about 10–14 days to reach most European destinations, letters five to seven days. Post boxes are bright yellow and are found in the main streets of all towns and villages. When sending items to North Cyprus, the code 'Mersin 10, Turkey' should always appear, otherwise they may be misdirected to Greek Cyprus.

NEWSPAPERS The most popular Turkish-language newspaper is *Kibris*, produced daily from Lefkoşa, while the oldest national daily is *Halkin Sesi*. For English-language readers, *Cyprus Today* and *Cyprus Observer* are published weekly while the *Cyprus Times* is a daily. *Essential Cyprus* is a glossy monthly magazine with a broad range of political, artistic and lifestyle features. Elsewhere, the Northern Cyprus Hoteliers Association publishes the dual-language *Tourism Monthly*, and *North Cyprus Magazine* can be found liberally distributed around hotels and restaurants.

TELEVISION AND RADIO Turkish Cypriot television and Turkish television channels are received. There is news in English, plus a few imported English

---

SUSTAINABLE TOURISM – HOPE FOR THE FUTURE?

Nigel Wallis

At first glance it might seem as if the tour operators and estate agents hold a monopoly on the North Cyprus tourism market, but dig a little deeper and it's clear that there's a small but steadily growing range of alternatives for those who want to go it alone and do things differently.

Most are out on the Karpas Peninsula, where package holidays are yet to penetrate and the rural way of life pervades. Doing more than anyone and deserving of a special mention is Lois Cemal, a Canadian expat who has settled in the village of Büyükkonuk with her Turkish Cypriot husband, Ismail. Together Lois and Ismail run **Delcraft** (*www.ecotourismcyprus.com*), an organisation devoted to the preservation of local traditions through a range of eco- and agro-tourism programmes, including wonderful day-long courses on bread baking, cheese making and olive oil extraction. You can also head further off the beaten track to the Yudi Natural Arch on a 4x4 excursion, or stay over in one of the four self-contained units – including one family suite (*B&B £30 per double room per night, or £180 per week*). The shop is open for locals to display homemade crafts, and operating under the principles of fair trade ensures the artisan earns a fair price for each sale. Development of the project is being directly supported by the UN, USAID, the Turkish Embassy and the local Büyükkonuk Municipality. Plans are afoot to double the number of beds and include facilities for backpackers, cyclists and the disabled; other improvements will encompass the whole town, creating North Cyprus's first eco-village. At the same time, after many years of active involvement in the community, Lois has developed something of a reputation for helping to empower local women in an otherwise staunchly male-dominated society. All Delcraft activities can be booked through local tour company Unique (☎ *366 50 32;* f *366 50 33;* e *ideal_cyprus@yahoo.com*).

Another example of sustainable development is the wonderful **Oasis at Ayfilon** (m *0533 868 55 91;* e *info@oasishotelkarpas.com; www.oasishotelkarpas.com*). Offering

programmes, usually soaps. The BBC World Service main frequency is 1323Khz MW. The British Forces Broadcasting Service in the Sovereign Bases in Greek Cyprus can be heard clearly in the Gazimağusa area on 99.6MHz and 95.3MHz, and in the Lefkoşa area on 89.7MHz and 91.7MHz. BFBS television broadcasts may also be received by those in Lefkoşa.

North Cyprus's main network is BRT, with both their radio and television studios located just outside Lefkoşa. Radio programmes (105MHz) are in English, Turkish and, for propaganda purposes, Greek.

PROPERTY DEVELOPMENT Nick Redmayne

In recent years the runaway development of holiday properties has become the saddest spectacle to visit the once tranquil shores of North Cyprus. The lessons learnt in other parts of the Mediterranean, not least Greek Cyprus, and known for so long, seem to have been forgotten so quickly by those hungry to make a fast buck. Indeed, to see the natural beauty of the island despoiled by cavalier developers whose obscene frenzy is fed by the dreams of naïve foreigners, can only be described as sickening.

Ignorance cannot excuse the crimes against North Cyprus's environment, for as well as Cypriot and Turkish businesses capitalising on the property boom, UK developers are here flying the flag. Though given the impact of this virulent outbreak of 'villamania', this is hardly cause for national pride. No doubt they'll be off to another place in the sun before their concrete has dried.

simple food and accommodation in breathtaking surroundings at Ayios Philon, the appeal of the project is for anyone disillusioned by the ongoing development of the island. It couldn't be further removed from the resorts around Girne. The long-term plan is to develop a separate, self-sufficient eco-friendly village on the Karpas Peninsula where tourists can experience the unfettered beauty that still remains in the more remote areas. Whether or not the project gets off the ground depends on the local authorities who, with their penchant for neon lights and tacky casinos, are yet to appreciate the full potential of ecotourism.

Elsewhere, not all is lost to the construction frenzy – there's a selection of well-designed specialist options, all low impact, from which to choose. Small, family-run restoration projects, such as the **Lefke Gardens Hotel** and **Karpaz Arch Houses**, are gaining popularity and provide viable alternatives to larger, traditional resort hotels, whilst the beach-shacks of the Karpas continue to draw visitors from far and wide. Tony and Maureen Hutchinson's much-loved flower walks continue to thrive, and even some UK tour operators will now take you on escorted trekking holidays through the mountains.

Various non-governmental organisations (NGOs) are active in North Cyprus, all promoting and aiming to preserve the wealth of natural beauty on offer. Details of current and upcoming projects can be obtained from the **Management Centre in Lefkoşa** (www.mc-med.org), or from any of the individuals mentioned above.

With the relaxation of border controls there's no reason for any independent traveller to be deterred from heading to North Cyprus. No longer restricted to flying via Turkey, it's a simple process to jet in to the south (Larnaca or Paphos) and cross over the divide at will. Not only are journey times reduced, but the wide availability of flights means cheaper airfares, and car hire can readily be organised on reaching the north.

Just a few years ago the very notion of having to encourage sustainable tourism in North Cyprus would have been laughable. Today, as a result of phenomenal growth and short-sighted planning, it seems essential for the long-term good of the country.

All around it's apparent that the infrastructure is feeling the strain of new demands. The road system around Girne illustrates one aspect of this whilst inadequate electricity and water systems continue to be problematic.

However, though previous reports of the development bubble having burst may have been wishful thinking, currently it does appear that a hiatus has been reached. At the time of writing an estimated 2,000 new holiday properties lie unfinished or unoccupied. Foreign purchasers' confidence may in part have been undermined by the emphatic victory of mainland Turkey's AK Party, which some suggest has a hidden Islamist agenda. Certainly events in Turkey seem to have made accession to the EU a more distant prospect and for the time being the level of speculation and investment in property has undoubtedly abated. Further unsettling news for holiday-home owners comes in the form of a ruling by a district court in Nicosia that British couple, Linda and David Orams, who have built a holiday villa in North Cyprus, must demolish it and return the land to its Greek Cypriot owner. Though southern rulings are not enforceable in North Cyprus, the case has since moved to the UK's High Court, involving Cherie Booth QC as council for the Orams, and thence on to the European Court of Justice. The resultant publicity can only create further unease for investors, developers and purchasers.

What the future now holds is dependent not only on demand for villas but also the overdue effective implementation of new building regulations, an impediment that developers have previously seemed all too adept at circumventing. One can only hope that the republic's government has woken up to the fact that North Cyprus's long-held allure runs the risk of being casually blighted by a chaotic and careless scramble for easy money and a bargain-basement place in the sun.

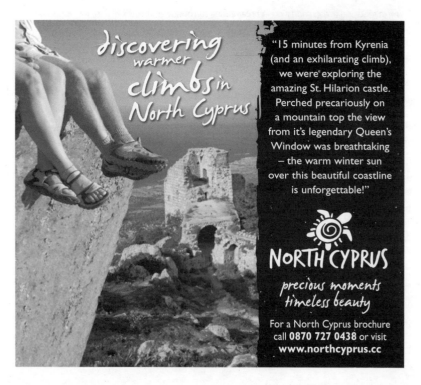

Part Two

THE GUIDE

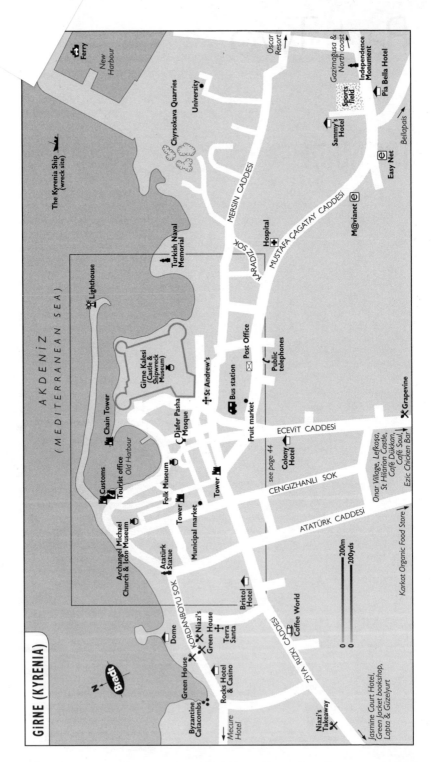

3

Girne (Kyrenia)

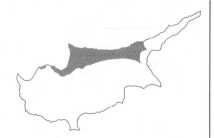

Despite having acquired many resort trappings, Girne remains the prettiest town on the island by virtue of its picturesque yacht-filled harbour and adjacent colossal Crusader castle. However, those arriving in search of a tranquil fishing village may be disappointed – for sure they're in the right place, just the wrong time. Nowhere in North Cyprus has the recent economic surge made a bigger impact. Officially the town is home to 14,000 residents, although when considering the outlying suburbs and transient student population, conservative estimates put this figure in excess of 25,000. During the evening, roads in and out of town regularly become choked and if you're heading into the old town, a ten-minute walk is preferable to half an hour sitting in traffic. That said, to wander the harbour in the calm of an early morning or take dinner along the waterfront in the evening is an uncomplicated pleasure to be savoured; there's nowhere else like it on the island.

The jagged Kyrenia Mountains lend a spectacular backdrop and the tiny, winding lanes around the Djafer Pasha Mosque convey images of the past. The shops on and around Ziya Rızkı Caddesi and Atatürk Caddesi continue to attract Turks from the mainland with their sophisticated range of choice, ever more so as North Cyprus opens up and international brands move in. Numerous bars and cafés offer friendly service for drinks and *meze*, whilst evening dining options are extensive, excellent value and of a generally admirable standard.

It is these qualities that will continue to attract visitors to Girne, and for many the town remains an excellent base for exploring the attractions of North Cyprus. Unspoiled it may no longer be, but a premier tourist destination it remains.

HISTORY

Today's population of Girne, officially 14,000, is double what it was before 1974. Many private houses were looted in the fighting and by 1976 only some 200 out of the original 2,500 British residents remained. Turks from the Limassol area were resettled here, and given land and property that had been Greek, in the same way that Greeks were given Turkish property in the south in compensation for their losses in the north. Some mainland Turks have also been brought across, which is how the population level has been restored.

Settlement from the Turkish mainland was how the Turkish Cypriot community first began on the island. After the defeat of the Venetians in 1571, the Turkish commander Lala Mustapha Pasha chose 12,000 infantry and 4,000 cavalrymen to stay behind as colonists. A further 22,000 decommissioned soldiers and their families also went to Cyprus, along with their livestock, tools for their crafts and all their possessions. They were given expatriate allowances and tax exemptions for the first three years to encourage them to settle, as was common practice by the Ottomans throughout their conquered territories. To help in the rebuilding and repopulating process, they favoured especially farmers, and thereafter a range of other skilled workers like weavers, cobblers, tailors, masons, coppersmiths, miners, etc. They also favoured families with young daughters. Many settlers came from the Black Sea coastal areas of Trabzon and Sinop, and the resettlement continued intermittently until the 18th century. By the time of the British administration in 1878, there were 95,000 Turkish Cypriots living on the island.

Girne's population in the past was subject to wild fluctuations depending on plagues, droughts and other disasters. In 1814 it was recorded that a mere 15 families lived in the town, all Greeks, and the ruling Turks would withdraw to the castle at night. From the 16th century, under the Ottoman administration, the population was fairly evenly balanced between Turks and Greeks. The Turks were traditionally landowners and farmers, while the Greeks were fishermen and shop owners. The Greeks tended to be the merchants. By 1900 the population had risen to some 1,500, and this gradually increased as Girne and the surrounding area became the favoured place of retirement for British colonial officials, living their lives of 'blameless monotony', as Lawrence Durrell put it in his *Bitter Lemons*. The British had taken on the administration of Cyprus from the Ottomans because of its strategic importance, since the 1869 opening of the Suez Canal, in the protection of their trade route to India. Five years later however, when Britain was also in military occupation of Egypt, Cyprus ceased to be vital and was subsequently neglected, with little financial investment.

GETTING THERE AND AROUND

BY ROAD Since the new road was built (with Saudi finance) the capital city of Lefkoşa (Nicosia) is just a 20-minute drive away, Ercan Airport is a 40-minute drive and Gazimağusa (Famagusta) is an hour and ten minutes. From Girne it takes one hour 45 minutes to reach Vouni, the westernmost point of interest, and three hours to reach Kastros at the easternmost tip of the Karpas, travelling on the new north coast road as far as Tatlısu.

If you choose to catch a taxi from Ercan Airport into Girne, it will probably cost you around £14 one-way, but most of the tour operators offer their own transfers.

Dolmuş buses (shared taxis) run fairly regularly until about 19.00, although not to a timetable, from the bus station in the centre of Girne to all the major towns in the north (sample fares: £1.20 to Lefkoşa, £1 to Lapta, £0.60 to Karaoğlanoğlu). They can also be flagged down on the main roads, although they often fill up before they leave the bus station itself.

BY SEA There are two main ferry companies, Akgünler and Fergün, running services from Kyrenia to the Turkish mainland. The **Fergün** agent (❁ *815 23 44*) is on the west side of Belediye Meydani. The **Akgünler** agent (❁ *815 35 10*) is on the southern side of Belediye Meydani. The ferry to Taşucu runs throughout the year and takes approximately two hours to complete the journey. The cost is currently £20 one-way, £40 return, though watch out for the port fees (£5/11 one-way/return) payable at the harbour. On a summer-only service, the other destination, Alanya, costs £26 one-way, £46 return plus port fees and is three and a half hours.

PRACTICALITIES

TOURIST OFFICE Situated on the harbour front, the tourist office is supposed to be open 09.00–17.00 daily but don't be surprised if it isn't. In any event this facility runs a poor second to your hotel when it comes to dispensing fulsome and accurate information.

POST OFFICE (⏰ *07.30–14.00 & 16.00–18.00 Mon–Fri, 09.00–12.00 Sat*) On M Çağatay Caddesi behind the bus station/car park.

TELEPHONE EXCHANGE Opposite the post office.

INTERNET Café Net is the most convenient and friendliest internet café, near to the harbour (*£0.60 for 30mins*). Opening hours are irregular, but generally are: 09.00–17.00 daily. Girne has half a dozen other internet cafés (including **B@rnet**, **M@vianet** and **Easy Net**), mostly cheaper than Café Net, although some of these cater to young men playing games and surfing uninhibited websites!

FOREIGN NEWSPAPERS Two doors up from HSBC on Ziya Rizki Caddesi is a small newsagent with the best selection of English- and other foreign-language newspapers, usually two or three days old at best.

WHERE TO STAY

The town and surrounding area offer the best range of accommodation in North Cyprus, from self-catering to five-star hotels. Unfortunately, an upsurge in investment over the last few years has led to a rash of building projects. The creeping development is sometimes unsightly and has made the fringes of Girne and parts of the coastline to the west somewhat tacky, with block formation hotels and gaudy casino lights. That said, the old harbour area has retained its charm and will be a favourite with many of its visitors.

The price codes refer to the cost of a double room with two people sharing including breakfast. These quotes are based on the high-season summer period, and therefore you may be pleasantly surprised by out-of-season bargains.

UPMARKET

🏠 **Mercure Hotel** (299 rooms) ☎ 650 25 00; f 650 25 59; e reservations@mercurecyprus.com; www.mercurecyprus.com. At the time of writing, it was very recently opened & a low level of finishing work was ongoing. Located outside the centre in Karaoğlanoğlu & constructed in a manner that echoes Girne's Crusader castle in style & proportion. Replete with 2 presidential suites, a casino & spa centre. Undoubtedly an upmarket property but currently aimed at a clientele of Turkish businessmen rather than Western tourists. $$$$$

🏠 **Rocks Hotel & Casino** (155 rooms) ☎ 815 22 38; f 815 57 12; e info@rockshotel.com; www.rockshotel.com. Formerly the Rock Hotel, now significantly redeveloped & expanded with all mod cons, but commanding premium rates as a result. Well-appointed rooms, a range of bars, restaurants & cafés, whilst the famous seawater pool & beach bar remain favourites. Stretch limos with 'Rocks' number plates available for high rollers. $$$$$

🏠 **The Colony** (90 rooms) ☎ 815 15 18; f 815 59 88; e thecolony@parkheritage.com; www.thecolonycyprus.com. One of Girne's newest & smartest hotels, though its location, well back from the harbour, & the adjoining glitzy casino initially suggests Turkish businessmen as major clientele. That said, increasing numbers of Western tourists are staying here, enjoying excellent food & service. All rooms come with personal entertainment centres (with DVD, video games, etc), internet access, minibar & AC. $$$$

🏠 **Jasmine Court Hotel** (192 rooms) ☎ 815 14 50; f 815 14 88; e info@jasminecourthotel.com; www.jasminecourthotel.com. Set in 30 acres of ground on its own private headland just to the west of Girne. Very high standard of self-catering apt, with fully equipped kitchen & satellite TV. Central facilities include pool, bars, restaurants, casino, shops, launderette, tennis courts & good facilities for children including a supervised crèche. Rocky cove for swimming & snorkelling. Courtesy bus to central Girne. $$$$

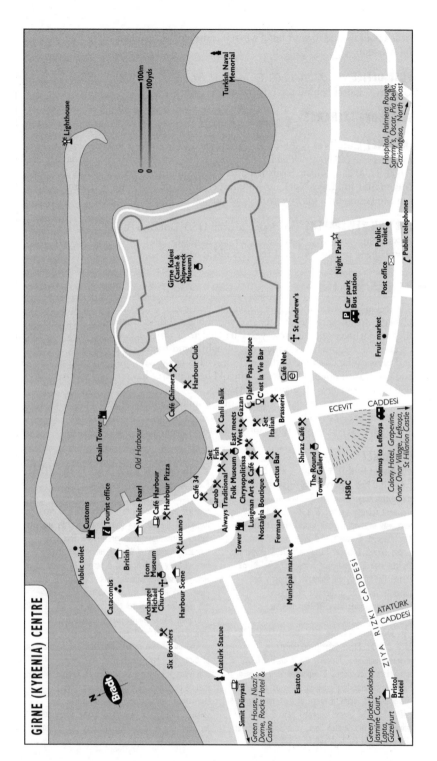

GİRNE (KYRENIA) CENTRE

Bradt

N

Lighthouse

Turkish Naval Memorial

100m
100yds
0
0

Girne Kalesi (Castle & Shipwreck Museum)

Public toilet

Chain Tower

Old Harbour

Customs

Tourist office

White Pearl

Café Harbour

Harbour Pizza

Luciano's

Café 34

Café Chimera

Harbour Club

Canli Balik

Set Fish

East meets West

Gazan

Carob

Always Traditional

Folk Museum

Chrysopolitissa

Set Italian

Brasserie

Djafer Paşa Mosque

C'est la Vie Bar

Café Net

St Andrew's

Catacombs

British

Icon Museum

Archangel Michael Church

Harbour Scene

Lusignan Art & Café

Nostalgia Boutique

Cactus Bar

Ferman

Shiraz Café

The Round Tower Gallery

HSBC

Night Park

Car park
Bus station

Fruit market

Post office

Public toilet

Public telephones

ECEVİT CADDESİ

Dolmuş to Lefkoşa

Colony Hotel, Grapevine,
Onar, Onar Village, Lefkoşa,
St Hilarion Castle

Hospital, Palmera Rouge,
Sammy's, Oscar, Pia Bella,
Gazimağusa, North coast

Six Brothers

Atatürk Statue

Tower

Municipal market

Esatto

Simit Dünyasi

Green House, Niazi's,
Dome, Rocks Hotel &
Casino

ZIYA RIZKI CADDESİ

ATATÜRK CADDESİ

Bristol Hotel

Green Jacket bookshop,
Jasmine Court,
Lapta,
Güzelyurt

44

MID-RANGE

🏠 **Dome Hotel** (161 rooms) ☎ 815 24 53; f 815 27 72; e thedome@kktc.net; www.thedomehotelcyprus.com. Girne's most famous & long-standing hotel, set on the seafront with its own rocky promontory for sunbathing & with ladders down into the sea. Large rooms with TV & minibar. Balconies overlooking sea or mountains. Busy cosmopolitan bar (offering the best brandy sours) & restaurant with international cuisine. Casino where all currencies are accepted, with roulette, blackjack & backgammon. Boating & fishing trips can be arranged. Still favoured by visiting dignitaries, although cynics would say that they're mostly Turkish officials who are sent to a hotel which is owned by the Turkish government! $$$

🏠 **Onar Village** (36 rooms) ☎ 815 58 50/1/2; f 815 58 53; e onarvillage@yahoo.com; www.onarvillage.com. Complex consisting of villas & hotel rooms, all set around a swimming pool on the hillside overlooking Girne. The family-run village offers a courtesy bus to town, restaurant, pool bar & a library, & even has its own private little museum. $$$

🏠 **Sammy's** (24 rooms) ☎ 815 62 79; f 815 62 80; e sammys@kktc.net. Once rumoured to be the hotel in Girne with the greatest number of repeat bookings. Still convenient for the town centre, but its peaceful location has been gobbled up by the spread of the town. On the inside though the owners make a real effort — full of the usual trappings including a lovely swimming pool, & as friendly as can be, this really is a lovely little place. Reductions for longer stays. $$$

🏠 **Oscar Resort** (229 rooms) ☎ 815 48 01; f 815 39 80; e info@oscar-resort.com; www.oscar-resort.com. Recently refurbished, this large complex is set on the outskirts of Girne. Less than scenic surroundings, but good facilities including AC, gym, swimming pools, restaurant, bar & the ubiquitous casino. Also self-catering villas & apts. $$

🏠 **White Pearl Hotel** (9 rooms) ☎ 815 04 30; f 816 01 10; e whitepearl@superonline.com; www.whitepearlhotel.com. Dbl & twin rooms, most with balcony, TV & AC & a superb setting on the eastern edge of Kyrenia harbour. Owner Bayram Bayramoğlu has made a considerable personal investment to produce a small but perfectly formed hotel. Superb panoramic views from roof terrace. Car hire & airport transfers. Currently no affiliation with travel agents & hence a great option for independent travellers. $$

BUDGET

🏠 **Bristol Hotel** (18 rooms) ☎ 815 65 70; f 815 73 65; e Bristol@northcyprus.net; www.cyprushotelbristol.com. Small, unassuming but friendly place on the main street. Rooms with bath or shower (shared toilet). Shady patio garden, restaurant & bar. $$

🏠 **British Hotel** (16 rooms) ☎ 815 22 40; f 815 27 42; e info@britishhotelcyprus.com; www.britishhotelcyprus.com. Rooms with balcony & good views to old harbour & Girne Castle. B&B only. Good simple base. $$

🏠 **Harbour Scene Hotel** (16 rooms) ☎ 815 68 55; f 815 68 57; e sertelb@kibris.net. Fairly large, anonymous but long-established hotel on the main shopping drag of Canbulat Sokak. Rooms are en suite & with TV, phone & a balcony. As with most in this budget category, cheap for what you get, but not exactly luxurious. $$

🏠 **Nostalgia Boutique Hotel** (28 rooms) ☎ 815 30 79; f 815 90 05; e kholidays@superonline.com; www.nostalgiahotel.com/tamco.html. Quaint hotel in quiet backstreet, just up from the Djafer Pasha Mosque. Traditional Cyprian décor in the rooms (inc 4-poster beds in some!) & attached restaurant. A reduction in the rates to offset the decline in tourism has made this perhaps the best value in central Girne. $$

🏠 **Pia Bella Hotel** (66 rooms) ☎ 815 53 21/2/3; f 815 53 24; e piabella@kktc.net; www.piabella.com. This hotel is perfectly set for exploring the town. Just a short walk from the harbourfront, it offers comfortable rooms with AC, 2 swimming pools, restaurant set amongst an attractive garden, pool tables, a large lounge & 2 bars. British holidaymakers, many who've been coming for years, seem in the majority. Friendly & knowledgeable staff. Free internet for guests. Currently building a large extension on the adjoining plot, so ask for a room away from the construction & the main road. $$

✗ WHERE TO EAT AND DRINK

SEAFRONT The seafront restaurants and bars are more expensive than others in town, but it is worth paying the extra. The harbour is a wonderful place to eat in the evening, the castle and boats light up and the atmosphere oozes calm and relaxation. In general, restaurants along the harbour have a fairly relaxed approach to opening – a late night will inevitably lead to a late opening. If in doubt, phone first.

✕ **Always Traditional** ↘ 815 66 61. On the harbourfront with tables by the water & inside. Couples with a head for heights, looking for quiet romantic balcony dining & a memorable overview of the harbour will find what they're after high up in the main building. £9

✕ **Café 34** ↘ 815 43 94. One of the most popular of the cafés along the harbourfront, tucked away in a corner but hugely popular in summer. £9

✕ **Café Chimera** ↘ 815 43 94. Nestling on the edge of the harbour closest to the castle you could sit here & watch the world go by all day long, relaxing on the terrace with a cocktail. The menu is extensive, French & Turkish dishes in the main, & if you can't decide, go for the *meze* feast – you certainly won't go hungry. Live music some nights. £8

⊡ **Café Harbour** ↘ 815 89 00. Serves more in the way of snacks & drinks, but is a comfortable place to sit & relax with an evening drink. There is often live music playing here. £5

✕ **Canli Balik** ↘ 815 11 23. Generally regarded as one of the better restaurants for fish along the harbourfront, & not as ridiculously overpriced as some along here. £10

✕ **Corner Restaurant** ↘ 815 3357. Next door to the Harbour Club, almost at the end of the frontage, towards the castle. Varied menus feature fresh fish & a good selection of Turkish dishes. £10

✕ **Carob** ↘ 815 62 77. The staff at Carob Restaurant will proudly tell you about the building, originally a carob warehouse, showing you around its beautiful interior & up the spiral stairs where you can eat up on the roof or on one of the balconies. A landmark of the harbour scene offering varied menus of both Turkish & continental cuisine. However, don't expect to occupy one of the upper floor tables just for a drink –

the waiters won't climb the stairs for anything less than a full meal. £8

✕ **Green House** ↘ 815 29 90. Ignore the naff green plastic chairs & grab a table at this large Mexican & Italian restaurant, with indoor seating next to Niazis & an *al fresco* area overlooking the sea opposite. A popular hangout with the young & noisy of Kyrenia, the portions are huge & the fajitas divine. £6

✕ **Harbour Club** ↘ 815 22 11. A popular place in the evenings for a more expensive meal. It has 2 sections, with 'upstairs' offering a large menu of French-style dishes (inc pork) & 'downstairs' a more traditional Turkish menu, with a good selection of mezes. £8

✕ **Harbour Pizza** ↘ 815 13 07. Another of the Harbour Group establishments, serving a standard range of pizzas & pastas, burgers & salads. In truth, it's hard to distinguish this place from any of the others at the east side of the harbour, whether in terms of service, quality or ambience. £5

✕ **Niazis** ↘ 815 21 60. Opposite the Dome Hotel. No harbour view but an excellent restaurant with great service. Deservedly a long-time favourite with everybody, from tourists to locals to Judith Chalmers (though don't let this put you off!). Specialises in the full kebab, prepared in front of you on an open BBQ. Once you've ordered, choice morsels just keep coming. – outstanding! £9

✕ **Set Fish** ↘ 815 23 36. On the harbour & unsurprisingly excels in a good value set fresh fish menu. Associated with the very good Set Italian Restaurant. £10

✕ **Six Brothers Restaurant** m 0533 832 13 18. Just outside the harbour. A handy place for a cup of çay (tea) & a snack. If you're so inclined, the adjoining Six Brothers Barber Shop will do a haircut & cut-throat razor shave for £6. A combined 'eat & shave' rate is sure to be available! £5

INLAND There are fewer big restaurants and bars behind the harbour but, by wandering around the cobbled streets, you are sure to come across smaller, friendly cafés with tables spilling out onto the street. A few of the better options are listed below.

✕ **Beyti** ↘ 815 25 73; ⊕ 24hrs. On Cengiz Hanlı Sokak (the 'street of the ironmongers' – turn left heading down Hürriyet Caddesi just after HSBC). This

busy little eating-place offers simple local fare of kebab & fish dishes with friendly service, low prices & generous helpings. £5

✕ **The Brasserie** ☎ 815 94 81. Situated behind the harbour on the cobbled steps just below Belediye Meydani & just above Djafer Pasha Mosque. Run by chef Guido Spina, this award-winning restaurant is one of the best in North Cyprus. During the day it may look rather sleepy but once night falls its Venetian-style façade is fashionably awakened by atmospheric lighting. Fine Italian à-la-carte meals, bar snacks & drinks. £10

✕ **Cactus Bar** m 0533 845 0955. Located just behind the harbour & popular both with expats & visitors alike. There's a cosy bar inside & a small courtyard at the back for summer evenings. Friendly service & simply prepared but excellent salads, sandwiches, quiches, pastas & curries – or maybe a cheese & pickle sandwich for a taste of home. Cat lovers take note – there's also a large adopted menagerie of friendly felines to be found here. Now also offering Sea Cactus boat tours in the harbour. £6

✕ **Café Dükkan** ☎ 815 58 85. Superb choice of salads, pastries & other lighter meals, this has become a firm favourite with locals since it opened, belying its incongruous location on the side of the main bypass to Karaoğlanoğlu. Live entertainment Sat evening. £7

☕ **Coffee World** ☎ 815 54 03. Being members of the 'Speciality Coffee Association of Europe', it's no surprise to find a comprehensive range of coffees in this little café off the main street, together with teas, beers, wines, spirits, snacks & cakes. Pull up a chair & join the British tourists whilst breathing in the aroma of freshly ground beans. £5

✕ **East Meets West** ☎ 815 82 66; ⌚ Tue–Sun. A simple idea – curries for those that like Eastern food & a range of Western dishes for those that don't. When we visited, the Western chef was out of commission but the chicken balti & dopiaza come highly recommended, cooked as they are to your own fiery preference. Recommended. £8

✕ **Esatto** ☎ 815 44 68. Popular with the younger clientele in Girne; you'll get a range of pizzas, pasta & chicken dishes served in a stylish outdoor-meets-indoor tent structure. With friendly service & one of the most relaxed atmospheres around, it's easy to while away a couple of hours here with a coffee or fresh orange juice at any time of day. £8

✕ **Ezic Chicken Bar** ☎ 815 26 17. Better than it sounds. On the main road to Karaoğlanoğlu, fast-food-style restaurant with an emphasis on chicken dishes. Always busy & a good option for families or for those passing through who don't want to head into town. £8

✕ **Ferman** ☎ 815 30 79. Only opened in 2004 but sharing the antiquated atmosphere of the adjoining Nostalgia Hotel. Ferman offers an eclectic assortment of Turkish, Indian, Italian & French dishes all served with a smile either in the cool dining room or the courtyard around the pool. £8

✕ **Gazan** ☎ 815 30 79. Also owned by the Nostalgia Hotel. Hidden in a small courtyard close to Djafer Pasha Mosque. Mostly Turkish dishes. £8

✕ **The Grapevine** ☎ 815 24 96. Long established, & despite an inauspicious location opposite a petrol station just off Ecevit Caddesi, the Grapevine is renowned for its duck dishes, though these have in the past received decidedly mixed reports. What is agreed, however, is that its T-bone steaks are amongst the finest in town. £9

✕ **Luciano's** ☎ 815 32 59; ⌚ Tue–Sun. English-run, cosy, intimate & friendly Italian restaurant just behind the Icon Museum, serving hearty, flavourful dishes. Delightful. £7

✕ **Set Italian Restaurant** ☎ 815 60 08. Beside the old mosque, situated in an exquisite Italianate split-level courtyard. Service is attentive & the pizzas are good. Has recently opened a swish fish restaurant on the harbour, Set Fish. £9

✕ **Shiraz Café** ☎ 816 05 11. Lacking the attractive location of other establishments but still a fine place to sit & watch the world go by over a decent-value kebab, pasta, soup or sandwich. £5

☕ **Simit Dünyasi** ☎ 815 09 07; ⌚ 05.30–24.00 daily. Part of a chain, café-cum-bakery with tasty pastries, breads & drinks. The shady roof terrace is a great place for a quick snack whilst you take in the view out to sea over the Atatürk statue, & it's got some of the longest opening hours in town.

NIGHTLIFE

While Girne's nightlife is not exactly buzzing, it's a great deal better than the rest of the island's. The premier club, **Night Park**, with its smart-casual dress code, sits by the entrance to the car park/bus station near the Belediye, and is probably the most highly recommended club in town.

Alternatively, there are plenty of bars where you can drink the night away, some right through until dawn if that's what you want. **C'est la Vie**, practically underneath Djafer Pasha Mosque, hosts some eclectic nights and regularly stays open to 06.00 and beyond. **Busters**, to the west of the Belediye, is a no-nonsense, unpretentious little bar that caters to the hordes of English tourists who arrive in summer, with quiz nights on Wednesdays, and karaoke and crib nights too. They also show Premiership football action.

There are two cinemas in Girne.

SHOPPING

Shops open at 08.00 or 09.00, often close for an hour from 13.00 to 14.00, and the majority then close at 17.30 or 18.00 in the winter. In the summer they close from 13.00 to 16.00, then reopen until 19.30 or 20.00. Distances are short, so a walk round the shops can be easily fitted in whenever you have the odd half-hour to spare. Of course, as with any other opening times in North Cyprus there's a great fluidity to how rigidly they are observed.

PLACES OF WORSHIP

Anglican services are held at the tiny **St Andrew's Church**, near Café Net by the southwest tower of the castle. A favourite with expats, there's Holy Communion at 08.00 on Sundays, followed by Family Communion and Sunday school at 10.00. The midweek service sees Holy Communion at 09.30 on a Thursday. The inside of the church is beautifully maintained and can make a cool, shady retreat from the midday sun. **Terra Santa**, the Roman Catholic church opposite the Dome Hotel, holds mass on the first Sunday of each month.

WHAT TO SEE AND DO

A WALK AROUND THE TOWN A stroll around Girne town offers a relaxing break from the beach or sightseeing. The pretty streets have a surprising range of shops, and souvenir hunting among them is a pleasure. Here and there you will come unexpectedly upon an old mosque or church or ancient tower, a relic of the town walls.

Medieval Girne was a walled town, and today the narrow wiggling streets and alleys behind the harbour still retain a slightly medieval feel, the houses huddled on top of each other. The variety fascinates: one moment you walk past a workshop where wood is crafted into furniture, the next you catch a glimpse into a private arcaded courtyard with tumbling jasmine and bougainvillea. The town walls themselves have been gradually dismantled and incorporated into other buildings, but you will still come across some of the towers, tucked a little incongruously beside a butcher's shop or a supermarket. The most obvious old tower is the one in the western corner of the harbour. The position of the others is shown on the map. The one beside the Municipal Market has now been converted to a crafts centre, the **Round Tower Gallery**, for the sale of traditional goods by locals and expats alike. It's a good place to shop for a souvenir or get hold of some local information, but it is probably most interesting for the chance it offers to see inside one of the best-preserved and most beautifully proportioned towers in Girne (✆ *815 63 77*).

Close behind the harbour you will find Girne's oldest mosque, the tiny **Djafer Pasha Mosque**, frequented by a handful of faithful worshippers. Turkish Cypriots are not known for their religious fervour, and a fairly relaxed view of Islam is taken on the island. The mosque was built by and named after a Turkish general shortly after the Ottoman takeover in 1570, and is a pleasant if unexciting example of early

Ottoman architecture. Beside the mosque, an ancient spring was converted to an area for the ritual ablutions before prayers and though the plumbing is still in evidence, hand and foot washing now takes place elsewhere.

Flights of steps connect the streets and in the area behind the mosque you will come across some very splendid old buildings, once private residences for the governor and wealthy citizens, now converted into bars and restaurants, like The Brasserie and Set Italian (see page 47).

Heading down towards the harbour from opposite Set Italian, as you continue along the narrow lane past the back of the Folk Museum (see page 50) you'll see, on your left, the dilapidated remains of Girne's oldest church, the **Chrysopolitissa**. Dating from around 1500, the whole edifice is now locked up, closed off and has been left to slip noiselessly into ruin. Indeed, why you can tell it was ever a building of some importance is the curious walled-up Gothic arch on its northern exterior – once, presumably, the church's main entrance.

The prominent bell tower of the Greek Orthodox church, **Archangel Michael**, forms a landmark from many parts of town, set up as it is on a rocky outcrop. It was built in 1860, with the Turks' blessing, and the bell was even donated by a Turkish resident. The church was locked from 1974, until it reopened in 1991 as an **icon museum** (*irregular hours, but supposedly* ⊕ *winter 09.00–13.00, 14.00–16.45 Mon–Fri, summer 09.00–14.00 Mon–Fri; £1.20/0.80 adults/students*) to display some of the icons from the churches of the Girne area, hitherto stored in the castle.

Opposite the street from the Greek Orthodox church you can see **Byzantine catacombs** cut into the brown limestone cliffs, with the attractive Perge Restaurant squatting on top of them. In the area between the Dome Hotel and the main shopping street inland, there are large numbers of these tombs, some 70 in all, the majority of them now covered by shops and modern buildings.

GIRNE HARBOUR The harbour must be one of the most picturesque in the Mediterranean. Besides providing a fine setting for a range of eating places, al fresco or indoors according to season, it also incorporates a number of curious relics of its ancient harbour within its modern one. The harbour is beautiful at all times of day, but is at its most bewitching at night. Many of the restaurants are open for food all day long.

The graceful horseshoe curve of Girne's harbour is an even more tranquil spot since it was closed to traffic by a barrier at the west end (except for a few hours in the morning to allow deliveries). A fair proportion of the buildings enclosing the harbour are Venetian, tastefully restored to shops and restaurants on their ground levels, with apartments or the owner's accommodation above. The **tourist office** is itself such a restored house, with a cavernous stone vaulted interior.

Above head height to the right of the Corner Restaurant as you face it, you can see large stones jutting out with holes in their centres. In the ancient harbour, ropes were threaded through these holes for hauling boats up onto the beach.

Sticking out of the water amongst the moored fishing boats and yachts, stands a semi-collapsed squat stone tower, approached by a crumbling causeway. On top of the tower is a smaller tower the size of a Roman column. This was the old chain tower, from which an iron chain was suspended across the harbour entrance to block hostile shipping. The chain, though huge, was but a tiny version of that used in Istanbul to control shipping in the Bosphorus. In the old wall that rises up behind the Café Chimera, careful observation will reveal the outline of a large Gothic archway, now blocked up. Before 1400, when the moat was still full, ships used to be dragged through this archway from the harbour into the castle moat for safety or simply for repair.

Walking towards the middle of the harbour, you come to the entrance of the **Folk Museum**, set in a typical 18th-century house just next to Set Fish Restaurant and overlooking the harbour to the front. It's reputed to be open weekdays 09.00–13.00 and 14.00–16.45 (closed weekends), although on several visits in the 2007 high season and 2008 early season I found it to be consistently closed. Entrance is free with a ticket from Girne Castle, otherwise it costs £1.20/0.80 adults/students. The house need only detain you for 15 minutes and is of interest less for its display of domestic equipment and costumes than for the chance to see inside one of the old city's three-storey buildings.

Strolling out along the harbour wall affords you the best view back to the **castle** and the difference in architectural styles is clearly visible. To the left (east) you have a good view for the first time of the taller Crusader tower, which is difficult to see from inside the castle or from the harbourfront. Its high squared medieval crenellations and arrow slits were built with quite a different style of warfare in mind – catapults and archery – from the later more advanced tower of the Venetians, round and squat, with no arrow slits but just a solitary gun port at sea level and others on top for the newly invented cannon. From the very end of the harbour wall you can also view the eastern wall of the castle.

Walking away from the horseshoe harbour towards the Dome Hotel, you will notice a solitary granite Roman column beside the children's playground on the seafront promenade. It is something of a mystery, for though there are several Roman stone fragments to be found incorporated into churches or other buildings in Girne, this is the only granite one. There is no indigenous granite in Cyprus, and this is one of the only pieces of granite found in the whole region.

BOAT TRIPS All along the harbourfront, you will find a whole host of boat owners offering day trips around the coastline, stopping at local bays for swimming and other water activities. Lunch and snacks are provided on board; most trips require advance booking and leave the harbour at 10.00, returning around 17.30. Costs at present are constant along the harbour at £20 per adult, with children at a reduced price. Some also offer sunset cruises with dinner included. **Sail Cyprus** (m *0533 876 3666;* e *info@sailcyprus; www.sailcyprus.com*) runs one of the larger gulets and offers a unique sunset 'curry' cruise.

INLAND GIRNE The outskirts of Girne will be familiar to most visitors simply as an area to pass through *en route* to somewhere else. There are few sights to detain the average tourist, but the increasing urbanisation provides a few more eating options and the photographic shops along the main Karaoğlanoğlu road (Bedreddin Demirel Caddesi) are the best bet for anyone wanting to develop a film or pick up a spare memory card.

From the roundabout on the edge of town, where the road heads over the mountains towards Lefkoşa, you can stroll in a westerly direction towards Karaoğlanoğlu. Immediately on the left is the old **British cemetery**, sandwiched as it is between new commercial properties, and now somewhat overgrown. Easily missed from the road, the graveyard is of little interest to anyone other than relatives and friends of those who are commemorated there. Continuing in the same direction, the recent retail outlets to both sides indicate the upturn in the economy of North Cyprus. You can pick up most things along here, from household appliances to ultra-stylish furniture. Should you fancy a house to go with them, you'll be spoilt for choice amongst all the estate agents who have made this road their home.

Girne's long-standing **Green Jacket Bookshop** is situated further still along Bedreddin Demirel Caddesi, shortly before the Jasmine Court Hotel. At this point, you can choose to cut back towards the sea by following the signs for the **Fine Arts Museum** on Paşa Bahçe Caddesi (☉ *winter 09.00–13.00 & 14.00–16.45 daily; summer 09.00–19.00; £1.20/0.80 adult/student*). The term 'fine' is employed loosely here. Many of the paintings are copies of unknown works, whilst elsewhere a motley collection of porcelain, glassware and silks is displayed in several dusty rooms, with no explanatory notes. When we visited, the curator had to cease watching television in order to unlock the doors and switch on the lights, so don't expect a queue to get in. The building itself is interesting from an architectural point of view, but the museum would best serve to fill half an hour on a rainy afternoon.

Leaving the gate of the Fine Arts Museum, to the left you will have a clear view of the sea. It appears that this is an excellent short cut back to the harbour, but don't be tempted to walk this way. The road leads only to the military base, and although it seems that locals come and go through the barriers at will, any tourist attempting so to do will very quickly be intercepted by rifle-toting soldiers. The best way back to the harbour is to head across to Atatürk Caddesi and then bear north. In doing so, those who are self-catering should take the opportunity to visit **Karkot Organic Food Store**, just opposite the primary school on İnönü Caddesi. A recent addition to Girne's range of epicurean options, Karkot stocks a delicious range of dried fruits, cereals, nuts, rice and wine, together with natural handmade soaps and cosmetics. If you keep your eyes peeled you might also see some of these products on sale in the large supermarkets.

GIRNE KALESI (KYRENIA CASTLE) As you approach the castle from the harbour, the sheer power of the walls impresses. The huge round tower that confronts you is the work of the Venetians. Such fortifications were their major legacy to Cyprus, for they always regarded it as a military outpost to protect and service their lust for trade.

Housed within the castle walls is the Girne Department of Antiquities, which took over custodianship of the castle in 1959. In some of the castle's locked rooms the Antiquities Department is keeping icons which were collected from churches in the Girne area pre-1974 and stored here for safe keeping. Some of these are now on display in the Archangel Michael Church.

Under British rule, the castle was also used as a police barracks and training school, and as a prison for members of EOKA, the Greek Cypriot resistance movement or the Nationalist Organisation of Cypriot Fighters (Ethniki Organosis Kyprion Agoniston). EOKA had begun in 1954, and from secret headquarters somewhere in the Troodos Mountains they organised a series of terrorist and sabotage attacks against British administration, to further their aim of union with Greece, or Enosis as this union was known. Pro-Enosis propaganda was concentrated in schools, where it was easy to sway feelings. Schoolteachers were mainly Greek-trained and full of Greek ideology. Although Enosis did not begin as an anti-British sentiment, it gradually became so, to the extent that anyone suspected of collaboration with the British was murdered. The Greek Orthodox Church, encouraged by Archbishop Makarios, retained a strong role in the conflict, refusing to give the sacrament to those who assisted the British police or who betrayed information on EOKA fighters. In the view of impartial observers, the majority of the population were intimidated and uncertain, simply wanting the end of military rule and the return of the old peaceful lifestyle. The Turkish Cypriots felt threatened by the prospect of union with Greece, and the seeds were sown for the inevitable intercommunal fighting. 'Greece and Turkey,' as AE Yalman, editor of the Turkish newspaper Vatan, wrote in 1960, 'have a common destiny. They are condemned either to be to be good neighbours, close friends, faithful allies or to commit suicide together.'

Touring the castle The ticket office sits at the head of the **drawbridge**, and can be reached either by steps from the harbour, or from inland, via the little police station with its navy blue Land Rovers (☺ *summer 09.00–19.00; winter 09.00–16.45*). You need to arrive at least an hour before closing to be allowed into the castle. The moat you cross to reach the main gateway was full of water until 1400, and provided an inner protected harbour at times of war. The entrance fee of £4.80 adults includes entry both to the Shipwreck Museum housed inside the castle and the Folk Museum on the harbour.

Once inside, the scale surprises, as you pass up a wide, almost ceremonial ramp, built by the Venetians to facilitate rolling the cannon up into place on the walls. An exit left leads off to a small Byzantine chapel (see page 6). Above the inner gateway, carved into the stone, is the **coat of arms** of the Crusader Lusignans, the Frankish baronial family who ruled Cyprus for 300 years in the Middle Ages, and who remodelled much of the original Byzantine fort when they took it over in 1191. This coat of arms is the best-preserved example on the island: it consists of three lions prancing on their hind legs, in contrast to the solitary Venetian winged lion to be found on the later walls and towers of Gazimağusa. Next to it, to the right, is a small room that provides a quick rundown of the history of the castle, including some interesting watercolours depicting how the harbour and town would have looked through the ages.

Just beyond the inner gateway stands the tomb of **Sadık Pasha**, the Turkish Ottoman admiral to whom the Venetians surrendered in 1570, and who died later the same year.

The path leads on into a dauntingly large open **courtyard** with a somewhat neglected garden at one end. Littering the ground are some Byzantine capitals and stones, many the size and shape of over-inflated beachballs, used in colossal catapult-like medieval weapons. Concerts are occasionally held in this courtyard, which is sheltered from the wind. In 1961 Sir John Barbirolli performed here with the Hallé Orchestra. Today's performances are usually somewhat more modest. There's also a small souvenir shop and simple café at the northern end of the courtyard.

A whole maze of steps, internal and external, interlink the Byzantine, Crusader and Venetian towers and ramparts of the castle. To the right of the entrance, dark foul-smelling steps set into the walls lead down into the dungeons, rarely empty in the complex series of plots and intrigues that make up the castle's past. The place was never taken by force throughout its history, though it was subjected to several lengthy sieges. The longest, in the 15th century, lasted nearly four years, and the unfortunate castle occupants were reduced to eating mice and rats. Today, rather too anatomically realistic models inhabit the place.

If you enjoy heights and a certain amount of scrambling, it is possible to walk a complete circuit of the ramparts, thereby gaining the full panorama. The most photogenic stretch is definitely the northwestern tower and the western wall, with stunning views down into the harbour. Peeping out from the thickness of the wall by the northwest tower is the little **Byzantine chapel**, still with its four ancient marble columns, thought to have been taken from the old Roman town that now lies buried under modern Girne. When built, in the 12th century, the chapel stood outside the castle walls, but the Venetians gave it an extra entrance and enclosed it in the 16th century within the tower. Hence its curious position today.

Walking along the western wall inland towards the **southwest tower** you will get fine views over the rooftops of Girne and the mountain pinnacles beyond. The tower itself is a remarkably advanced example of military design, built, like Gazimağusa's Martinengo Bastion, with three different heights of embrasure to allow three staggered levels of gunfire across the moat. These impressive Venetian fortifications are still in excellent condition, for they were never put to the test. In 1570, at the first confrontation since being completed around 1500, the Venetians at Girne surrendered to the Turks without a single shot being fired. They had heard of the bloody fall of Lefkoşa, and their surrender spared them the devastating siege that Gazimağusa endured. Had they not surrendered, we would doubtless not be looking at such a well-preserved monument today. The rusting gun emplacements along the ramparts are the relics of the castle's modern role in the intercommunal fighting of this century.

Alongside this western wall are the roofless yet elegant remains of the Gothic-style **royal apartments** of the castle, where the French Lusignan family resided at times of unrest or during their battles with the Genoese, their maritime rivals.

From the far **southeast tower** you can look down onto the rocky town beach tucked underneath the castle walls, with its own pretty café terrace. Pre-1974 this swimming spot was known as **The Slab**, and you had to be a member of the Country Club to use it. The Country Club is the building set up amid the greenery by itself above the bay, now called the **Halk Evi** or People's House. In the area in front of the Halk Evi and west towards the Anglican church, is the **old Turkish cemetery**. Excavations carried out here a few years ago revealed the elusive Roman town of Corineum, whose relics in the form of reused columns and capitals are visible here and there throughout the modern town.

Back down in the courtyard, rusting yellow signs point the way to various displays, from the dungeons to the right of the entrance, to the display of armour and weapons in the Lusignan tower (including some early prototype machine guns, one with the shot still stuck in one of the barrels). Next door to this tower is a room displaying the finds from various archaeological sites such as the Akdeniz village tomb (see page 74), the Neolithic settlement at Vrysi, and the Kirni Bronze Age tomb. The jewellery and glassware from Akdeniz in particular are exquisite.

The Shipwreck Museum Built into a couple of the great halls along the eastern wall of the castle is the much-praised Shipwreck Museum, where a 2,300-year-old Greek trading vessel is on display, together with its complete cargo. It is the oldest ship yet recovered from the seabed anywhere.

The ship was first discovered in 1965 by a Girne sponge diver some 2km off the coast from the castle. Over the course of 1968 and 1969 a team of 50 underwater archaeologists from the University of Pennsylvania Museum raised the vessel systematically from the seabed and it then took a further six years to reconstruct. Its cargo consisted of some 400 wine amphorae from Rhodes, 29 stone grain-mills, lead weights and a staggering 9,000 almonds as food for the crew. It was these that enabled the carbon-dating of the ship. The reconstructed vessel is now in a separate temperature-controlled room. The Aleppo pine timbers had to be soaked in a preservative bath, then dried, and the hull was sheathed in lead. No skeletons were found, so the crew are thought to have swum to safety when the ship sank.

The museum is well laid out and is enhanced by the setting inside the lovely Gothic halls which form the main surviving domestic rooms of the castle. The museum was opened after the division of the island in March 1976, though most of the work was in fact completed pre-1974.

SOUTH FROM GIRNE

Two sites south of Girne town make excellent excursions. Bellapais Abbey is an enchanting place, with its mountain location, Gothic archways and sense of calm. St Hilarion Castle is well worth the climb; it is the best preserved of the three mountain-top Crusader castles of North Cyprus and also the most romantic.

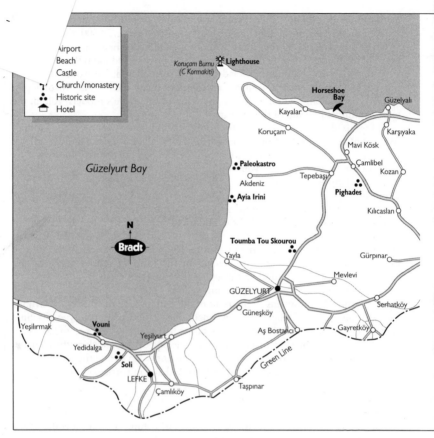

WHERE TO STAY

Bella View (21 rooms) ☎ 816 11 55; f 816 11 99; e info@bellaview.net; www.bellaview.net. A new property on the way up to Bellapais Abbey from Girne. Bills itself as 'The only registered boutique hotel of northern Cyprus' & certainly it exudes quality, both in its rooms & its relaxed professional service. Fine dining á-la-carte restaurant featuring both Turkish & European cuisine, bar & swimming pool. Children under 15 are not encouraged, so worth considering if you're looking for an upmarket child-free base outside Girne. $$$$

Bellapais Gardens (18 bungalows) ☎ 815 60 66; f 815 76 67; e bgarden@superonline.com; www.bellapaisgardens.com. Hanging on to the hillside below the abbey, set amidst orange & lemon groves, & with views down to the coast. Comprehensive facilities including AC, satellite TV, minibar, kitchen facilities & private balcony or terrace. Spring-fed swimming pool & splendid clifftop lounge, & a log

fire affords a welcoming glow in the cooler months. Private parking but the hilly location could cause difficulties for the elderly or infirm. $$$

Abbey Inn at Bellapais (10 rooms) ☎ 815 94 44; f 815 94 46; e abbeyinn@kktc.net. This small hotel is not easy to find, hiding as it does behind an archway down the little narrow cobbled street by the side of the abbey. Nevertheless, it's a lovely little place, with great food (the owner is a gourmet chef) & pretty rooms, all furnished with antiques, & each with a balcony overlooking the freshwater swimming pool. Not suitable for children under 16. $$$

Bellapais Monastery Village (63 rooms) ☎ 815 91 71; f 815 90 58; e info@ bellapaismonasteryvillage.com; www.bellapaismonasteryvillage.com. On the road up to Bellapais, more akin to a resort than any other hotel in the area, with 2 pools, jacuzzi, sauna, steam room, massage, 2 restaurants, bars & entertainment all on offer. All rooms have AC, satellite TV, minibar

AKDENİZ
(MEDITERRANEAN SEA)

Kantara,
Karpas Peninsula,
(see page 132)

Denizkızı
Beach
Celebrity
Escape
Peace and Freedom
Museum
Karaoğlanoğlu
Mecure Hotel
Riviera
Club Acapulco
Kharcha
Denizkızı
Royal
LAPTA Alsancak Yeşiltepe
Karakum
Acapulco
Lara
Alagadi
Esentepe
Hideaway Club
Ship Inn GiRNE
Hazreti Ömer
Tekke (shrine)
Vrysi
Karaağaç
Antiphonitis
İncesu Edremit
▲ Selvili Tepe
1024m
Karaman
St Hilarion
Çatalköy
Beşparmak
Akçiçek
Boğazköy
Komando Tepe
▲936m
Çatalköy
Riding Club
Sourp Magar
Körmürcü
Bellapais
Bellapais
Abbey
Buffavento
Şirinevler
Dağyolu
Aş Dikmen
Güngör
Değirmenlik
Yılmazköy
Türkeli
Panayia
Absinthiotissa
Kanlıköy Gönyeli
Hamitköy
Alayköy
LEFKOŞA
Gazıköy
Green Line
Ercan
Paşaköy

0   10km
0   10 miles

& safe. Courtesy shuttle bus to Girne, but it's a long walk up to Bellapais village. $$$

The Gardens of Irini (2 cottages) ☏ 815 2820; e deirdremairi@yahoo.com; www.gardensofirini.com. Up the hill, close to Laurence Durrell's former residence, artist & long-time resident Deirdre Guthrie rents a cottage & converted studio both suitable for couples. This bargain bohemian hideaway is well suited to those in search of a tranquil redoubt away from the hubbub of Girne. Minimum 7-night stay; £245 per week for either cottage.

✕ **WHERE TO EAT** Bellapais village in the hills above Girne boasts several good restaurants; a couple of the more well known are:

✕ **Bella Moon** ☏ 815 43 11; m 0542 851 68 98. Excellent family-run restaurant with peaceful courtyard setting & panoramic roof terrace overlooking the abbey. Friendly & attentive service & a hearty selection of *meze* & traditional Cypriot dishes, cooked in an open kitchen next to the dining terrace. *Kleftiko* special on Fri nights. Free taxi service from Girne. £8

✕ **Kybele** ☏ 815 7531; f 815 75 32; e kybele@kybele.biz; www.kybele.biz. Here the ambience is the best thing on the menu. The restaurant is the only one within the abbey grounds & its array of outdoor tables, one balcony table above all, offer breathtaking views towards Girne & the coast. Particularly beautiful in the evening when atmospheric lighting of the abbey ruins adds to an already unique setting. £8

✕ **Tree of Idleness** (Huzur Ağaç) ☏ 815 33 80; e treeofidleness@hotmail.com. Situated in front of the abbey & serving local & international cuisine. The balcony tables are cool & comfortable & offer relief from summertime heat. Beware of lingering too long

under the Tree of Idleness, one of 2 that claim to
be Durrell's original shady spot; a restful contentment

may just give way to lethargy. Live music & dancing
Sat. Free taxi service from Girne. £8

ST HILARION CASTLE (⊕ *09.00–18.00 daily; £2.80/1.00 adults/students*) This castle
and royal summer palace makes an exciting and mildly strenuous half-day trip
from Girne. '*Dieu d'Amour*' was the name the Frankish knights bestowed upon it,
and certainly from afar its extravagantly crenellated walls and towers tumbling over
the craggy hilltop evoke a fairy-tale vision of bygone chivalry. From within, the
paths and steps wind up through the three castle sections, one superimposed on
the other, and culminating in the royal apartments ingeniously sheltered in their
own natural courtyard of rock. Rose Macaulay, author of *The Towers of Trebizond*,
described it as 'a picture book castle for elf kings', and Walt Disney is said to have
used it as inspiration for the palace in *Snow White and the Seven Dwarfs*.

The path to the uppermost section of the castle is steep and slippery when wet,
and not suitable for anyone with wobbly legs or balance. One Canadian tourist
slipped and fell to his death here in recent years. Choose appropriate footwear.

A drive of 15 minutes from Girne brings you to the car park at the foot of St
Hilarion; from here the walk up to the summit takes a good 20 minutes. Allow at
least two hours to explore all the different levels of the castle. There's no
restaurant, though simple refreshments (coffee, tea, soft drinks and sweets) are on
sale both outside by the entrance and, during the summer, inside the castle at the
Great Hall. The energetic could carry a picnic to the 732m summit.

On the drive back down the mountain, don't panic if the army patrol stops you
next to the monument just near the military base. Far from being suspicious of
what you're doing, it's much more likely that they'll simply ask you to wait whilst
a tour bus winds its way up the road below.

A word of warning though. Even if you feel sufficiently energised to trek up to
the summit, don't be tempted to walk from the main road. One couple who did
were afforded a very frosty reception when they reached the army barracks at the
halfway point, subjected to a severe interrogation and forced to car-share with the
next passing tourists. Stick to the car, or coach, and don't stop under any
circumstances.

Touring St Hilarion Castle From Girne you take the main road out towards
Lefkoşa, and as you leave the town behind, you can already pick out the distinctive
shape of the Hilarion peak above you a little to the right. It was Durrell who first
used the word 'Gothic' to describe the Kyrenia range, and their sharp pinnacles do
lend them a fine Gothic silhouette. The Troodos on the other hand, rounder and
more rolling, are more naturally allied to the domes of Byzantine inspiration.

The much improved road network of the north is now such that a drive of just
ten minutes brings you to the turn-off for St Hilarion, marked by a yellow sign to
the right, shortly before the summit of the Lefkoşa pass.

From here, after appearing to double back on itself, the narrow tarmac road
winds for 2–3km and you will catch glimpses above of a soldier perched on a lofty
crag, gun poised. He reveals himself on closer inspection to be made of metal. On
the drive up, your eye may also have been caught by a prominent white building
alone on its crag among the thickly forested hills towards Bellapais – not a
magnificent private villa, but a military headquarters. The military is never far away
in North Cyprus, and it is as well to accustom yourself to the idea and regard it as
an interesting extra dimension to the island's sights. Don't be tempted to park in
the car park you come to; this is for the military base opposite. Instead, continue
on the winding road. Cresting a hill, the road swoops down and on the left is a
large flat terrace, now the army's rifle range – appropriately enough, for it was here

top Alagadi Beach is a favourite spot for nesting turtles (JC) page 80

above left and right Young loggerhead turtles (*Caretta caretta*) make their way to the sea (ZY) page 14

below Karşiyaka near Girne (ZY) page 57

top	The beauty of 14th-century Bellapais Abbey is legendary (NR) page 60
above left	The intricate geometric designs of the mosaic floor at Ayia Trias are striking (ZY) page 138
above right	Venetian lion in a white marble gabled plaque, Othello's Tower, Gazimağusa (NR) page 113
below	Buffavento Castle has the most dramatic setting of any ruin on the island (ZY) page 81

above   The theatre at Salamis still hosts crowds for regular music and theatre performances (NW) page 124

below left   Kantara Castle offers splendid views to the sea (HT) page 89

below right   The Queen's Window at St Hilarion Castle (NR) page 58

top left   Basket shop, Edremit (SJ) page 30

above   Making chairs, Lefkoşa (NW) page 30

left   Nuts and pulses, Bandabulya market, Lefkoşa (NW)

below   On the Karpas Peninsula, local traditions such as bread baking are being preserved (ZY) page 38

above left   School children in Lefkoşa (JC)

above right   Lefkara lacework is a traditional craft (JC) page 30

right   Beware the evil eye! These talismans are used for protection and safety (NW) page 32

below   Harvest time in the orange groves near Güzelyurt (JC) page 28

above	Starred agama lizard *Agama stelio* (RC) page 14
left	European Chameleon (*Chamaeleo chamaeleon*) in a plant pot (JC) page 14
below	Cypriot donkeys roam freely in the Karpas Peninsula (ZY) page 15

above	Escaping the afternoon sun beneath a jacaranda tree (RC)
right	Wild flowers abound in the Cypriot countryside, Karaman (JC) page 78
below left	Star clover (*Trifolium stellatum*) ((RC) page 12
below right	Golden drops *Onosma fruticosa* are endemic to the island (RC) page 12

that the knights held jousts and tournaments, watched by the ladies of the court waving coloured favours from the battlements.

The tarmac road terminates in a small car park where you will find the ticket kiosk. To the west you will notice the road continuing along the ridge of the mountains as it heads off to reach Karşiyaka. There is also a footpath from here down to the pretty village of Karmi (Turkish Karaman). The road of 29km to Karşiyaka has been improved with a new tarmac surface and crash barriers, which infinitely improve the enjoyment of what used to be a painfully slow and bumpy journey. It is now perfectly possible to enjoy the spectacular mountain scenery and abundant wildlife without worrying about falling off the road, something that the driver of an abandoned Turkish tank clearly couldn't manage. The tank ran off the road a few years ago near Karşiyaka, irrecoverably, and is now the subject of much local interest and several postcards. By taking a picnic, a morning visit to the castle could be followed by this drive, thereby turning the outing into a day trip. Halfway along the track is a crossroads forking left for Akçiçek and right for Lapta, but you continue straight on for Karşiyaka. To the right of the road above Karşiyaka you can spot a heavily ruined monastery.

Back at St Hilarion, the first section of the ascent through the castle now begins up well-laid steps and concrete paths. The **main gate** and **outer walls** were built originally by the Byzantines in the 11th century for extra defence, and these lowest parts were for the men-at-arms and the horses. In the many long sieges of medieval times this area and its cisterns were invaluable. The castle had its exposure to modern warfare too, serving in 1964 as a stronghold for Turkish Cypriots. Such were the castle's defences, even in ruin, that a garrison of boys was able to ward off the Greek attack. The Turkish army still used the castle until relatively recently, before moving out to their camp along the ridge.

As the path climbs up it passes one of the **cisterns**, still in use, built up against the wall, and at the first corner where the path bends and forks to the right, you can see the **stables** where the animals were kept. After a few minutes' climb you reach the **main gatehouse**, a huge and powerful arched structure which originally closed with a drawbridge.

Entering the passage, a set of steps leads off to the **church**, quite well preserved and still with traces of **12th-century paintings** on the south (car-park) side of the wall. Some restoration work was done here in 1959. It is larger than you would expect for a castle chapel, and this is because it belonged originally to a 10th-century monastery built here by the Byzantines to honour St Hilarion, a hermit who had fled to Cyprus from the Holy Land to escape persecution. He died here in a nearby cave. An old man, 'unclean in person but very holy', he sought out refuge in the mountain, with its ample water supplies. Cypriot peasantry has long believed in evil spirits, *kalikantzaroi* as they call them, which take weird and wonderful forms and have to be appeased at certain times of year by being thrown freshly baked honey doughnuts. The demons who, by popular account, had until then held possession of this mountain-top, watched the hermit's arrival with dismay and conspired to drive him off with hideous noises. His hearing was such, however, that he merely thanked them for welcoming him with music and settled down to his solitary life, leaving the nonplussed demons to look elsewhere for their doughnuts.

The area all around the church was originally the monastery, and the series of rooms to the north and east of it were the refectory, **cellars** and **kitchen**, and a belvedere. The **refectory**, the largest room in this group by far, was used in Lusignan Crusader times as a banqueting hall, and has now been restored as a modest café selling tea and coffee, soft drinks and homemade honey. The walls are currently home to a display of wildflower photographs, the work of the café's proprietor Mustafa Gürsel. The echoing walls and huge vaulted ceiling and rafters of the hall preserve an atmosphere of bygone days, with its smoke-blackened fireplace at the far end. Doors lead on to its narrow vertiginous balcony with benches and small tables offering a splendid panorama down over Girne and the coast. On a hot day this as an excellent spot to enjoy an ever-present cool breeze, sink one of Mustafa's cool drinks, take a rest and absorb the view. On clear days, especially in winter, the snow-covered Taurus Mountains of mainland Turkey can be seen, some 100km distant. Ongoing renovation work in some rooms has included the fitting of new windows and the provision of electricity, allowing the installation of various static tableaux illustrating life in the castle during its heyday.

Immediately below is another series of rooms, thought to be **barracks** built for the Crusader knights in the 14th century. They are best reached by the stone steps that lead down from the main path just beyond the refectory, and are curious in that their floors follow the contours of the natural bedrock below.

From the refectory in the central, middle section of the castle, you now continue to the uppermost and in many ways the most intriguing part, the **royal apartments** and **watchtowers**. The path zigzags steeply up on uneven rock steps. In the heavy rains and floods of 1968 it was washed away completely, and access to the castle summit was impossible. Just as the path begins, notice below you to the right a huge open cistern designed to collect winter rainfall.

At the top of the path, turn right and you now enter the royal area by passing through a **Crusader archway** guarded by a tower. Heavily overgrown with trees and bushes, this area was the main courtyard, cleverly sheltered by being wedged between the twin peaks of the summit. These peaks gave the mountain its first name of Didymos (Greek for twin), from which the non-Greek-speaking Crusaders arrived at the corruption 'Dieu d'Amour'.

The tumbledown buildings immediately to your right on entering are the **royal kitchens** and **waiting rooms**. In the centre of the courtyard you may stumble across, but hopefully not into (thankfully it's railed off), a stagnant cistern sunk into the rock, and beyond it, at the farthest end, are the royal apartments themselves, closing off the western side of the courtyard.

To reach these you follow the little path straight on through the undergrowth. The staircase which used to lead up to the first-floor gallery on the south side has recently caved in, but that on the northern (sea) side is still safe, if somewhat overgrown. From it you emerge onto what is certainly the most evocative spot in the castle, a partly collapsed but elegant gallery, still retaining two Gothic tracery windows, the further one with charming stone window seats on either side. Popularly known as the **Queen's Window**, it is here that Queen Eleanor, the scheming queen of the Lusignans, is said to have sat. Today the view over to the west is a spectacular one, with the little white picture-book village, still known by its Greek name of Karmi, though more properly Karaman, in the foreground.The village was leased by the Ministry of Tourism to foreigners wishing to restore and live in old-style village houses (see page 78).

Returning to the front part of the courtyard, the sure-footed can now climb the rugged steps and clamber along the ramparts and ruined tower to the southern peak, the highest point at 732m. You'll know when you've arrived as there's a reassuringly congratulatory sign to this effect. The rickety iron railings have been replaced with a chunkier, more robust handrail that makes the ascent an altogether less daunting prospect than used to be the case.

Just outside the courtyard area as you begin the descent, another set of rough steps leads off to your right to ascend the 14th-century **Prince John's Tower**, a powerfully built watchtower on a rocky crag. It was from here that the gullible Prince John of Antioch in 1373 flung his faithful Bulgarian guards to their death, after receiving a fabricated warning about them from Queen Eleanor. All but one were dashed on the rocks below and it was he who survived to tell the tale.

In the structure of the castle, each of the three defensive sections was self-supporting, with its own cisterns and supply depots. All of the three castles in the Kyrenia range – St Hilarion, Buffavento and Kantara – were originally built as defence from Arab raids. From the 7th to the 10th century, the Arabs launched a succession of raids on Cyprus and all along the coast of Turkey. The worst was that conducted in 806 by the Caliph Haroun ar-Rashid of *One Thousand and One Nights* fame, in which the Arabs ravaged much of the island and abducted 16,000 as prisoners, including the archbishop and many other ecclesiastics. The goal of the raids was booty and prisoners, never to conquer and rule. The Arab armies still had many Bedouin in whom the tradition of 'raiding' (Arabic *ghazwa*) was deeply rooted as a way of life. With the fighting for the Arab empire largely over, they had to find an alternative outlet for their energies and these raids were sanctioned by their leaders as a convenient method of keeping the armies fit and trained. The continuing raids had a marked effect on the population distribution, causing people to leave the coast and move inland to the hills.

St Hilarion Castle served as a place of refuge and summer residence for the island's kings for some 400 years after this. It was not only to escape the heat of Nicosia that they came here, but sometimes also to flee great plagues. In the summer of 1349 the Black Death swept the island and the royal entourage beat a hasty retreat from Nicosia to the safe and healthy heights of Hilarion. Estimates of the number of people who died range from a quarter to half the island's population. The castle has, like its sisters Buffavento and Kantara, been a ruin since the 16th century, when the merchants of Venice, whose preoccupations always lay with the sea, methodically dismantled it to deter any troublesome insurrections that might arise in the island's interior and thus distract them from their trading activities.

'Happy is the country that has no history' runs the saying. Cyprus, Gordon Home's 'unhappy shuttlecock', has too much (see *Further information*, page 146). Its geographical location, stepping stone to the East from the Western viewpoint, and to the West from the Eastern viewpoint, has condemned it always to be the victim of predatory powers. Throughout its long past, Cyprus raised revolts against its rulers of the day, but they were nearly always quashed. Only on two occasions before 1960 did Cyprus experience independence. The first was in 367BC under the first king of the island, Evagoras, and the second was in 1184 under Isaac Comnenus.

Independence was, however, not necessarily any better for the Cypriots themselves, and it was in fact under the despotic rule of Isaac Comnenus that they suffered especially. Yet by a twist of fate, the rashness of this despot led to the Crusaders becoming rulers of the island. Cyprus was ruled at that time from Constantinople, by a Byzantine official sent to the island as local governor. Even so, the island continued to be unceremoniously raided, three times in the 12th century, first by Raymond of Chatillon, then by Egyptian bandits, then by Raymond Prince of Antioch.

Isaac Comnenus was the nephew of the Byzantine emperor, and after a family dispute he fled to Cyprus and had himself proclaimed, through force and guile, the ruler of the island. He starved and robbed the wealthy, murdered, and ravished young virgins at whim. His tyrannical seven-year rule was thus chronicled:

> The island groaned beneath this scourge of fate, and he reduced the Cypriots to such a state of despair that all were ready to welcome anything which afforded a means of escape from such tyranny.

His violence and temper met their match, however, in the person of Richard the Lionheart. Richard was on his way to the Holy Land in the Third Crusade in 1191 when some of his ships were wrecked off the Cypriot coast. Isaac Comnenus rushed to the scene and seized the booty. In the process however, he unwisely insulted two of the passengers, Berengaria, Richard's betrothed, and Joanna, his favourite sister. Enraged at Isaac's effrontery, Richard, who had had no intention of conquering Cyprus, pursued Comnenus and unceremoniously defeated him. Isaac's daughter was locked up in St Hilarion. Richard despatched his knights to take the rest of the island and in turn helped himself to large quantities of booty, as was customary. He stayed on the island long enough to marry the dark-eyed Berengaria, daughter of the King of Navarre, and one tradition recounts that Isaac, gift-wrapped in gilt chains, was brought to the queen as a wedding present.

Though generally presented as a hero, Richard was in fact not much different from Cyprus's previous rulers. The Archbishop of Sinai, chronicling events in 1766, described him as a 'bloodthirsty beast', lamenting that the poor Cypriots 'had escaped the wolf to fall into the jaws of the bear'.

On leaving the island, Richard sold it to the Knights Templar for 100,000 byzants (the medieval gold currency of Europe), to raise money for his army and the crusade. The knights, however, found it more of a handful than they bargained for, and after only a year they besought Richard to buy it back.

The English king had already received nearly half the sale price and did not wish to lose his money. Instead, he persuaded Guy de Lusignan, a Frankish nobleman who had been King of Jerusalem before it was lost to Saladin, to take it on in compensation for the loss of the Kingdom of Jerusalem. De Lusignan accepted, and his family retained the kingship of the island for the next three centuries, until 1489.

De Lusignan's reign was always feudal in style, and did not represent an improvement for the Cypriots themselves. They were serfs with no rights or privileges, working the land and heavily taxed to pay for the extravagances of the nobles. Some were even bartered by their masters in exchange for dogs or horses.

Also subjugated at this time was the Greek Orthodox Church of Cyprus, scorned by the French-speaking Latin Catholic rulers. Its treasures were robbed and its bishops burnt as heretics when they refused to bow to Catholic dominance and recognise the Pope in Rome as head of all Christendom. The appointment of an Orthodox archbishop was banned, and it was in these centuries that the Greek Orthodox monasteries, hidden away in the mountain ranges, were established. Cyprus had long been a refuge for Christianity during difficult times in the Holy Land, and when the last Christian stronghold of Acre fell in 1191, Cyprus took on the role of Latin Christianity's easternmost outpost, becoming the trading centre of the eastern Mediterranean, and bringing its rulers much wealth and prosperity. The relics of this prosperity are left to us today in the cathedrals of Lefkoşa and Gazimağusa, the castles of St Hilarion, Buffavento and Kantara, and the unrivalled Bellapais Abbey.

BELLAPAIS ABBEY (*Entry to the abbey is by ticket at the kiosk;* ☉ *daily 09.00–19.00 summer, daily 09.00–17.00 winter; £3.60/1.00 adults/students*) The beauty of Bellapais is legendary. When Lawrence Durrell bought a house here, he felt 'guilty of an act of fearful temerity in trying to settle in so fantastic a place'. Set in the mountains just ten minutes above Girne, this magnificent 14th-century Crusader abbey with its fabulous location and pervasive atmosphere of calm is a must-see.

Those who knew Bellapais before the 1950s speak disparagingly of the encroaching commercialisation of the abbey. There are indeed several cafés and souvenir shops beside the abbey, and even a restaurant inside it, but they can all be counted on the fingers of one hand, and the narrow streets of the village will scarcely permit more than this. Parking can sometimes be a little tricky, particularly if your visit coincides with a classic-car rally, though there is a large and free open parking area just beyond the abbey. Beware of sitting under the famous **Tree of Idleness**, an ancient mulberry by the abbey entrance, one of two trees claiming the title, lest you are struck down with the indolence for which the villagers are famed. Bellapais, Durrell was told, was synonymous with laziness and the villagers lived for so long that even the gravedigger was out of a job.

At least two hours should be allowed for the visit, starting from Girne, and the most special time is sunset, when the place is alive with the glowing silhouettes of arches. 'The dawns and the sunsets in Cyprus,' wrote Durrell, 'are unforgettable – better even than those of Rhodes which I always believed were unique in their slow Tiberian magnificence.' Durrell himself would frequently see the dawn, for when he ran out of money for renovating his house, he took a job teaching English in a Lefkoşa school which meant he had to get up at 04.30.

Any time from mid-morning to late afternoon should be avoided if at all possible, as the abbey is swamped with tour parties and the seductive atmosphere of calm is lost amidst a frenzy of clicking camera shutters. If, however, you have no other means of transport such a tour may be your only option of reaching the village. In this instance, it should be noted that most buses eject passengers near the army camp, leaving a long uphill trek of about ten to 15 minutes to reach the abbey itself.

If you are especially fortunate, your visit may coincide with one of the concerts occasionally held in the abbey refectory: a more picturesque musical backdrop is hard to imagine. Later, after a stroll, you could stay on for dinner at one of the nearby restaurants, and soak up the abbey, illuminated in its own surrealistic halo. Sipping wine on the terrace, you may wonder if you are hallucinating as a tractor trundles by towing a grand piano.

The annual **Bellapais Music Festival** (*www.bellapaisfestival.com*) is held in May and June and continues to gather momentum, attracting a diverse range of classical performers from as far afield as Taiwan, Korea and Bosnia & Herzegovina. Tickets are generally available in the village at Hotel Bellapais Gardens as well as the abbey ticket office, and in Girne at the Green Jacket Bookshop, Dome Hotel and Deniz Plaza. If the concert isn't sold out, tickets can also be bought on the door. If you can get into a recital, the atmosphere and location are likely to rival anything you may have experienced elsewhere.

Touring Bellapais Abbey 'Bellapais' is actually a corruption of 'Abbaye de la Paix', or Abbey of Peace. Climbing the 5km drive from Girne through olive and carob groves and ever-increasing development, few are prepared for the vista that hits them as they round the last corner before Bellapais village. There, rising up from the mountain on its natural terrace, like a mirage, is the Gothic masterpiece of the island, and indeed of all the Levant. Rarely has a place so lived up to its name, for this remarkable 14th-century abbey is imbued with a sense of tranquillity and peace so powerful it is almost tangible. The road winds through the narrow streets of Bellapais village to reach the tiny square in front of the abbey. From here the path leads in from the ticket kiosk past the main entrance of the church (see page 62) to the abbey enclosure through a pretty and colourful garden, to what was once the abbey kitchen, and is now a restaurant and café, tastefully tucked into the side and with excellent views of the abbey and down over the coastline. In the abbey courtyard, the fine pencilled cypress trees, 'emblems of grief and eternity' as eminent travel writer Colin Thubron called them, were planted only in 1940, but now they are home to hundreds of sparrows whose incessant chirping is usually the only sound to greet you as you enter.

Thoughtfully placed at the refectory door, by the lovely tracery windows of the cloister, lies a fine white **marble sarcophagus** of the 2nd century AD, carved with dainty figures and foliage. Here, the fastidious monks would wash their hands before meals. The first monks here were Augustinians, displaced from their custody of the Holy Sepulchre Church in Jerusalem by the arrival of Saladin in 1187. Fleeing with them were some canons of the Order of St Norbert, whose white habits lent Bellapais its other name of the White Abbey. Initially, the strictness of the abbey was exemplary, and converts were drawn from far afield.

Gradually, however, worldly values began to infiltrate. The mellow beauty of the abbey was not the natural bedfellow of asceticism, as Thubron wryly observed on his first visit: 'The spirit here feels more like a ripe fruit than a soldier of God.' Stories of the monks' misdeeds gathered momentum, as they took not just one, but two and three wives, and would accept only their own sons as novices. By the time the Genoese arrived in 1373, the abbey was ripe for pillaging, and much of its treasure was abducted. The Ottoman invasion of the 16th century destroyed more of the abbey, but the Turks allowed the Greeks to use the church after the monks were driven out. The abbey church in fact continued to be used as the village church until 1974.

Prior to the Ottoman takeover, the village of Bellapais had scarcely existed, but its numbers were swelled by the sudden influx of Greeks fleeing Kyrenia. The daughters of the monks also played their role in the growing population.

Though the church was still used, the abbey itself was a ruin from the 16th century onwards, for what the Turks did not destroy, the arriving Greeks plundered as a most convenient quarry for building their new houses. Early travellers observed cows grazing in the cloisters. The British army made its contribution by using the place as a military hospital after 1878, cementing over the refectory floor.

This **refectory**, with its lovely fan-vaulted ceiling and perfect proportions, must have been one of the finest dining halls in the East. Carved into the thickness of the wall is a pulpit from which the monks were addressed throughout meals. High on the end wall, a rose window casts an attractive patterned light. On the marble lintel above the entrance, are three well-carved sets of coats of arms – the prancing lions of the Lusignans on the right, Jerusalem in the centre, and the royal quarterings of Cyprus on the left. The abbey **church**, which runs the length of the cloister on the opposite side of the refectory, is still used now for occasional services, and has been opened to the public again, revealing the lovely iconostasis (wooden partition separating the nave from the altar area) and wooden carving on the pulpits. Pre-1974 accounts describe it as remarkably unchanged from its original 13th-century structure, apart from the iconostasis which was added by the Greek Orthodox Church in the 16th century.

There are three stairways up to the **abbey roof**: one is near the church entrance on the garden side, and the other two are long straight vaulted staircases running up on the church side of the cloister. One of these latter was the nightstair, used by the monks to come down from their dormitories at midnight for prayers. Today the roof forms an excellent viewing and vantage point from which to look down on the cloister with its melancholy cypresses and colourful garden, and across to the sea beyond.

From the car park behind the abbey to the east, you have the best view of the heavily ruined **undercroft** with its simple vaulting and damaged rose window to the north. Beside it in the southeast corner, is the **chapter house**, used like an administration office for the abbey, which merits closer inspection because of its eccentric Gothic stone carving, featuring wriggling sirens, monsters embracing or fighting, and a monkey and cat in the foliage of a pear tree.

The **village of Bellapais** still boasts a fair number of foreigners among its residents, especially in the newer villas that have grown up on the outskirts. Its closeness to Girne and natural beauty and tranquillity make it an obvious choice, and its image and popularity were certainly enhanced by Lawrence Durrell's purchase of a house here in 1953, and his subsequent book about the island and its troubles, *Bitter Lemons*, published in 1957. Durrell's house still stands at the top of the steep road that runs up from the Tree of Idleness, opposite the 1953 water trough, and is now the poshest house in the village, lovingly restored and superbly maintained by the current owner. The well-designed Ambelia village self-catering complex was built nearby in 1973, and more recently the sprawling village of Ozanköy beneath Bellapais has also become fashionable for foreigners purchasing and converting traditional homes. Those with accommodation in Bellapais may be interested to know that the village has two **car-hire agencies**: Driver Rent-a-Car (✆ *815 88 51;* e *info@driverrentals.com; www.driverrentals.com*) and Bellapais Rent-a-Car (✆ *815 75 10;* e *info@bellapaisrentacar.com; www.bellapaisrentacar.com*), together with a couple of small bars and the Tatlisulu grocery shop. A gentle stroll through the backstreets will reveal these and other places of interest. Keep an eye out for Nirvana Bar, a simple place offering toasted sandwiches and salads, and a local hotbed of campaigning to counter the Greek Cypriot propaganda on the never-ending land rights issue.

WEST FROM GIRNE

A day or two spent trundling off to the west of Girne offers the chance to see a different kind of Cypriot scenery, notably the highly fertile plain of Güzelyurt with its citrus and banana plantations. There are many good swimming beaches, and there is a wide variety of sites to see, ranging from the sultry hilltop Persian palace of Vouni, to the Bronze Age sanctuary at Pighades and the Roman fish tanks at Lapta. None of the antiquities are in themselves spectacular, but they are all from different periods and offer an interesting diversity.

Distances are mercifully short in northern Cyprus, and driving at a gentle pace it takes no more than an hour to reach Güzelyurt, and a further 45 minutes to arrive at the Persian palace of Vouni. This rocky summit is the westernmost place to visit, and the best policy on a day's outing from Girne is to drive first to this, then to work your way back eastwards, That way, if you run out of daylight and still have some places to visit, they will at least be closer to home for subsequent visits. In the summer months it is perfectly realistic to make leisurely morning visits to Vouni and Soli, then to take lunch at one of the beach restaurants near Soli (at Yedidalga). After lunch there will still be time to see Lefke, Güzelyurt, Pighades and probably Lapta on the way home. In winter, with shorter daylight hours, the afternoon itinerary may have to be curtailed, as it is too dark after 17.00 to do any sightseeing.

 WHERE TO STAY
Karaoğlanoğlu, Edremit, Karaman and around

⌂ **The Hideaway Club** (31 suites) ✆ 822 26 20/1/2; f 822 31 33; e info@hideawayclub.com; www.hideawayclub.com. 3 miles west of Girne, this is a truly lovely, smart yet informal place with a divine 22m freshwater pool & very comfortable, wonderfully appointed 'Connoisseur suites', each with fridge/minibar, phone, TV, AC & a balcony or terrace. Recommended. $$

⌂ **Hilarion Village** (10 studios & 8 villas) ✆ 822 27 72; f 822 27 67; e management@

hilarion-cyprus.com; www.hilarion-cyprus.com. On the road up to Karaman (Karmi). Tranquil, leafy surroundings with a good restaurant & large swimming pool. A good out-of-town base. $$

⌂ **Pine Bay Club** (12 apts) ✆ 822 30 32; f 822 30 35; e info@pinebayclub.com; www.pinebayclub.com. Located on the western edge of Karaoğlanoğlu & run by a former policeman from England. Accommodation-wise, the club's villas, each painted a different colour, are divided into spacious, en-suite apts which come equipped with TV, phone, AC & fridge. The club also boasts 2 pools & an à-la-carte restaurant. $$

🏠 **The Ship Inn** (79 rooms) ☎ 815 67 01/4; f 815 67 05; e info@theshipinn.com; www.theshipinn.com. Tudor-style pub with good rooms & self-catering villas. It has a large pool & children's pool, tennis courts & beer garden. One mile west of Girne centre. Good restaurant. $$

Alsancak and around

🏠 **Denizkızı Royal** (54 rooms) & **Denizkızı Hotel** (57 rooms) ☎ 821 26 76; f 821 27 27; e info@denizkizi.com; www.denizkizi.com. A 4-star hotel with 3-star neighbour 8 miles west of Girne, overlooking a picturesque beach. The Royal boasts some suites with jacuzzis; both offer swimming pools & watersports facilities. $$$ & $$

🏠 **Almond Holiday Village** (21 bungalows & 7 rooms) ☎ 821 28 85; f 821 28 89; e info@almond-holidays.com; www.almond-holidays.com. A very friendly place to the west of Lapta, with smart bungalows built round a pool & set back 200m from main road to avoid the din of the traffic. The bungalows are actually split-level apts, with a dining/kitchen/lounge area downstairs, & the bedroom/bathroom on the 1st floor. Facilities include AC, TV, fridge, & a hotplate for those who'd rather cook for themselves. Recommended. $$

🏠 **Citrus Tree Gardens** (17 bungalows) ☎ 821 28 72; f 821 28 75; e citrus@kktc.net;

🏠 **Top Set** (77 rooms) ☎ 822 22 04; f 822 24 78; e info@topsethotel.com; www.topsethotel.com. Situated on the sea-side of the road near the centre of Karaoğlanoğlu, this is a very hospitable little place with a variety of rooms, many overlooking the beach. All rooms are centrally heated & have AC, shower & WC, minibar, phone & TV with international channels. $$

www.citrus-tree.com. Small, family-run complex 9km from Girne with a pool & highly respected restaurant. Minimum booking 3 nights. $$

🏠 **King's Court** (24 bungalows & studios) ☎ 821 84 95; f 821 22 20; www.kings-hotel.com. A short walk from the sea, these self-catering bungalows & studios are set amongst pretty gardens on the main road. There is a bus service to Girne & airport transfers are available from both Ercan & Larnaca. British-run, friendly. Pre-school & fully qualified childcare available on site. $$

🏠 **Villa Club** (31 rooms) ☎ 821 84 00; f 821 80 47; www.villa-club.com/cyprus. Tucked away behind the King's Court amongst orange groves, this quiet little idyll is surrounded by fountains that provide the welcome, cooling sound of running water during the hot summer months. Rooms are equipped with bath or shower, TV, phone, minibar & AC. Minimum 7 nights. $$

Lapta and beyond The three hotels (Celebrity, Lapethos and LA) on Lapta's main drag appear to be little more than appendages to the casinos, and as such this area tends to appeal more to Turkish holidaymakers than Westerners. Nevertheless there are plenty of good restaurants (and a couple of more Western-orientated hotels) in the vicinity and in the height of the season the area does have a certain buzz.

🏠 **LA Hotel & Resort** (aka LAS Holiday Centre) (101 rooms) ☎ 821 88 84; f 821 89 92; e info@la-hotel-cyprus.com; www.la-hotel-cyprus.com. The best of the 3 on Lapta's main drag, its rooms are equipped with TV, AC, shower, minibar & phone. Has its own sandy beach. $$$

🏠 **Celebrity Hotel** (84 rooms) ☎ 821 87 51; e celebrity@kktc.net; www.celebrity-hotel.com. On the beach in Lapta. Majority Turkish clientele but increasing numbers of English & German tourists too. 3 restaurants, swimming pool plus range of watersports, including an on-site dive school run by an English couple. $$

🏠 **Club Lapethos** (105 rooms) ☎ 821 89 61; f 821 89 66; e info@lapethos.com;

www.lapethos.com. Flashy-looking place in the heart of Lapta surrounded by swimming pools & catering mainly to Turkish holidaymakers. Rooms with AC, bars, swimming pool, sauna, beach & watersports. Restaurants serving homegrown organic vegetables. $$

🏠 **Lefke Gardens** (21 rooms) ☎ 728 82 23; f 728 82 22; e info@lefkegardens.com. This is a real jewel tucked away below the main road in Lefke. The main front building is an Ottoman house dating from 1923. It has been restored & tastefully decorated, with a well-stocked bar, by the current owners, the Taskin family. The rooms at the back of the courtyard behind the swimming pool are new, but still very homely & not without character. All accommodation is en suite & comes with a huge TV, minibar & AC. $$

🏠 **Hotel Sempati** (34 rooms) ↘ 821 27 70; f 821 27 74; e info@hotelsempati.com; www.hotelsempati.com. Located 12km from Girne, this 3-star hotel lies down a rough track, just 150m from the beach. All rooms are en suite & have satellite TV, AC, phone & minibar. $$

🏠 **Soli Inn** (16 rooms & 5 bungalows) ↘ 727 75 75; f 727 82 10; e soliinn@northcyprus.net. Situated in Güzelyurt Bay, 500m to the east of the turn-off to the Soli ruins, this seaside hotel offers facilities for watersports, a swimming pool out front. There are also 2-bedroom self-catering apts on the 1st floor. $

✖ **WHERE TO EAT** The coastline west from Girne is the most developed stretch in the north, and restaurants and hotels are here in abundance. The following are just a select few.

Karaoğlanoğlu, Edremit, Karaman (Karmi) & around

✖ **The Address** ↘ 822 35 37. Still one of the smartest places in North Cyprus, the long-running Address continues to pull in the crowds thanks partly to its location right on the beach in Karaoğlanoğlu, & fairly priced (albeit expensive) local & international menu. Call to book. £12

✖ **Chinese House** ↘ 815 21 30. Popular with the expatriate community, this lovely Chinese restaurant is situated opposite The Ship Inn on the main road. £8.50

✖ **Cousin's Brasserie** ↘ 821 26 39. A slightly out-of-the-way location in Alsancak is the only fault I could find with this excellent smart restaurant serving international & local dishes, including a fine beef stroganoff. £8

♀ **Crow's Nest** ↘ 822 25 67. Located at the heart of Karaman (Karmi) in more ways than one, this friendly pub is a fine example, not of assimilation but sympathetic coexistence by Karmi's expatriate community. Cold beer, light snacks & free Karmi water. £5

✖ **Dünya** ↘ 822 23 92. Formerly an upholstery shop & still run by the same guy, the ever-genial Hasan, Dünya on the main coast road is the place in Karaoğlanoğlu for a plentiful meze (currently £16 inclusive of local drinks). Opening hours & days can be erratic, & it can get busy when it is open, so booking ahead is advised. £10

✖ **Follow Me** ↘ 815 38 03; 🕐 from 17.00 only; give them a call if you're planning on coming. The restaurant, belonging to North Cyprus's foremost walking guide, Yuçel Asan, is a rustic treat lying at the end of a dirt track on the way to Edremit. Much of the menu is homegrown & homemade, from the wine to the halloumi cheese. They also produce excellent wild honey (£2.40 per jar). £15

✖ **Halfway House** ↘ 822 33 14. A lovely little stop if you're walking to or from Karaman (Karmi), the Halfway House is another meze place where the

beer's always cold & the welcome friendly. Worth calling ahead. £10

✖ **The Hideaway Club** ↘ 822 26 20. In Edremit has its own swimming pool & a varied lunchtime menu, topped off with cocktails & local brandy sours. £6

✖ **Jashan's** ↘ 822 20 27. Regarded as the best Indian restaurant in North Cyprus, Jashan's, recently relocated on the Karaoğlanoğlu road, serves some pretty authentic subcontinental dishes — though those who love spicy food will find their regular curries a little bland; if you want it hot, insist that they make it hot. £6.50

✖ **Levant Bar & Restaurant** ↘ 822 25 59. Karaman's (Karmi's) other bar, attracting a younger & more mixed crowd than the Crow's Nest. Snacks & light meals. £7

✖ **Missina** ↘ 822 38 44. Flashy establishment on the seafront in Karaoğlanoğlu, recently opened amidst a blaze of local publicity. Specialising in excellent fish dishes, although the service at times struggles to justify the prices. £18

✖ **The Ship Inn** ↘ 815 67 01. Family-run traditional English bar between Karaoğlanoğlu & Girne serving an excellent selection of international & local cuisine, cocktails & beers. Live entertainment on Fri with a set menu package. Booking is advised. £6.50

✖ **Stonegrill Restaurant** ↘ 822 20 02. With its less than flattering location next to the main road & somewhat sterile interior, what this place lacks in charisma it makes up for with great steaks which you cook yourself on a hot stone at the table. More expensive than some places & it seems to cater mostly for tourists but a sociable way to eat nonetheless. The generous meze is almost a meal in itself so make sure you go with an appetite. £10

✖ **Treasure** ↘ 822 24 00; 🕐 Thu–Tue. Situated at the entrance to Karaman (Karmi) village, this restaurant, previously a schoolhouse, doubles as a simple but interesting art gallery. It serves Cypriot & English cuisine (inc some fantastic local soups) & has an open log fire & panoramic terrace. £8

Alsancak and around

✖ **Altınkaya I** ☏ 821 83 41. Overlooking the sea near Invasion Beach, 8km from Girne, & reckoned to be the best & longest-established speciality fish restaurant on the island. It is very popular with the local people & offers a set *meze* with your own choice of fish. £16

✖ **Çenap** ☏ 821 84 17. Up the hill in the heart of Alsancak, a simple local place serving BBQs & the most authentic & mouth-watering *meze*. £12

✖ **The Veranda** ☏ 822 20 53. Restaurant & beach bar in Karaoğlanoğlu serving international cuisine. Beautiful seafront location. £8

✖ **Saint Tropez** ☏ 821 83 24. Reputed to be the best restaurant on the island, the Saint Tropez – easy to find thanks to its 8m mock-up of the Eiffel Tower in the front yard – serves up a wide selection of French & other continental dishes, many slathered with very rich sauces. New grill restaurant just opened on 2nd floor. Reliable & still the place to be seen in North Cyprus. £10

Lapta and beyond Though the situation is improving, west of Lapta eating-places are few and far between. There is, however, a pleasant cluster of beach restaurants near Yedidalga, before Vouni, offering a simple fare of *meze*, kebabs and fish, with willing service.

✖ **The Hut** ☏ 821 8990; ⏱ lunch only. Recently taken over by English couple Sue & Chris Hall. The Hut is a no-nonsense bar/restaurant by the side of the road a few hundred metres to the east of the Celebrity Hotel, with one of the best views on the north coast. Access to the sea via an unmaintained track. Lovely pasta & steak sandwiches, perfect for a lunch break between sunbathing. £6

✖ **Şevket's** ☏ 821 8077. West of Silver Rocks, this place specialises in Turkish Cypriot cuisine, offering

fresh fish, kebabs & *meze*. It also has vegetarian specialities & cocktails. £8

✖ **Silver Rocks** (formerly Shirley Valentine's) ☏ 821 89 22. Situated in a lovely spot almost on the beach just to the west of Lapta, this is a popular place, recently taken over by Ibrahim Seyhun, that serves a wide variety of Turkish & European dishes. 1- & 2-bedroom bungalows available for rental too. £7

BEACHES

Riviera Beach (*free entry*) Situated 4km from Girne, near Karaoğlanoğlu and signposted from the main road. Small sandy bay for children, but otherwise rocky, with a small jetty for swimming off. There is a restaurant and showers.

Escape Beach Club (*Entry £5 includes a soft drink & a shade umbrella*) 8km west, below the Altınkaya. You can drive the car right down to the beach, by following the sign for Yavaz Cikartma, just west of Altınkaya Restaurant from the main road. The Sunset Restaurant and Beach Bar is at the end of the long sandy bay. The water is shallow and safe for children desperate to use air-mattresses and dinghies – there is an island, known as Golden Rock, protecting the entrance to the bay. It is so close that you can wade across to it.

Denizkızı (*Entry £4 allows use of beach & swimming pool*) Belonging to the hotel of the same name, but open, like all the hotel beaches, to fee-paying non-residents (see page 64). 9km from Girne, a sandy bay with safe, sheltered swimming. There are bamboo umbrellas, showers and changing cabins, as well as a beach café and children's play area. A variety of watersports offered by Dolphin Cyprus (see page 34).

Celebrity (*Entry £2.50*) The hotel beach, but very small. 14km west with all amenities.

LA (*Entry £4.50*) Just beyond the Celebrity complex, with sunbeds, umbrellas and a snack bar.

Horseshoe Bay (*Entry £4*) 20km west of Girne and 3km before Kayalar. A shingle beach with pretty coloured pebbles, good for snorkelling but not suitable for young children. There is a simple beach restaurant.

TOWARDS KORUÇAM BURNU (CAPE KORMAKITI)

All along this stretch of wild coastline, west from Kayalar, there are small sandy and rocky bays backed by the cliffs. Attractive, deserted and secluded, they are also often difficult to reach, involving a scramble down from the road and a longish walk. The area around the cape itself near the lighthouse used to be military and prohibited, but was demilitarised a few years ago and is now approachable.

If you're driving from the Girne direction the turn-off towards Kayalar signifies the end of the north coast development and the start of how things used to be. As the road sweeps round the coastline, affording superb panoramic views, it's a welcome relief to see open land ahead and, by local standards, an absence of litter. Driving here is a joy, and will definitely act to lift the spirits of anyone who wondered just where the 'real' North Cyprus actually was.

Shortly after leaving the main road, the **Horseshoe Beach Restaurant** makes a pleasant place to stop for a drink or simple kebab lunch. Pressing further on it's clear to see why locals and visitors alike favour this stretch of road, meandering as it does towards old Kayalar. Unfortunately, even here the builders have been busy and the old village now sits in uneasy proximity to the new development that has been thrown up by the roadside.

WHAT TO SEE AND DO The description given here starts with a brief account of the route westwards to Vouni, then gives the site details starting from Vouni and working eastwards back towards Girne. As throughout North Cyprus, the roads are in good condition, with the towns and sites being clearly signposted.

The road first follows the thin coastal strip for 20km or so, before it then begins to climb as it winds inland through wooded hillsides. Leaving the valleys behind, you have a fine view below to a new dam, one of many which the north Cypriots are now building to harness the water that is lost in a flash after a heavy downpour: no river in Cyprus flows all year round and water is a scarce resource. For most of the year it comes from the mains for only two hours a day, and in July and August sometimes not at all. Residents and hotels get round this by having extremely large tanks on the roof.

At the top of the climb you arrive at **Çamlıbel**, a heavily garrisoned town whose military camp hides the mysterious Mavi Köşk (see box on page 69), where there is a major fork in the road: straight on to Lefkoşa, and right to Güzelyurt and Lefke. The road straight on is the one you need to take to visit Pighades, just 2km away, on the return journey, but for now, you fork right.

Leaving Çamlıbel on its hilltop, the road drops down into the adjacent valley. **Güzelyurt** is set in the heart of this vast and fertile river plain, the centre for the island's citrus plantations. Your arrival at Güzelyurt is marked by a fine example of 20th-century British engineering – a 1904 tank engine, rusting gently just to the left of the road. This curiosity is a leftover of the line built by the British that used to run from Gazimağusa via Lefkoşa to Morphou. The last train ran in 1951. Continuing straight along the main road, you reach the centre of town with the unmistakable Byzantine dome of the Ayias Mamas Church and the municipal museum beside it, both set in the centre of a huge roundabout (and both described in detail on the return journey). The forks to the left from the roundabout lead back towards Lefkoşa, but you continue straight on, following signs for Lefke.

From Güzelyurt the drive on, through lush plantations, takes a further half-hour to reach the sweep of **Güzelyurt Körfezi** (Morphou Bay) with its distinctive **iron jetties**, relics of the copper-mining operations. Ships would tie up alongside these jetties and be loaded with copper for export, mainly to West Germany. Copper was Cyprus's most important natural resource, and the Greek name for it, *kupros*, is even thought to be taken from the name of the island. Cyprus was known throughout ancient times for its copper, supplying the Egyptian pharaohs and producing more than any other Mediterranean country. The rich mines here of Skouriotissa and Mavrovouni were first worked by the ancient Greeks and then the Romans, but after that lay disused for centuries until they were reopened in 1923. The Cyprus Mines Corporation, an American outfit, worked the mines until partition, when the ore was nearly exhausted anyway. Their supervisors marvelled at the extent of the Roman diggings, and the depth of their galleries and shafts, especially in view of the lack of ventilation. Slaves were used, of course, to work the mines, so safety standards were hardly a consideration. In Roman times Christians from Palestine who refused to renounce their faith were also sent down the mines. Careful observation of the landscape will reveal it to be largely composed of Roman slagheaps, for they are said to have left more than a million tons of slag behind. 'Our Lady of the Slag Heaps' is one rough translation of Skouriotissa.

Shortly after the mining sites, but before the village of Yedidalga, the Roman theatre and basilica of **Soli** lie on a hillside just 200m inland from the road, signposted as usual with one of the tourist service's clear yellow signs. **Vouni**, too, about 8km further west along the coast road, is clearly signposted.

First the road passes a cluster of beach restaurants west of Soli, where you can eat and swim, before a steep winding ascent begins of a colossal hilly outcrop on the sea edge. Vouni Palace lies on the summit of this outcrop. The last three minutes are along a narrow track. Near the foot of the hill, incidentally, about halfway between Soli and Vouni, is the shell of a **modern Greek church** built in a sheltered nook to the right of the road, but badly destroyed inside. It appears never to have been completed and is covered inside and out with the vain exhortation 'Please keep tidy'. Most mosques in Greek Cyprus are, by contrast, kept locked and clean, but the record for tolerance is poor on both sides: 117 mosques were destroyed between 1955 and 1974 by zealous Greek Cypriots.

At the foot of the Vouni hill, the main road continues westwards to the village of **Yeşilirmak**, just beyond which is another simple beach restaurant. This is the westernmost point you can reach before the edge of north Cypriot territory, though some 8km further west, inaccessible and surrounded by Greek Cypriot territory, is the curious Turkish Cypriot pocket of **Erenköy** (Greek Kokkina). Today only troops live in this fiercely Turkish Cypriot enclave, all the original villagers having been evacuated to Yeni Erenköy on the Karpas Peninsula. These villagers had bravely resisted an attack by General Grivas and 3,000 Greek soldiers in 1964 and were supported in their struggle by student volunteers who included a young Rauf Denktash, the former TRNC president.

Having arrived at the westernmost point, the site descriptions now begin from Vouni eastwards.

VOUNI (*ticket kiosk ⊕ around 09.00–16.45 daily, though as the site isn't gated, departure from the specified opening times shouldn't inconvenience; £2.00/0.60 adults/students*) This is

Nick Redmayne

The heavily guarded perimeter fences of Çamlıbel's army camp hide a secret whose precise origins, though hardly ancient, have been lost in an obfuscating mêlée of conflict and hastily rewritten recent history. To investigate the mystery you'll need photo ID, and just two words, 'Mavi Köşk', to pass beyond the gun-toting sentries and into a twilight zone of Cyprus's past. Mavi Köşk or the Blue House is testament to one man, Byron Pavlides, though for all their amiable manner it's likely that your Turkish military guides will be unsure even of this fact. The army's story is that Pavlides was a gunrunner for Greek Cypriot EOKA terrorists and the house was sited in its lofty position in order to oversee the arrival of weapons shipments at the coast below. They will also state that the building contains secret escape passages and storage rooms concurrent with its usage as a hub for terrorist activity. It's further suggested that rather like a paranoid pharaoh, Pavlides ordered the house's architect, his own brother, and the unfortunate workforce to be shot upon its completion. Given extreme circumstances one could perhaps sympathise with Pavlides's sentiment if not his actions in this excess. However, there's little evidence to support the story. What's beyond dispute is Pavlides's eccentric nature, manifest in the unique design and colour scheme of Mavi Köşk. Exploring the house, it'll be for you to judge whether the blue walls, blue-painted furniture, kitsch mock taverna with colour-coded tables and chairs, combined with a multitude of '70s-style bathrooms, sunken fountains and, for its time, sophisticated air conditioning reflect a ruthless and violent criminal mastermind.

What is known is that Byron Pavlides was a wealthy businessman, holding the dealership franchises for a number of automotive manufacturers across Cyprus. The house was built in 1973 and was not the first 'coloured' house that Pavlides was responsible for, having first conceived the 'White House' near St Hilarion, now also in the domain of the Turkish military.

Returning to the myth, following the 1974 invasion Pavlides escaped from Mavi Köşk by the skin of his teeth via a bespoke escape tunnel. All Turkish soldiers found was a locked safe that proved to contain a single golden key, whose significance remains tantalisingly unknown to this day. Byron was not heard of again till 1986 when a rumour arose that he had died in Sicily, shot dead at a Mafia meeting by a Turk.

the only Persian palace in Cyprus, indeed in the Mediterranean, and it lies on a spectacular hilltop overlooking the sea. However, the remains of the palace are scant, and the imagination has to be called into play.

The dizzy views down to the sea on the way up are stunning, with the rocky island of Petra Tou Limniti in the foreground. It was on this island that Cyprus's earliest inhabitants lived, and traces of a pre-Neolithic settlement were found there by the same Swedish expedition in the 1920s that excavated Vouni and Soli. Local folklore holds that this is the rock (as indeed are all the small rock islands off Cyprus's shore) that the hero Dighenis tossed onto the ships of the Arab raiders of the 7th century.

As with most of these historical sites, in return for your entrance fee you get a handy sheet of A4 explaining the site. There is no refreshments stall here, so bring your own supplies, especially liquid in the summer months. Vouni is a good spot for a picnic. Allow 45 minutes for a full walk round.

Touring Vouni The name Vouni means mountain peak, and it was built on this summit specifically to dominate and spy on the city kingdom of Soli down below, which had at that time aligned itself with the Greeks in a revolt against Persia. The palace was only in use for some 70 years, for in 380BC it was destroyed by fire and not lived in again.

Reduced today to little more than its foundations, the 5th-century BC palace of Vouni may disappoint at first. Do not dismiss it too quickly though, for if you take the trouble to walk round slowly, you will be surprised how it can be transformed, by careful observation and a little imagination, into a magnificent royal residence. The yellow signs may help to obliterate any 'palatial' atmosphere, but they do at least provide a handy guide as to what rooms went where in the palace. Ruined but gracious walkways, broad stairways and ample courtyards all hint at the opulent oriental lifestyle enjoyed here, and the elaborate water system is a marvel of 5th-century BC engineering. Everywhere there are ingeniously cut channels and very deep wells, ensuring running water in all the main rooms. In the extreme northwest corner, there is a water closet beside a deep cistern, which in its day was probably far more luxurious than its modern counterpart could ever aspire to be. Lower down the hill are the baths, with one of the earliest-known saunas. There were 137 rooms in all.

The path from the ticket office leads first straight into the area identified as the royal apartments, and from these a broad flight of seven steps leads down into the huge open courtyard which is the generally photographed view of Vouni. At its farthest end stands the strange carved stone stele which resembles an altar but was in fact designed to hold a windlass over the cistern wellhead. In the bulbous centre of the stone is an unfinished likeness of Athene.

The Swedish excavators made a series of finds in the palace that testified to the lavish lifestyle of the occupants. As well as statues and bronzes they discovered quantities of silver and gold treasure in the form of bracelets, bowls and coins. One local story tells of noblemen dining here and leaving their silver spoons behind, and villagers still refer to it as 'the eating-place of the lords'. Much silver treasure was found in a terracotta jar that seemed to have been deliberately hidden under a staircase. Some of this treasure, including Persian-style snake-head bracelets, can be seen in the Cyprus Museum of Greek Nicosia.

Beyond the palace area, at the highest point of the hill, stands a military trigonometry point, 250m above the sea, and nearby are the scant remains of a temple to Athena where the Swedish excavators found several sculptures, notably an endearing bronze cow, now also in the Cyprus Museum.

The serene and lovely location encourages much wildlife. Lizards up to a foot long leap around on the walls and butterflies sun themselves gaily in sheltered corners. All around, the yellow aromatic Johanniskreuz bush flourishes, well known for its stomach-calming qualities when drunk as a tea.

SOLI (*ticket kiosk* ⊕ *09.00–19.00; £2.80/£1.20 adults/students*) The Roman site of Soli boasts the best-preserved mosaic and marble floor in northern Cyprus in its basilica, and nearby beach restaurants offer a pleasant stop for lunch and a swim.

The site lacks grandeur and its setting, though raised up overlooking the bay, is a bit scruffy and uninspiring. The theatre is the only other monument to have been excavated besides the basilica, and has been rather over-restored.

About 45 minutes should be allowed for a tour. There are no refreshments available, and Soli is not a particularly good picnic spot.

Touring Soli Coming from Vouni, look out for the yellow Soli sign to the right just after the village of Yedidalga. (The turn-off lies directly opposite the rusting iron jetty, hovering above the water like a swan's neck, leaning forlornly over the sea.)

Just to the left of the ticket kiosk you can see the **cathedral/basilica**, with its beautiful **mosaic** and **marble floor**. Among the marble remnants, you can still see some magnificent colours: columns in deep brick-red marble with swirls of white, or cool greeny-white slabs on the floor.

The majority of the mosaics are geometric in design, with red, white and dark blue as the predominant colours. Sadly, these colours have faded due to long exposure to the sun (the roof was only erected in the late 1990s). Near the centre, the main area of mosaic is chained off in token protection. The centrepiece is a lovely white swan or goose-like bird surrounded by flower motifs, with four small blue dolphins and a pretty multi-coloured duck.

At the far end of the basilica a huge tumbled column gives some idea of the size of the whole structure, whose full length must have been close to 200m. The baptistry area was also mosaic, but only with geometric patterns. In the apse itself is a Greek inscription set in an oblong panel, entirely in mosaic. Nearby is a deep well, and scattered all around are thousands of fragments of marble flooring.

The **theatre**, dating from the 3rd century AD, lies a few minutes' walk higher up the hill, approached by the tree-lined path. Facing out to sea, it stands on the same site as the theatre of the original Greek city of Soli before it, which had a similar capacity, some 4,000. The town had reached its zenith under the Romans, but was destroyed in the Arab raids of the 7th century. The heavy restoration carried out in the 1960s by the Cyprus Department of Antiquities has somewhat ruined the atmosphere. Everything was reconstructed except the orchestra floor and the platform of the stage buildings, so the seats, rebuilt to diazoma level (ie: halfway), are all new. The original seats, it is said, were carried off in the last century to help build the quaysides of Port Said. Local school performances are occasionally held here.

Above the theatre on the nearby hill to the west are the extremely scant remains of a **temple to Aphrodite and Isis**, and it was here that the famous, if armless, 2nd-century BC statue of Aphrodite was laid bare by a Canadian team of archaeologists. She is now on display in the Cyprus Museum, Greek Nicosia. Her likeness is often to be seen on wine bottles, stamps and such like – Aphrodite, goddess of Love, symbol of Cyprus, born from the waves breaking on the shore near Paphos. The other theory, that she was born of Uranus's castrated testicles, is not nearly so widely advertised…

> Love hath an island,
> And I would be there;
> Love hath an island,
> And nurtureth there
> For men the Delights
> The beguilers of care,
> Cyprus, Love's island;
> And I would be there.
> *Euripides,* The Bacchae

Nothing of the original 6th-century BC Greek city remains today, and the theatre and basilica are the only visible parts from the Roman city. The rest awaits excavation.

LEFKE Set in one of the lushest and most fertile pockets of the island, Lefke is a pretty and unspoilt rural Turkish town that pays little attention to tourists but boasts a new university and three mosques, an unusually large number for North Cyprus. Its citrus fruits are said to be the juiciest on the island, from the abundance of water. The nearby reservoir is a favourite spot for local picnics.

Lefke is about 5km inland from Soli and the total detour from the coast road to see it need take only about 40 minutes. There is one excellent hotel in Lefke – perhaps the best outside Girne – though no restaurants of note.

Touring Lefke Following the sign from the settlement of Gemikonaği that points inland about 1km east of the Soli ruins, you fork right again at the T-junction that comes 300m later. The approach to the town is heralded by an incongruously stately stretch of dual carriageway with well-tended gardens at the side and a cloaked Atatürk (the founding father of modern Turkey) on horseback rearing up as the centrepiece. This ceremonial entry lasts about 500m, and the town proper then begins as the road winds first down and then up again to reach the core of the town. Predominantly Turkish since well before 1974, its 3,800 inhabitants have suffered no displacement or uprooting. Lefke today remains a relaxed and friendly place, sprawling over several hillsides.

The best way to see it is therefore by car. Arriving at the centre you come to a fine colonnaded building on the right, constructed as a **British storehouse** and now doing a good impression of the café that time forgot, then a curious circular stone monument, built to commemorate the coronation of King George VI in 1937. By turning off the main street to the left just opposite this monument, you can wiggle down through a whole maze of narrow lanes lined with picturesque old houses. One lane passes a fine old **aqueduct** some 4m high. Water is everywhere in Lefke, and gurgles in little water channels that run beside the streets.

Returning to the main street, you will see, as you begin to drive out of the village, an **old mosque** in sandy-coloured stone surrounded by colourful gardens, its minaret topped with an aluminium cone. This is Lefke's main mosque, and in its garden lies one of the loveliest Turkish tombs in Cyprus, the **tomb of Piri Osman Pasha** who died in 1839. Built of white, elaborately carved marble in the dervish style with tall turbaned top, its centre is blackened from the smoke of candles, for every time the women of the village ask a favour of the local saint – a husband, a male child, a cure for illness – they leave a lighted candle on the tomb.

Taking the time to drive a little further afield in Lefke, especially down in the valley, you will cross a wide riverbed beside which stands a derelict small Greek chapel, raised up next to a grand and excellently maintained house, evidently the seat of the local landowner.

GÜZELYURT (MORPHOU) The Turkish name of Güzelyurt means 'beautiful place'. It is referring less to the town itself than to the surrounding area, where beauty is virtually synonymous with fertility. Some 80% of the island's citrus groves were concentrated here, and in the first few years after 1974, the Turkish Cypriots had neither the manpower nor the expertise to tend them. Many trees died from neglect or disease, but by 1980 the situation was under control, and exports of citrus fruits began an upward trend. Sunzest, the juice and canning factory of Asil Nadir, Turkish Cypriot fugitive millionaire, is conspicuous at the town's outskirts. Unfortunately, as the citrus groves increased in size and number, the development of irrigation techniques could not keep up, leading to water contamination along the coastline.

Touring Güzelyurt Arriving at the large central roundabout of the town, you drive into the little car park in front of the museum, beside the Ayias Mamas Church. The **Güzelyurt Museum** is open daily from 08.00 to 19.00, and the museum guardian has the key to the church (*£2.50/1.20 adult/student for entry to museum & church*). A visit to both takes about an hour or so.

The museum opened in 1979 and contains downstairs a remarkable assortment of stuffed animals of the island, including pelicans and other birds, reptiles, foxes, rabbits and sheep. Particularly memorable, if somewhat grotesque, are the aberrant lambs, freaks of nature, one with eight legs, one with two heads on its tiny frail body. Upstairs is the archaeological section, with finds from nearby Bronze Age sites, notably Toumba tou Skourou. The room in the far corner is the most interesting, containing both a 2nd-century statue of Artemis, whose unusual, multi-breasted form will be familiar to anyone who has visited Ephesus on Turkey's west coast, and some exquisite, and remarkably well-preserved gold jewellery.

Outside, the guardian will, on request, take you across the courtyard of **Ayias Mamas Church**, round the edge of what are now the disused 18th-century monastic cells. A modern wing of this accommodation was, pre-1974, one of the Bishop of Girne's residences.

Inside the church, it is as if the service had only just finished. The walls and iconostasis are resplendent with icons, many of them Venetian, and all of them in excellent condition. Behind the iconostasis, the cupboards still bulge with silver and gilt cups and chalices, and lavish richly coloured robes. One reader describes the church perfectly: 'a Miss Havisham of a church, frozen in time'.

The **tomb of Ayias Mamas** himself is on a side wall beside the entrance, draped in red curtains. In the centre of the sarcophagus is a wooden flap which lifts to reveal two holes where, according to the guardian, 'the Greeks poured oil inside'. Tradition held that the saint's body exuded an oil which cured earache and calmed stormy seas, an oil which was collected from these two holes. Ears, in silver and in wax, still hang beside the tomb, their owners waiting patiently to be healed.

Ayias Mamas himself was a popular saint who earned the undying respect of the Cypriot peasantry in the 12th century by refusing to pay his poll tax. He is always shown in icons riding on a lion, because the story goes that when his Byzantine ruler sent for him to be brought before the court and punished, the saint rode in astride a wild lion and was promptly exempted from his taxes for life. Around 14 churches are dedicated to him throughout the island.

To the north of the town it's difficult to miss the large construction on the barren hill overlooking the area. The **University of the Eastern Mediterranean** has chosen Güzelyurt as the location for its new campus, reflecting the continued investment in education in North Cyprus and suggesting a welcome diversification for a local economy that relies so heavily on citrus fruits.

TOUMBA TOU SKOUROU The site of this Bronze Age town, like so many Bronze Age settlements, is not of interest to the layman, and only merits the detour for the real archaeological enthusiast. Its name is known from its finds displayed in the Güzelyurt Museum. There is no guardian so the site is always accessible. The visit will detain you about an hour from the point where you turn off the main road.

Touring Toumba Tou Skourou Leaving Güzelyurt in the direction of Girne, look out for the yellow sign pointing along an old tarmac road leading off to the left opposite a juice stall. Taking a right by another signpost, you'll find this track ends in a clearing; immediately after this are the ruins as excavated by Harvard University and the Museum of Fine Arts from 1971 to 1974. The area all around is littered with potsherds, and the huge holes left by the giant *pithoi* (earthenware jars) are in some ways more impressive than the *pithoi* themselves. Also found on the site was Minoan pottery, Syrian cylinder seals and some African ostrich eggs. The setting, surrounded by citrus trees a long way from any village, lends a certain charm to the site.

The main road continues east across the plain before climbing up to the village of Kalkanli. From here a steep descent begins, winding down into the next valley, followed by a shorter climb up to Çamlıbel and Tepebaşi.

PALEOKASTRO AND AYIA IRINI As you approach the mound of Tepebaşi a tarmac road leads off to the left towards the bay of Güzelyurt, signposted Akdeniz, just next to the petrol station. This is the road you must take to reach these two sites.

Both are remarkable for what was found at them, but since these finds have been removed to museums, there is little of interest left for anyone except the specialist. The 2,000 clay figures from Ayia Irini are one of the most intriguing exhibits on display in the Cyprus Museum of Greek Nicosia. Near Paleokastro, however, is an unusual undergound rock tomb, only recently discovered.

Although Paleokastro lies in an attractive spot on a clifftop overlooking the sea, it is not suitable for swimming or picnicking as it is encompassed by a military camp. Depending on the officer in charge, however, it can sometimes be visited, and you may even be offered a guided tour, followed by tea.

It is 15km from the main road to Paleokastro and the total return visit from this point will take about one and a half hours. The military camp is always manned, so you can visit any time in daylight hours. There are no refreshment facilities anywhere along the road, although the petrol station at the junction with the main road has a refrigerator and soft drinks.

Touring Paleokastro Following the sign to Akdeniz, you begin a drive through heavily militarised countryside. Akdeniz itself, contrary to its name (which means Mediterranean), is not on the coast but some 2km short of it. Its Greek name was Ayia Irini, and this is the name that is well known from the Ayia Irini sanctuary displays in the Cyprus Museum in Greek Nicosia. The sanctuary where these extraordinary terracotta votive figures, all 2,000 of them, were found was not in Ayia Irini village itself, but on a hillock on the coast, at the site which is called Paleokastro.

To reach this you must drive through the semi-deserted village to where the tarmac road stops. At the far edge of the village stands the forlorn shell of a Greek church beside some sheep pens, and at this point you fork to the right along the dirt track, heading towards the sea. The track is well used because of military traffic and quite straightforward for a saloon car. After some 2km you can see the headland on the coast a little to the right, with the military camp on its summit. If you drive right up to the gates, soldiers will soon come running. Don't panic that you are about to be arrested; they are simply delighted to have visitors, a distraction from the routine of the day. Most of the soldiers are on their two-year military service stint from the Turkish mainland, rather than native islanders. The Turkish army is highly disciplined, and so as long as you are courteous and decently dressed, there will be no problems, even as an all-female party. You leave the car parked outside the gates, and go in on foot.

A soldier will escort you round the **temple site** of Paleokastro, probably displaying a surprising amount of knowledge. To the layman the site today is no more than a huddle of foundations with one deepish well from which a tunnel is said to have led off towards the sea below. Excavated in 1929, the 2,000 votive figures were found round the temple altar. Of these, only two were female, a few hermaphrodite and the remainder male, most of them shown wearing conical helmets. They have been dated to 750–500BC.

The coastline here is magnificent, with rocky coves beside the fine sandy sweep of Güzelyurt Bay. Currently deserted, there is talk of hotel projects at some unspecified future point.

More interesting to most than the Paleokastro foundations, however, is a nearby **rock tomb**, discovered only in 1988 by Turkish archaeologists. It is thought to belong to a king, as gold and treasure were found inside. The tomb lies about 1km back along the track towards Ayia Irini, some 200m to the left of the road. Although no longer in a military area, it is difficult to find without the help of the soldiers since it lies underground and is not visible till you are virtually upon it. Built of large well-crafted blocks, the entrance leads down steps into a main chamber with alcoves off it for the sarcophagi of the family members. It is quite likely that more tombs of this sort will be found in the vicinity.

Having returned to the main Girne–Güzelyurt road, you could take the small fork up into the village of **Tepebaşi**, just for some variation in the route. This and Koruçam (to the northwest on the Cape Kormakiti Peninsula) were both Maronite Christian villages, and Tepebaşi was badly damaged in the intercommunal fighting. Many of the village houses near the centre are derelict and crumbling. Higher up the hill, close to the main road, the large domed modern church now serves as a hospital and clinic for the military. **Koruçam** remains the main Maronite village on the island, and these Lebanese Christians continue to use their huge church of Ayios Georgios freely: the Turks never had any quarrel with the Maronites. It's not a problem to visit the church. If it's locked (the side door is usually open) ask around the nearby cafés for the key.

ÇAMLIBEL AND PIGHADES The short detour through Çamlıbel gives you a chance to see the monastery of Ayios Panteleimon briefly from the outside, and then soon after, the charming little Bronze Age sanctuary of Pighades, in Cretan-Minoan style, attractively set by itself in the midst of fields. Ayios Panteleimon cannot be visited as it lies within a military headquarters. The road passes very close by it, so you must content yourself with having a good peer from the car.

Pighades is only 2km outside Çamlıbel, so the total detour including the visit need take only about 40 minutes. There is no site guardian so you can visit any time. It goes without saying that there are no refreshment facilities.

Touring Çamlıbel Arriving at Çamlıbel from Güzelyurt, you reach the T-junction with its army post, but fork right towards Lefkoşa rather than left towards Girne. This road takes you almost immediately past the **Ayios Panteleimon Monastery** on the right, now within the boundaries of the military camp that seems to encompass most of Çamlıbel. Ayios Panteleimon was the patron saint of doctors. In his pagan youth he had studied medicine at Constantinople, but after his conversion to Christianity he cured the deaf, the blind and the lame by prayer alone. Following his martyrdom, his healing powers were said to have transferred themselves to his silver gilt icon at the monastery. The church was heavily restored in the 1920s, when the monastery was the residence of the Bishop of Kyrenia, and very little of any age or interest remained beyond a few icons of the saint dated 1770. The church was closed in the 1950s and is badly run-down. Also of interest, within the military camp but accessible upon the production of photo ID, is **Mavi Köşk**, former home of the intriguing eccentric, Byron Pavlides. Whether he was a successful businessman, gunrunner or harmless eccentric, it's not clear, but he remains a man of mystery (see box, page 69).

Touring Pighades If you're not in a hurry a short detour will encompass this small Bronze Age sanctuary. It lies scarcely 2km along the same road that passes Ayios Panteleimon on the way to Lefkoşa. It is signposted, the sign pointing along a 200m track by a row of cypress trees before reaching a cluster of them set in the middle of fields.

Amongst these trees lies the **Temple of Pighades** (1600–1050BC), with its centrepiece of a small step pyramid-shaped altar, some 3m high, built from large stone blocks. It is topped with two stones in the shape of a bull's horns, strongly reminiscent of the Cretan-Minoan horns of consecration with which it is contemporary. The excavated area has revealed a double courtyard with cisterns, all surprisingly well constructed for this early date.

The road that continues southeast towards Lefkoşa across the plain is heavily militarised, each village along the way having been largely transformed into a military camp.

At Yilmazköy (Greek Skylloura) a small road forks to the right through the village towards Gürpinar. Pre-partition maps will show the Prophitis Elias Monastery here on the hillside behind the village, but the area is now a military camp, and the road terminates at the barrier, leaving the monastery tantalisingly in view beyond.

Forking left at Yilmazköy, a road leads off towards Şirinevler, and beyond to the heavily ruined village of Akçiçek with its vandalised church. After Akçiçek, a rough dirt track leads over the mountain range passing through an area of blasting and quarrying, and bringing you eventually, bruised and battered, to Lapta from the rear. This route is not for the faint-hearted, starting out rough and just getting rougher. If you're in a Jeep and are not afraid to use it then this route makes a memorable excursion. However, take a wrong turn in a non-4x4 car and you might find yourself looking at a long walk in search of tractor with a tow rope.

LAPTA Lapta is one of the most picturesque towns in the north of the island, with a superb setting on several mountain terraces overlooking the sea. Formerly Greek, there are three churches in the town, either locked or ruined. Its sister town of Lambousa on the coast below served in Roman times as its port, and some remains of harbour installations, like the harbour wall and fish tanks, are still worth a quick visit. Nearby are two pretty churches which can be seen from the outside though they are firmly within the confines of a military camp and not visitable. This is a shame as one of them has an early mosaic floor.

A drive around the town of Lapta will take about 30 minutes, as the road network is positively labyrinthine. The visit to the Roman fish tanks at Lambousa will take an hour to an hour and a half as you have to walk along the coast from the Mare Monte Hotel.

Touring Lapta Lapta lies about halfway between Çamlıbel and Girne, and the turn-off to it is well signposted from the main road. The town is reached after about 2km, but the maze of roads leading up and down and all over the various levels of terraces amount to at least a further 5km. These terraces are a natural geological formation, relics of the higher sea levels, and interspersed with huge rocky outcrops, ravines and chasms. One moment you glimpse a church set up above on a cliff edge, and your next view of it is from above surrounded by orchards and still seemingly inaccessible.

Water seems to gush in abundance all over Lapta, in one place more like a waterfall than a stream, making it one of the most fertile spots in Cyprus, famous for its orange and lemon groves. A perennial spring (one of the very few on the island) issues from a rock above the town, at an altitude of some 280m, reached by the road which continues on above the town.

Under the Romans Lapta was one of the four administrative capitals of the island. It grew still further in the 7th century, when its sister town of Lambousa on the coast was being regularly pillaged by raiding Arabs, like most coastal settlements. When the population moved up the hillside, they carried with them many of the stones from Lambousa to build their new houses at Lapta.

Today you can still visit the ruins of **Lambousa** on a headland near the Mare Monte Hotel. From the main Girne road, follow the large sign to the hotel that points off close to the Alsancak turning. Leaving the car at the hotel car park, follow the sign pointing westward. The dirt track splits by the sea, with the left fork leading to the nearby farm, while the right fork heads towards the beach and the ruins. Once you hit the beach, turn left and walk west until you come to the ruins. The total time to reach the site from the hotel is 15 minutes at a leisurely pace. This is no longer within the grounds of the hotel, and shepherds are often to be found grazing their sheep in the ruins. It is best therefore to put on something rather more than your swimsuit, to prevent any misunderstandings.

You come first to the **Roman fish tanks** on the headland, the largest of which are the size of a good hotel pool, about 30m by 15m. Guests at the hotel who had stumbled on them during their evening strolls, considered them to be precisely that: the pools of a hotel since pulled down or never finished. They are cut into the rock beside the harbour, and were used by the Roman fishermen to keep their catch alive and therefore fresh for market. Waves splashing over the rock ensured the water was cool and constantly renewed, and intake channels specially positioned to tally with the tides and prevailing winds guaranteed that clean water entered the tanks, while another suitably positioned exit channel guided out the staler warmer water. These tanks are one of the first examples of Roman fish tanks to be found.

Inland from them, on the other side of the path, are the scant remains of Lambousa, sprawling over the headland. The overwhelming impression at first sight is of mounds of rubble everywhere, but this is not so much the work of Arab raiders as of illicit treasure seekers, digging for their fortunes. Lambousa in fact means 'brilliant', a name justified by the quantities of Roman and Byzantine treasure found here, notably the famous early 7th-century silver plates depicting the story of David, some of which are still to be seen in the Cyprus Museum. The place was abandoned completely in the 13th century.

The original town was founded by the Greeks in the 12th century BC, but it was the Romans who made it into a major trading centre, establishing a naval base and dockyard here. The **Roman harbour wall** is quite well preserved, visible as you walk a little further round the headland. It is still in use with a handful of small fishing boats.

Just 200m beyond the headland to the west, you can see the little churches of Akhiropitos Monastery and Ayios Eulalios, now unfortunately firmly within a military camp. You can get a good view of the latter from The **Hut Restaurant** (see page 66). This section of coastline can also be reached from the main road, by driving down the tarmac fork that runs to the sea directly opposite the sign pointing inland to Alsancak.

The closest church, set in the military exercise ground, is the charming little single-domed **Ayios Eulalios**, named after one of Lambousa's bishops. The outer structure dates from the 15th century, but inside it has an early mosaic floor and fine grey marble columns supporting the nave. The **Akhiropitos Monastery** is within the camp proper and is much more difficult to see. Its name means 'built without hands' in Greek, from the story, somewhat ironic in the circumstances, that it was transported here intact overnight from Asia Minor to save it from Muslim desecration. It was founded in the 12th century and rebuilt in the 14th century. Disused for some time, the monastery cells were occupied in the 1960s by animals and shepherds. Rising damp had been threatening the buildings for some time before partition, but now the problem requires urgent attention.

ALSANCAK TO KARAMAN The 15km of coastline between Alsancak and Girne are now fairly developed, passing a series of hotels, motels and holiday villages. Inland from Alsancak, a short detour will bring you to Malatya, a hill village with a fine gorge and permanent waterfall in a grotto on its eastern edge.

Some 9km west of Girne, just beside the Denizkizi Royal Hotel and the Altınkaya Restaurant, is a monument reminiscent of fascist architecture, its sloping concrete fingers stretching inland towards the mountains. It marks the spot referred to by the Greeks as Invasion Beach, and by the Turks as the point from which the 1974 Turkish Peace Operation was launched. Close by is the **Peace and**

Freedom Museum (☉ *winter 09.00–12.30 & 13.30–16.45 Mon–Fri; summer 09.00–14.00 Mon–Fri; £1.20/free adults/students*), with an open-air display of guns and tanks, both Greek and Turkish, used in intercommunal fighting from 1955 to the present. It was hereabouts that Colonel Karaoğlanoğlu, after whom a village is now named, and his soldiers were killed in the early days of the fighting in 1974.

Nearby, a small **sculpture** on the seafront commemorates the Peace Operation, whilst a helpful sign by the roadside explains the imagery. Most visitors will pass by here without a second thought, but for some it represents something of a pilgrimage. For Turkish tourists it's a must-see, and you're quite likely to encounter coach loads of sightseers taking group photographs and laying flowers at one of the 70 headstones commemorating fallen comrades. Such visits are obviously pre-arranged, as a young Turkish soldier will then deliver a rousing speech which will be followed by a hearty round of applause and more group photography.

The road inland to Karaman forks off at the sprawling little village of **Karaoğlanoğlu**, once known as Tiger Bay by the British, and having a number of good supermarkets and restaurants. It lies just 5km west of Girne. From here the road climbs some 4km up into the mountains, passing *en route* the village of **Edremit** with its photogenic basket shop.

Karaman (Karmi) The road ends at the picture-book village of Karaman, magnificently set beneath the outcrop of St Hilarion. Curiosity is the main thing that will push you to visit this little mountain village, curiosity to see the only village in North Cyprus that has been entirely renovated by foreigners. It also boasts a small Bronze Age site, a couple of good bars and two restaurants (see page 65 for details).

Karaman is a 20-minute drive from Girne, and the last part is up a narrow winding road that climbs to the village and stops there. You might time your visit to coincide with lunch or dinner, or outside the summer heat allow an extra hour or so to walk up the mountain path towards St Hilarion Castle (see pages 56–60), set just above the village.

Formerly a Greek village, it was badly damaged in the fighting, and after partition the Turkish Cypriot government leased the entire village to the Ministry of Tourism for development. The Ministry of Tourism in turn leased the houses to foreigners for renovation, and the whole place has consequently been rebuilt in old village style, inhabited by expats, most of whom have chosen to retire here. The names of some of the roads – Mulberry Way and Geranium Lane for example – and the traditional British Crow's Nest pub in the centre of the village give a clue as to the nationality of the majority of the residents, though Swiss, French, Germans, Canadians and Belgians have also chosen Karaman as their home.

The 19th-century **church** is pretty much as it was pre-1974 and, although it no longer holds services, it is the venue for occasional village events. The neighbouring village of İlgaz has also been redeveloped on a similar model though not under the auspices of the Ministry of Tourism. The **Bronze Age cemetery** lies about a kilometre below Karmi. A signpost by a bend in the road points along a path leading to an enclosure boasting a number of tombs which have been dated 1900–1800BC, making them older than the Royal Tombs at Salamis. In the roofed-over Tomb 6 you can just about make out the oldest funerary relief on the island – that of a primitive fertility goddess, heavily weathered.

EAST FROM GIRNE

The excursions described in this section are among the highpoints of any visit to northern Cyprus and should not be missed by anyone who loves walking and mountain scenery.

The two Crusader castles of Buffavento and Kantara are in spectacular settings perched on craggy summits, and the derelict monasteries of Sourp Magar, Antiphonitis and Panayia Ahsinthiotissa are nestled in gentle folds deep in the pine forests of the Kyrenia range. As well as the beauty of the settings, the sites themselves are also of great intrinsic interest.

The drive to the mountain monasteries involves a bit of bumping along forest tracks, but nothing that a saloon car driven slowly cannot handle. Access to Buffavento, once 4x4 only, has recently been upgraded and though a single and precipitous gravel track, it's currently no problem for a normal saloon car. The walk to Kantara and the monasteries is straightforward and gentle, while the climb to Buffavento is via steps recently constructed by the military, taking a good 45 minutes for the young and averagely fit. There are no refreshment facilities at any of these places, and it is best to go equipped with your own food and drink.

The trips to Buffavento and to the mountain monasteries can be done in half that time, and whilst it is possible, if you are feeling energetic, to do all in the same day, it is preferable and more in keeping with the gentle pace of the island to reserve the excursions for separate days. The journey along the coast to Kantara certainly requires a full day, as the drive one-way takes a good two hours.

WHERE TO STAY
Upmarket

⌂ **Acapulco Beach Club & Resort Hotel** (470 rooms) ☎ 824 41 11; f 824 44 55; e acapulco@acapulco.com.tr; www.acapulco.com.tr. 10km east of Girne, an enormous bungalow village offering one of the cleanest & best-maintained beaches around Girne. Rooms & bungalows are available on an HB basis only, which makes this a less attractive option for those wanting to explore the island. However, excellent facilities for families & for anyone who enjoys sport. Watersports, tennis, volleyball, basketball, swimming pool, aqua park, spa, jacuzzi, Turkish bath & last but not least, you guessed it... a casino. Courtesy bus to Girne. $$$$

⌂ **The Dedeman Olive Tree Resort** (105 rooms) ☎ 824 42 00; f 824 42 09; e olivetree@dedeman.com; www.dedeman.com. Considered one of the most luxurious holiday villages on the island. Huge pool, tennis & fitness facilities together with ubiquitous casino. Located above Çatalköy. $$$$

Mid-range

⌂ **Altınkaya** (69 rooms) ☎ 815 50 01/2; f 815 50 03; e altinkaya@altinkaya-cyprus.net; www.altinkaya-cyprus.com. Set in the charming village of Ozanköy, this complex has a pool & associated restaurant. $$

⌂ **Ambelia Village** (52 rooms) ☎ 815 36 55; f 815 77 01; e managment@cyprus-ambelia.com; www.cyprus-ambelia.com. Set in the mountains near Bellapais, 5km from Girne. Features 2- or 4-bedroom studios & villas in a setting of mature trees & flowering shrubs, with fine views. Central bar & restaurant promoting organic produce as well as a bar set around a small pool. $$

Budget

⌂ **Club Tropicana** (14 rooms) ☎ 815 51 88; f 815 16 35; e info@cyprus-tropicana.com; www.cyprus-tropicana.com. Small, family-run complex, 10mins' walk from the pretty Ozanköy village. Swimming pool, attractive gardens, poolside bar, traditional home cooking & self-catering apts available. $

⌂ **Courtyard Inn** (4 bungalows) ☎/f 815 33 43; e enquiries@courtyard-inn-cyprus.com; www.courtyard-inn-cyprus.com. Situated in pleasant, tree-shaded grounds near Karakum, 2km from Girne, this smallish hotel-cum-restaurant is signposted right off the main road. All rooms are equipped with AC, TV & fridge, & there's the obligatory pool too. $

⌂ **The Fez** (13 rooms) ☎ 824 46 00; e thefezcatalkoy@yahoo.co.uk; www.thefez.biz. Situated by the entrance to Çatalköy, this delightful restaurant, bar & pool also has rooms for rent. Guests speak of a wonderfully friendly welcome. A room-only bargain! $

✖ WHERE TO EAT

✖ **China Garden** ☎ 824 43 98. Situated 5km from Girne, this restaurant offers evening dining in a beautiful setting. As its name suggests, a purveyor of oriental cuisine with some Turkish dishes thrown in. £5

✖ **Courtyard Inn** (contact details as above) Now run by Mohammed, owner of Mo's Balti House in Kyrenia, this attractive restaurant has undergone a few changes of ownership over the past few years, but has kept its high standards & reputation throughout. As befits the new owner, the food now includes a number of dishes from the subcontinent alongside the usual English staples (roast dinners, fish & chips, etc). Unpretentious & reasonable value. £6.50

✖ **Erol's** ☎ 815 91 36. Popular restaurant near the centre of Ozanköy offering a largely grill-based menu with a huge selection of *meze* dishes. Soups come highly recommended too. Book ahead in summer. £8

✖ **Paradise Restaurant** ☎ 824 43 97. 5km from Girne in Ozanköy to the left (sea-side) of the coastal road. Boasts daily fresh fish, *meze*, kebabs & *kleftiko*. It also has a bar, swimming pool & some bungalows to rent. £8

Small restaurants are slowly popping up along the northern coast road towards the Karpas:

✖ **Ani** ☎ 824 43 55. Superb *meze* & fish dishes served by brothers Menteş & Fuat on the eastern edge of Çatalköy. The special for 4 or more is large fish, oven baked in rock salt. £4.50

✖ **The Lemon Tree** ☎ 824 40 45. In Çatalköy, serving fresh fish & traditional food. It also has live music on Fri & Sat nights. £8

✖ **Taner's Secret Terrace** (formerly Taner's) ☎ 815 80 13; m 0533 841 05 50. On the left, about half a mile past the speed camera... An unstoppable torrent of delicious *meze* continues to be the speciality, now complemented by a varied menu of traditional Cypriot dishes. £9

After these, there is little else until Alagadi, 18km from Girne:

✖ **Benöz** ☎ 0533 863 38 23. At Alagadi, after the power station but before the turtle beach, & serves up simple but satisfying *meze*, fish & kebabs. £6.50

✖ **St Kathleen's Restaurant & Bar** ☎ 0533 861 76 40. Serves simple kebabs & snacks. It is named after the ruined basilica between it & the sea. £6

BEACHES

Karakum A small horseshoe cove of sand ideal for young children, just 3km east of Girne. You'll need a keen sense of direction to get down to the water in the right place, before branching right to follow the coast to the cove.

Acapulco (*Entry £6*) Belongs to the holiday village, Club Acapulco, 10km east of Girne. Probably the best beach on the north coast for children with its shallow water and gentle shelving. It's also one of the most expensive, and features a long stretch of clean sand bounded by rocky promontories. Straw umbrellas, sunbeds and watersports are available. On the eastern promontory stands the excavated Neolithic site of Vrysi (see page 87). There's a self-service beach restaurant, children's playground and a tennis court.

Lara (*Entry £4*) 2km east of Acapulco and, though it may feel as though you're heading for the power station, a very pretty bay with rock and sand lies at the end of the track. Sometimes a little 'tarry'. There's an attractive restaurant with picnic area. Fine for children, but adults may prefer the area of smooth limestone rock slabs and rock pools beyond the western edge of the sandy bay. The cliffs behind these rock slabs are also fun to explore, with caves and other weird formations.

Alagadi (*Entry free*) 18km from Girne, this is the longest stretch of sand on the north coast and unquestionably one of the most beautiful spots on the island – it has now been designated a 'Halk Plaj' (public beach), so there's no access fee. Inland the view looks directly onto the five peaks of Beşparmak Mountain (see page 88). Access from the main road is from a metalled road leading to a large, well-defined car park. Alagadi is often referred to as 'Turtle Beach' as it is a favoured spot for loggerhead turtles to come ashore and lay their eggs (see pages 14–15). Volunteers try to keep the beach clean and access is limited to guided turtle-watching groups between 20.00 and 08.00.

Karaağaç (*Entry free*) 25.5km from Girne just before Esentepe, there's a small secluded shingly bay not visible from the road. The track off is marked by a small group of stone farm buildings, but is too rocky to be driven far. The walk to the sea takes about ten minutes, and passes through the ruins of ancient Kharcha (see page 88), for which this beach was once the harbour.

Yalı Gazinosu (*Entry free*) 53km from Girne, a cluster of small sandy beaches visible from the road. No amenities.

Kaplıca (*Entry free*) 69km from Girne, a long, remarkably clean sandy beach just before the turn-off to Kaplica and Kantara Castle, whose outline can be seen on the crest of the mountains above. A large recently developed hotel stands in front of it (*www.kaplicabeach.8m.com*). Good picnic spot *en route* to Kantara.

Yeni Erenköy (*Entry free*) 67km east of Girne, soon after the town of Yeni Erenköy, a track leads down onto this sandy Halk Plaj or public beach, which has a restaurant, showers and cabins that function from April to October.

Karpaz Plaj (*Entry free*) 2km beyond Yeni Erenköy at the Deks Restaurant. Swimming is possible, though a bit tricky, in the rocky bay below. There are three abandoned Greek churches here.

Ayios Philon (*Entry free*) Some 4km beyond Dipkarpaz, this sandy bay below the ruined basilica was once the harbour of ancient Karpasia. Now it's the new home to Oasis at Ayfilon (see page 134).

Aphendrika (*Entry free*) 10km beyond Dipkarpaz, at the end of the road on the northern coastline, where a group of three picturesque ruined churches stand. The walk to the sea is a long one, 1.5km to the east of the ruins across the fields. The beach is sandy with advancing dunes and is utterly deserted.

The southern coastline of the Karpas has many beaches, often sandy, but most are difficult to reach and have no amenities. The most magnificent stretch of all lies close to the tip, a few kilometres before the Apostolos Andreas Monastery. It is known as **Golden Sands** (though the wild dunes often look more red than golden) and is a major breeding ground for sea turtles. It is marred only by tar and accumulated sea debris. The tip of the peninsula itself is rocky and swimming is very tricky.

WHAT TO SEE AND DO

Buffavento An essential outing for all who love heights, castles and adventure. This is the highest of the island's three Crusader fortresses, and the most difficult to reach. However, its setting is the most dramatic of any ruin on the entire island and well worth the trip. Remember to pack your head for heights, as the final 8km of the approach is along a precipitous gravel road. The steep climb from where the gravel road ends to the summit takes about 45 minutes, often on a concrete pathway and steps, with very little shade.

There is no longer any guardian at the castle, so in theory you can visit any time and although the military has been known to restrict visiting days in the past, no evidence of this practice was apparent at the time of writing. The drive from Girne to where the gravel road ends below the castle takes about 45 minutes.

Touring Buffavento The distinctive shape of Buffavento's rocky crag dominates the northern coastline, and hovers ever present, beckoning seductively for most of the approach drive. Its outline bulges upwards, as if an unseen hand has struck the brow of the mountain range, making the terrain come up in an almighty bump. The only road approach is by a gravel road from the east. The really masochistic can, however, make a whole day of it, ascending from Bellapais by donkey on a 12km (7.5 mile) track, having made arrangements at the village beforehand.

By car, you leave Girne on the Gazimağusa road, following the coastal strip eastwards for some 10km, until you reach the fork left towards Esentepe and the Karpas. You stay on the main Gazimağusa road as it heads inland and begins to climb up into the mountains, approaching the distinctive Beşparmak Mountain to the left of the road, with its five rocky fingers reaching to the sky. Immediately at the brow of the pass, two stony, signposted tracks head off to the left and right. To the left is the path to the Sourp Magar Monastery. To the right, and also signposted, is the Buffavento track which you must follow for some 8km as it runs along the ridge of the mountains, giving fine views to the south over the Nicosia plain.

From leaving the tarmac, it takes a maximum of 30 minutes to reach the point where the track ends, at an open space with a well under a shady olive tree. Emphasising the rugged nature of the terrain, there's also a battered memorial listing those who perished in a 1988 Turkish Airlines crash. During the final 2km you will notice that the land immediately below you belongs to a military camp, and red signs proclaim it as military and forbidden. At one point the shooting range is uncomfortably close, but from your higher vantage point, it is perfectly clear whether or not it is in use. The road you are on is in no way forbidden territory, and as long as you stay on it and never venture downhill, you are perfectly safe. But pay attention: the Turkish army have created a number of paths across the mountainside and the turning for the final ascent towards the olive tree is easy to miss. Look for the easternmost right-hand track, a hairpin that sits at the junction of four tracks. The junction is marked with a yellow sign for the castle, but gives no indication of the correct direction.

On emerging from the car at the olive tree, the sheer silence of the place is striking. Above you on the summit are the distant crenellations which are your goal, and down below you are aware of the military presence in its incongruous headquarters, the **Ayios Chrysostomos Monastery**. The monastery itself is not actually visible until you have reached the first level of the castle. From that higher vantage point, you can see the yellow ochre painted walls peeping out from behind the hill which obscures it when viewed from lower down, and a tall old cypress tree stands by its door. According to local tradition, a queen who suffered from leprosy lived apart in the high castle, and her dog, her only companion, caught the disease from her. Slowly, however, he was cured, for he had discovered at the foot of the mountain, a mineral spring with miraculous healing powers. The queen followed him to the spring and was herself cured, whereupon she had the monastery built beside it in gratitude. Today, some of the oldest henna plants on the island are said to grow around the monastery.

Other traditions have the Empress Helena, mother of Constantine, as founder, but at any rate what remains of the monastery is now largely modern. The double church still has some frescoes of the 11th and 12th centuries which are among the most important on the island. It also retains a magnificent double door, built entirely without nails and set in a frame of carved marble, dated to the 16th century. The monastery is not accessible to visitors these days, but a North Cyprus television documentary revealed the inside to viewers. It showed the frescoes whitewashed up to a height of 1.7m; this was, according to the military, a deliberate act to protect them. The frescoes were restored in 1972 with great skill by the Dumbarton Oaks Byzantine Institute of Harvard University, and their condition under the whitewash is therefore likely to be good. Any faces of Apostles that appeared higher than 1.7m had wallpaper put over their eyes by the soldiers, in accordance with the Muslim belief that the Apostles must be blinded. Also out of bounds is the 12th-century church, now heavily ruined, lower down the hill below Chrysostomos, on the road to Güngor (Koutsovendis), with its faded fresco of the *Lamentation over the Body of Christ*.

From leaving the car, the steep walk up to the first gateway takes 30 minutes. The path is rocky, so appropriate footwear should be worn. Like St Hilarion, the castle is divided into an upper and a lower ward, though the ruins are far less complete here than at Hilarion. From the gateway, the climb up to the summit, mainly on steps and often wonderfully vertiginous, takes a further 15–20 minutes. The summit is 955m, and even the Chrysostomos Monastery at 620m is nearly three times higher than Bellapais. In the last century the ascent was distinctly trickier than it is on today's path, as witness the following description by a Spanish traveller:

The peak itself is a rock nearly perpendicular on every side. There was no further trace of a path, so we climbed this natural wall, taking advantage of jutting rocks, projections, holes, anything to which our hands and feet would cling. Sometimes we had to help one another with a stick, or the guide would stop to see where he could get the best foothold, so as to get over the parapet in front of him; and to complete the picture, we had always beside us a horrible precipice.

Disparaging comments are often made about the paltry nature of the ruins at Buffavento, along with jokes about its name 'buffetted by the wind' meaning that everything on the summit has been blown away. Yet the ascent to Buffavento, because of the terrain and the stupendous location, makes if anything an even deeper impression than the other two Crusader castles, and the wonder is how anything was ever built up here at all. For a time in the early 1970s a guardian was posted up here, but he has since abandoned his lonely job. Indeed, at the time of writing, in tourist high season, no other visitors were apparent apart from lizards and birds; Buffavento's only resident was a large black publicity-shy snake.

You arrive now at the deserted first section of the castle, entered by a fine **arched gateway**. Inside is a cluster of chambers, one of which is built over a cistern. The red tiles used in the arches around the doorways are reminiscent of the Seljuk style of mainland Turkey.

Right on the summit are the remains of a **chapel** and a few other buildings, but most memorable are the staggering views, often through wisps of cloud, over the coast and back towards Lefkoşa and the Troodos Mountains beyond.

Like Hilarion and Kantara, Buffavento was constructed as part of a chain of defence against the Arab raids in Byzantine times. The Byzantine despot king of the island, Isaac Comnenus, fled here to escape the clutches of Richard the Lionheart at the time of the Third Crusade. Isaac's daughter surrendered it and herself to Richard in 1191, and the castle was thereafter fortified by the Lusignan Frankish knights and maintained as a prison called Château du Lion. The Venetians dismantled it fairly thoroughly in the 16th century to deny the islanders any chance of using the inland stronghold in any revolt against them. The Venetians' own interest was restricted to the coast, and they had no desire to maintain costly garrisons in these inland castles.

The mountain monasteries The ruined monasteries of Sourp Magar, Antiphonitis and Panayia Absinthiotissa all have superb settings deep in the forest of the Kyrenia Mountains, and make wonderful spots for peaceful picnics and mountain walks. Sourp Magar has some interesting decorative features, and Antiphonitis still has extensive frescoes. A couple of other ruined monasteries in the area don't really justify a visit.

Much of the driving is on earthy forest tracks, which present no problem for saloon cars unless there has been recent rain. The final 1km of track to all the monasteries is quite steep in gradient, and sometimes deep ruts created by previous rainfall make driving tricky. When this is the case, it is best to walk the final kilometre. Should you break down, you are a long way from help. The drive from Girne to Sourp Magar is about 55 minutes. From here there used to be a track that continued along the mountain ridge to Antiphonitis, though in recent years this has been closed. Assuming there has been no reopening, you'll have to return to the main Girne–Gazimağusa road, take a left towards Gazimağusa and take a left towards the herbarium and Esentepe. Including time for walking and full exploration, as well as a picnic, a total of four hours for the excursion should be allowed. From Esentepe you can then drop down to the coast road and continue west back to Girne. As for the third monastery, Panayia Absinthiotissa, this sits in a different part of the Kyrenia range, though is still easily accessible by taking the main dual carriageway Girne–Lefkoşa road, forking off east at Bogazköy through Aşaği Dikmen. From there the monastery is clearly visible, though you may want to ask for directions in the village as there are plenty of paths leading off the correct track.

The trip to see these monasteries is worthwhile not only for the monasteries, of which only one is in a reasonable condition, but also to savour the tranquillity and beauty of the forest. Once you have forked off the main Gazimağusa road, you may well not encounter another car till you return to tarmac above Esentepe. Indeed the only time the mountains get busy is on summer weekends, when the picnic tables at the nearby Alevkaya (Halevga) Forest Station can be full of local families having an outing. Very few, however, visit the monasteries, which are also utterly abandoned save for a guardian at Antiphonitis, there to protect the frescoes.

Sourp Magar Monastery If you have visited Buffavento in the morning, and are still feeling robust and ripe for adventure, all you need to do to visit Sourp Magar is cross the tarmac road at the brow of the hill and continue eastwards along the crest of the range. (You may want to stop at the timbered restaurant sitting by the turn-off, which does good-value local cuisine and sits in a pleasant, if somewhat chilly location.)

The narrow road has been recently resurfaced and makes for a pleasant drive into the forest, with far-reaching views down to the sea. The turn-off to the monastery can easily be missed, hidden as it is amongst the trees of a picnic site. Should you arrive at a T-junction, just nearby to the Alevkaya (Halevga) Forest Station, then you've gone about 100m too far. The atmosphere and superb location, nestling into the crook of the wooded mountains with distant views of the sea, make this monastery an unforgettable spot. Yet as you step down into the terraced courtyard, the desolation that greets you is enough to make you weep. Here in the beauty and silence of the mountains lies this gutted carcass, traces of its former splendour apparent at every turn – in the smashed tiles, the neglected citrus trees and the broken stairways.

Although the last monks left early in the 20th century, a resident guardian ensured, until 1974, that the place was maintained, and it was even possible for visitors and mountain wayfarers to spend the night in the monks' old rooms. The Armenian community in Nicosia used it as a summer resort, and orphans of the 1895–96 massacres in Turkey were sent here to be educated by the monks. On Sourp Magar's feast day, the first Sunday in May, the place was the scene of much festivity. The monastery used to own 10,000 donums (a donum is about a third of an acre) of land covered in carob, olive and pine trees, and crops and vegetables were grown on the terracing below, with the help of an elaborately constructed irrigation system. Now abandoned and unguarded, the monastery has been the victim of wanton vandalism. The monastery church has had its altar hacked to pieces and the Armenian tilework, the only decorative ornamentation left here, has been prised off the floor and smashed.

First founded in the year 1000, the current buildings date from the 19th and 20th centuries. The Armenian name Sourp Magar refers to the Egyptian hermit Saint Makarios (309–404), whose Coptic (Egyptian Christian) monastery still stands in the Wadi Natrun between Cairo and Alexandria. This Cypriot monastery too was originally a Coptic one, but was passed to the Armenian Church c1425.

Mystery Monastery In the mountains some 15 minutes' walk above the road from the Armenian monastery is an unnamed monastery, heavily ruined, and thought to date from the 12th century. Beside it is a very old and unusual tree tethered with iron ropes. The spot is difficult to find without a local guide.

Antiphonitis Monastery (⊕ *09.00–16.00 daily; £2.00/1.20 adults/students. This is the only monastery of the 3 with an entrance fee which goes towards the upkeep of the monastery & the provision of facilities – café & toilet*) Coming from Sourp Magar, take a left at the T-junction near the forest station, then a few minutes later another left to turn onto the road to the **Alevkaya North Cyprus herbarium**, a little museum of 800 local plant specimens pressed or preserved by Dr Deryck Viney, an expatriate resident of Karmi. It is open from 08.00 until 16.00, and was a project aided by the Forestry Department.

For Antiphonitis, continue past the herbarium and down the hill on the winding forest track for 8km until you reach a junction at a bend in the road where a dirt track heads off right. A signpost points out that this is the way to Antiphonitis. Follow this picturesque track as it winds and climbs for some 6km until it reaches a huge incongruous electricity pylon. Straight on is unsignposted, as is the smaller track that drops steeply downhill to the left of it, and it is this latter track that will lead you directly down to Antiphonitis, nestling below in a fold of the mountain, its red-tiled dome protruding unmistakably from the surrounding green. The steep track is driveable with care in a saloon car, unless there has been recent rainfall, but if you prefer to walk, it will take only 15 minutes.

Architecturally, Antiphonitis is of far greater merit than Sourp Magar, and the lovely **Byzantine church**, centre of the monastery until 1965, dates to the 12th century when it was built by a monk from Asia Minor. The porch and graceful **Gothic loggia** (open arcade) were added in the 15th century under the Lusignans, and inside the derelict shell you are staggered to see exquisite **frescoes** still preserving their colour surprisingly well. It was in the wall paintings of such tiny rustic churches, tucked away in remote places, and often financed by private donors, that Cypriot Christian art achieved its own distinctive style, and such frescoes are today their finest legacy.

The dome reveals itself, on close examination, not to be a perfect circle, but its disproportionately large size gives it fine acoustics, if you fancy a bit of chanting. Appropriately, the name Antiphonitis means, loosely translated, Christ who Responds. High up in the dome is the lovely deep blue background of the *Christ Pantokrator*, and on the south wall is the unusual *Last Judgement* scene, both from the 15th century. In the southwest corner are the main, early 12th-century frescoes. In recent years two professional attempts have been made, probably by locals under the instruction of international art dealers, to steal sections of these frescoes. These two sections can be identified quite clearly, squares of about half a metre each way, cut into the walls. One of the attempts failed, and the cut-out section crumbled, disintegrating into pieces on the ground. The other is now probably part of a private Byzantine art collection in some distant part of the world.

From Antiphonitis you can, if you are based in Gazimağusa, take the forest track eastwards from the pylon for 500m to reach a further crossroads at which you continue straight on. Some 300m later there is yet another junction, and from here you can fork to the right, downhill some 6km to reach the village of Tirmen where the tarmac begins again. This dramatic descent can be driven with care in a saloon car, though the villagers are generally rather startled to see visitors approach from the mountain heights.

If you are based in Girne, the more likely return is back down on the northern slope of the mountains towards Esentepe. Returning from this direction, you may spot, about halfway back along the forest track, the forlorn little red dome of a derelict Greek church, overgrown with scrub, with no apparent way to it.

Apati Monastery This church is in fact all that remains of the 16th-century Apati Monastery, and as you get closer and pass underneath it, you will notice a poor but driveable track fork off to the left which brings you to within a five-minute scramble of it. Set on a wide grassy terrace, it is empty of frescoes and full of goat droppings.

The old village of Esentepe (Greek Ayios Amvrosios), just 15 minutes' drive below Antiphonitis, was noted for its weaving and woodwork. Beside the church in the village square are a couple of restaurants offering simple fare. From here the drive back to Girne takes 25 minutes.

Panayia Absinthiotissa Monastery This is the least visited of the mountain monasteries, lying as it does on the southern flank of the Kyrenia range and therefore difficult to incorporate into another itinerary. The only maps to mark it are old Greek ones: none of the currently available maps admit to it at all. The monastery itself was originally Byzantine and stands on a platform at a height of 510m (1,700ft), directly above the village, previously Maronite, of Taşkent (Vouno), now inhabited largely by Turkish refugees from the south. In the centre is a small museum displaying photos of atrocities committed during an attack on the village by Greek Cypriot EOKA fighters in 1963.

From the top of the village a tarmac road leads north and after about half a kilometre a dirt track forks off to the right near a gravel pit, then right again opposite a water tower. Round the corner another rough track forks up to the monastery plateau with the bump of Buffavento lowering to the right. A carefully driven saloon car can manage it all the way to the monastery, though a Jeep is preferable. The walk from the tarmac road is in any event only about 15 minutes.

All around the monastery church are numerous outbuildings indicating that quite a prosperous monastic community once flourished here. The church itself is mainly 15th century and is in a good state of repair following some restoration work in the 1960s. Inside are a few heavily defaced frescoes, the main murals having been stolen post-1974, probably by professional black-market traders.

Coastal route to Kantara The 77km drive to Kantara is a magnificent one eastwards taking the Esentepe turn-off along the scenic coast. Development here, although steadily increasing, is nothing in comparison with the shoreline west of Girne. Undoubtedly you will be sharing the road with a regular flow of construction traffic, but in the main a feeling of freedom envelops you as you escape the congestion of the town. The castle of Kantara itself makes a fitting climax to the .trip, perched dramatically astride the ridge, facing the sea on both sides.

The new north coast road here is superb to drive, and a considerable improvement on the old single-track route, although it continues to be the centre of fervent environmental debate for its impact on turtle-nesting beaches and the expedition of further property development. At the time of writing the new road runs as far as Tatlısu, meaning that this section of the journey can now comfortably be completed in 30 minutes. Currently from here, a mixture of the old road and new road bed goes as far as the Mersinlik turn off. Expect another one and a half hours to reach Kantara.

Of course, the drawback of a fast road is that it becomes all too easy to get detached from the landscape through which you are driving. There are plenty of tracks running down to the sea, some of which comprise parts of the old road, and beaches offering countless swimming or picnic opportunities. The temptation is to stay on the tarmac and race through to your destination, but time spent exploring the side roads will yield some worthwhile discoveries.

Hazreti Ömer Tekke (⊕ *09.00–16.00 Sat–Thu*) Some 4km east of Girne, a green sign just before the go-kart circuit points off left towards the coast to 'Hz. Ömer Tekkesi', a delightful little Ottoman mausoleum set on a headland, where seven Muslim saints are buried. The tarmac track leads down some 2km to the whitewashed domes of the shrine, at the end of a rocky bay.

Vrysi Leaving the main Gazimağusa road which heads inland, you continue straight on along the coast, following the signpost to Esentepe. Barely 1km later, after passing a military camp, you come to Acapulco Beach, a pretty bay which has been developed into a hotel bungalow and restaurant complex. The open-air self-service beach restaurant here offers reasonable food and the sandy beach is kept clean and has excellent swimming, safe even for the youngest children. The complex also boasts one of the north's few tennis courts. The fee for non-residents gives use of showers, changing rooms and sunbeds.

On the eastern headland of the bay, just behind the nightclub, is the Neolithic site of Vrysi, excavated from 1969 to 1973 by Glasgow University. Clusters of primitive stone houses were uncovered, thought to have been inhabited between 4000 and 3000BC by Neolithic people from Cilicia on the Mediterranean coast of Turkey opposite Cyprus. Among the finds, 250 bone needles and 62,000 fragments of pottery indicated that the Vrysins were weavers and potters rather than fishermen. To the layman today, the site is of little interest, and almost looks more impressive from below when swimming in the sea. The protective fence has fallen over, and visitors are, alas, free to clamber about on the fast-crumbling walls.

Alagadi Soon after Acapulco Beach, you will pass the signs to Lara Beach, a pretty cove of mixed sand and pebbles, a restaurant and a picnic area. After this, there is no village or restaurant along the coast until you reach the area known as Alagadi, some 18km from Girne, heralded by a couple of simple restaurants set down by the sea. The potential for this stretch of coastline, the longest stretch of sandy beach on the northern coast, and in a beautifully wild setting with the Beşparmak Mountain as backdrop, is enormous. The area is also characterised by extensive sand dunes.

For a number of years conservationists have been concerned about development of the area around Alagadi, because of the threat to turtles who currently favour it to come ashore and bury their eggs in the sand. The construction of the new north coast road disturbed several nesting beaches, and the improved access to the area is now expediting the rate of property development. Although these loggerhead sea turtles are now the subject of several active conservationist projects, it is too soon to say what the long-term impact of the development will be.

There's now a metalled road, identified by signs for the turtle conservation project, leading to a clearly defined parking area, complete with litter barrels! There's also a barrier that closes off the beach to public access from 20.00 to 08.00 during the May to October turtle-nesting season (see pages 14–15 for more details). The long sandy beach is quite magnificent, dominated by the spectacular Beşparmak Mountain. Two local legends surround this five-fingered mountain. Sometimes it is seen as the handprint of the Greek hero Dighenis, left behind as he grabbed hold of boulders to toss onto the Arab pirates; sometimes as a testimony to woman's fickleness: the handful of mud that the man threw at the woman when she rejected him. Another track leads off to the small village of Beşparmak at the foot of the mountain, and the energetic can, if they wish, make an assault on its northern face.

Peeping round the western headland, a significant disfigurement to the landscape is the ugly electric power station, built unconscionably close to the sea, the first one of several planned in North Cyprus. The north of the island currently gets its electricity from the south, in exchange for water, but this situation will change once the north has completed more power stations.

Kharcha ruins Another pretty beach, which has the added interest of archaeological ruins, is some 22km from Girne, just 1km west of the sign inland to the village of Karaağaç. Not signposted, it is more suitable for a day trip from Girne than as a stop *en route* to Kantara, since it takes a good 15 minutes to walk down to the beach from the road. The track to it turns off from the main road beside an old stone farm building. It is too rocky to drive anything more than the first 100m, and then the path descends to the pebbly bay. On the eastern side of the bay is an old Roman jetty and a section of narrow sunken road. All around are fragments of pottery and crafted stone blocks.

This is the harbour and ancient town of Kharcha, traces of which lie scattered over the hillside to the east of the path. With time and patience you can still see, among the scrub and rocks, cisterns and tombs cut into the rock. One tomb, difficult to find and set underground, still bears a carved face on its lintel.

Along the coast, as you drive further east, you will notice ruined shells of large buildings such as that near Esentepe, just where the fork goes off inland. These are old storehouses for carobs and generally date to the 19th century when carobs were exported in large quantities (see box opposite).

Panayia Pergaminiotissa Some 2km east of the Esentepe fork, you may notice, if you are looking out for it, a large whitewashed church set in the fields about 1km off the road. A dirt track leads to it and arrives at the derelict monks' cells, for this was the monastery of Melandryna. The church lies down in a little dip and has now been incorporated into a local farmer's outbuildings, its floor thick with dung. It is nevertheless impressive, and still has the frame of its wooden iconostasis, with fragments of gold, blue and red paint. The interior is whitewashed, with no frescoes. The unusual buttresses were added in 1731 as a strengthening device.

Aphrodision and Galounia The pretty drive meanders eastwards along the coastline, passing a few modern ruins, the large hulks of buildings which were going to be hotels, bought by Greeks pre-1974, but now abandoned for lack of trade along this lonely shore. Old maps mark an ancient site called Aphrodision here on the coast, just at a kink in the road near the fork to Tatlısu, but nothing remains of it save a few rubble foundations. The same is true of Galounia, 18km further east, at the point where the road heads inland. Both are said to be the capital of the Hittite kingdom of Cyprus in 700BC.

Some 8km beyond the Tatlısu fork you drive through an area where the road is flanked by extensive greenhouses, or long plastic sheds to be more precise. If you look inland at this point you will notice peeping out above the undergrowth about 500m from the road, a tiny single-domed church built from grey stone. A rough track leads across to it, which you can bump along in the car or walk in ten minutes.

This delicate church, with its tiny ground area in relation to its height, has an almost Armenian feel to it. Scattered all around it are the ruined fragments of what were presumably once its monastery outbuildings. The church entrance has been completely walled up as a measure to preserve the frescoes inside. By standing on tiptoe on stone blocks you can still peer inside just enough to make out some traces on the walls.

Still further eastwards the road passes another ruined chapel set beside a group of abandoned houses. Today the chapel is used to pen lambs.

Kantara At Kaplıca the road forks inland towards Kantara, just after passing the recently resurrected Kaplıca Beach Hotel set on its own lovely sandy beach, a good spot for lunch and a swim (see map page 81). You then turn up the pine-lined street towards the beacon-like white minaret of the new Rauf Denktash Mosque. You can see the castle beckoning from its ridge up above, and the winding drive from here up a narrow twisting road to reach it takes another 30 minutes.

As you reach the summit of the ridge, you enter the little village of Kantara, strongly reminiscent of the Greek summer resorts of the Troodos. There used to be hotels here, but the decline in visitors since 1974 has meant that only the Kantara Restaurant, not a bad option for lunch, is now left. There are no refreshments at the castle itself, so if you do not bring a picnic, this is your only option.

A narrow tarmac road now runs a further 4km eastwards along the top of the ridge to end below the castle walls by the ticket office. If the guardian is there, you might well find him cooking on his gas stove or playing backgammon with his friend from the mountain fire rescue team. A more convivial place to work is hard to imagine. From here a path, a mixture of steps and earthy ground, brings you to the main castle gateway in just five minutes.

Kantara Castle (⊕ *09.00–18.00 every day supposedly, but don't be surprised if the guardian's not there. In any case it doesn't matter as the castle isn't locked. £2.00/1.20 adult/student*) The relative ease of the approach makes Kantara Castle in some ways less exciting than its two sister castles of St Hilarion and Buffavento and its altitude, at 724m, is also the lowest of the three. It is, however, unique in having splendid views to the sea on both sides, being sited as it is on the beginning of the island's tapering peninsula, the 'Panhandle', or more correctly, the Karpas (Turkish

3

Kirpaşa). On clear days, especially early in the morning, you can glimpse the distant mountains of mainland Turkey, and even, in winter, the snows of Lebanon, 160km away. The word *kantara* is Arabic for arch, and accurately describes the sheer rock walls on which the castle is built, making it accessible only from the east. Here, the entrance is guarded by twin towers, and steps climb up to the iron gate which leads into the castle enclosure.

Inside, the castle is surprisingly elusive, as the ground plan had to adapt to the rocky contours. Locally the castle was referred to as the House of 101 Rooms, and the popular Muslim belief was that anyone who entered the 101st room would suddenly find themselves in paradise and unable to go back through the door. Unlike its sister castles, it is not divided into upper and lower wards, but the summit of the mountain rising up in the centre means that the western half of the castle is not visible at all as you enter. Having clambered up to the summit, you will discover paths leading off through the trees and undergrowth to reach a group of three chambers, the living quarters, one of which has an emergency exit from the castle. Underneath are two large cisterns still full of water.

Returning along the southern wall, the first building you reach is a medieval latrine, barely visible now. The best views and photos are to be had from the roof of the huge northeast tower, the highest constructed point, and which can be reached with a bit of clambering by those who enjoy heights. This tower is the best preserved of any in the island's three mountain castles, with a fine row of arrow slits in its thick windowless walls.

From the ruined chamber at the very summit, messages were transmitted using a system of flares after dark, first to Buffavento, and thence to St Hilarion. At its solitary Gothic window, villagers claimed to see a queen sitting gazing out towards her lost country. She has been there, they say, for the last 500 years, since the castle was abandoned. For 50-odd years in the 19th century, she shared the castle with a hermit called Simeon. The orientation of the castle is towards Gazimağusa, an hour's horseride away, and when the Genoese had seized Gazimağusa from the Lusignans in the 14th century, Kantara was a refuge for many a prisoner who escaped.

The Lusignan lords lived in true feudal style on the island, and on fleeing from Palestine brought with them their semi-oriental ways and habits. With the fall of Acre in 1291, the last Crusader foothold in the Holy Land was lost, but the knights had grown accustomed to their Eastern titles and luxurious lifestyles. Here in the grand quarters of their castles, princes of Antioch, Tyre and Galilee, and counts of Jaffa, Beirut and Caesaria, pursued the pleasures of the chase, hunting moufflon (mountain goats) with tame leopards. The manes and tails of the horses were dyed red with exotic henna, as were the tails of the hunting hounds. One count of Jaffa had more than 500 hounds, with a servant tending to each pair.

Also somewhere within this enclosure, 13 Greek monks were sentenced to death by the Lusignan Crusaders who established the Catholic Church as the official church of the island. The Greek Orthodox bishops were therefore forced to comply with Catholic beliefs, and when the outspoken ones did not, they were, as a contemporary historian described it, 'condemned to be tied by the feet to the tails of horses and mules, and thus dragged over the rough stones in the market place, or the river bed, until the flesh was torn from their bones, and then burnt.'

It is from this time that most of the remoter mountain monasteries date, built far away in the mountains, where the devoted could pursue their faith safe from Catholic interference and persecution.

Alternative return route If you are based at Boğaz, a drive of 35 minutes brings you out, via the villages of Turnalar and Yarköy, to the coast at Boğaztepe. If you are at Gazimağusa or Salamis, the more direct route is via Ardahan and İskele.

4

Lefkoşa (Nicosia)

In the featureless Mesaoria Plain that surrounds Lefkoşa, there is little to detain the visitor. Lefkoşa itself is the worthwhile destination, with a fascinating collection of Crusader Gothic and Turkish Ottoman monuments set within the old Venetian fortifications. Selimiye Camii and the cluster of half a dozen or so buildings in this immediate area form the heart of old Lefkoşa. They were nearly all originally Christian Crusader structures, converted by the Ottomans in the 16th century to Muslim or secular functions. Lefkoşa was the Gothic capital of the Lusignan kings, and they graced it with magnificent palaces, churches and gardens. Much was destroyed in pillaging through the centuries by Venetians, Genoese, Egyptians and Turks, and earthquakes helped wreak the final havoc.

The end result, with its medley of Christian and Muslim, cathedrals turned into mosques, Greek foundations topped by Turkish roofs, churches reworked as public baths, archbishops' palaces reincarnated as municipal offices, is what makes Lefkoşa memorable today.

Anyone who is attracted by things Turkish should spend a day in Lefkoşa. Here, within the walls of the old city, are concentrated the island's major Ottoman monuments, many of them either still in use, or renovated as museums. Lefkoşa is divided into Greek and Turkish sectors by the euphemistically named 'Green Line', erected by the UN, an ugly barrier built from barbed wire and corrugated iron, cutting across the heart of the old walled city. (The Green Line gets its name from the fact that it was originally drawn on a map in green ink by a British army officer.) The sight of streets barricaded and houses bisected has a certain eerie fascination and few will visit Lefkoşa without taking a look at the Green Line. Of course, it's now possible to cross over to the south, and those that do so will be struck by the difference. Where Turkish Lefkoşa retains an old-world charm and sense of individuality, Greek Nicosia is rapidly pursuing the EU dream, with a liberal sprinkling of international coffee shops, high-street boutiques and fast-food outlets providing every tourist with a home-from-home experience. But like all facelifts, the effect is only skin deep – the heart of Greek Nicosia has long since relocated from inside the walls to the new high-rise suburbs of the commercial city.

GETTING THERE AND AROUND

On the main highway funded by the Saudi Arabians, it takes a mere 20 minutes from Girne to Lefkoşa, and many people who work in Lefkoşa commute with ease in half an hour from Girne. Gazimağusa is a 50-minute drive away. It is therefore possible, especially from a Girne base, to visit the major monuments of Lefkoşa in a half-day, but it will be more leisurely and enjoyable to spend a whole day there.

Dolmuş run regularly to Lefkoşa from the other major towns in North Cyprus. Currently, it will cost you only about £1.20 from Girne, £2 return. Dolmuş run from the bus station to Lefkoşa's terminal at the south end of town. Alternatively,

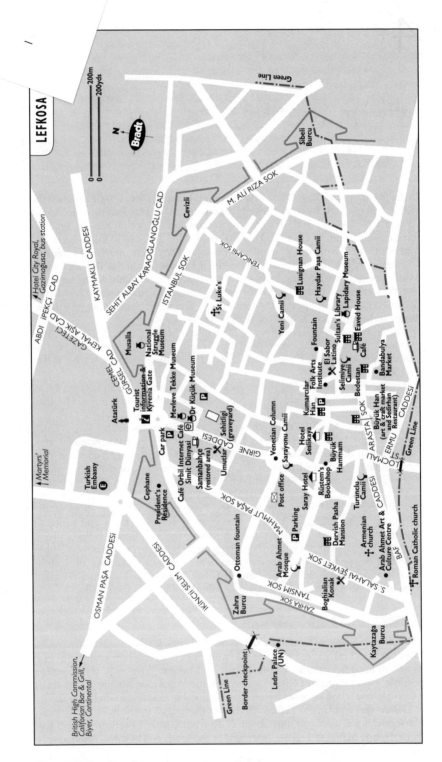

LEFKOSA

Green Line

British High Commission,
Califonian Bar & Grill,
Biyer, Continental

Martyrs'
Memorial

Hotel City Royal,
Gazimağusa, bus station

0   200m
0   200yds

N

Bradt

ABDI İPEKÇİ CAD
GAZETECI CEMEL CAD
KEMAL AŞIK CAD
KAYMAKLI CADDESİ
GÜRSEL CAD
ŞEHİT ALBAY KARAOĞLANOĞLU CAD
İSTANBUL SOK

OSMAN PAŞA CADDESİ
İKINCİ SELİM CADDESİ

Turkish Embassy

President's Residence

Cephane

Atatürk

Tourist Information & Kyrenia Gate

Musalla

National Struggle Museum

Mevleve Tekke Museum

Dr Küçük Museum

Car park

Café Orbil Internet Café
Simit Dünyası

Samanbahçe (restored area)

Şehitliği (graveyard)

Umurtlar CADDESİ

Venetian Column

Sarayonu Camii

Hotel Seslikaya

GIRNE CADDESİ

Ottoman fountain

Post office

Parking

Şaray Hotel

Rüstem's Bookshop

Dervish Pasha Mansion

Arab Ahmet Mosque

Boghjialian Konak

ZAHRA SOK
TANSIM SOK
MAHMUT PAŞA SOK
S. SALAHI ŞEVKET SOK

Zahra Burcu

Kaytazağa Burcu

Ledra Palace (UN)

Border checkpoint

Green Line

Green Line

St Luke's

Yeni Camii

YENİCAMİİ SOK

M. ALİ RIZA SOK

Cevizli

Lusignan House
Haydar Paşa Camii
Lapidary Museum
Eaved House
Sultan's Library

Fountain
El Sabor Latino
Selimiye Camii
Café
Bedestan
Bandabulya Market

Kumarcılar Han
Folk Arts Institute
Büyük Han (art & craft market and Sedirhan ERMU Restaurant)
Büyük Hammam

LOCMALI ARASTA SOK
ERMU CADDESİ

Turuncu Camii

Armenian church

Arab Ahmet Art & Culture Centre

BAF

Roman Catholic church

Sibeli Burcu

92

across the Belediye Meydani in Girne (the central roundabout with the sculpture of the doves in the middle), *dolmuş* charge the same but sometimes drive into the heart of the old city, saving you a ten-minute walk in Lefkoşa.

Traffic around Lefkoşa can be heavy but **driving** into town is still straightforward. From Girne, head directly over the first roundabout with the Gazimağusa road and look for and follow the signs for Ledra Palace. The road passes through the suburb of Ortaköy before eventually widening to four lanes – branch right and you'll arrive at the Kyrenia Gate on your left. Passing through the gate there are several options for parking, one almost immediately off to the left a little way up Girne Caddesi. However, for those keen to dive straight in, continue straight up towards the Venetian column, bear left just after the column and then a right towards the Kumarcılar Han. As you arrive, an 'Oto Park' sign will point the final few yards. The car park behind the Han currently charges £1.20 for four hours and is open from 07.00 to 20.00.

It is fairly easy to **walk** around the walled parts of Lefkoşa, and the main attractions are closely packed together. Distances are small and the twin minarets of the Selimiye Camii, always rising above the rooftops, act as dependable homing beacons. The major monuments are clustered around the Selimiye so a leisurely circuit of them need take no more than three or four hours. Take heed that depending on which map you use, streets and places of interest may well have different names, which all adds to the challenge of competent navigation. It is worth noting that Lefkoşa is blessed with the highest temperatures in the north, but with humidity and its inland position making it a very uncomfortable place over midday.

WHERE TO STAY

The choice of places to stay in Lefkoşa is minimal but there are a couple of hotels providing a convenient base for shopping and exploring the old parts of town. Indeed, the following are the only two hotels that even feature in the official accommodation guide.

🏠 **Hotel City Royal** (86 rooms) ☎ 228 76 21; f 228 75 80; e crhotel@kktc.net; www.city-royal.com. Just up from the bus station, another hotel-cum-casino, but efficiently run &, though it's not really saying much, the smartest address in Lefkoşa. $$$

🏠 **Saray Hotel** (60 rooms) ☎ 228 31 15; f 228 48 08; e saray.hotel@superonline.com. Rather featureless, dreary hotel in town centre, but well placed for the old city. Rooftop bar & restaurant (on 8th floor) with average food but excellent views across to southern Cyprus. Disco & casino. $$$

In addition to these two, there are a number of cheaper pensions in the walled city, close to the Saray Hotel; one of these with some international guests and air-conditioned rooms is the **Hotel Seslikaya** (☎ 227 4192; e seslikayaturizm@hotmail.com. $ room only).

WHERE TO EAT

Eating options are slowly expanding in Lefkoşa, and, whilst the choice might not match Girne, there are restaurants that merit a special visit even if you're not in town, although some lie outside of the old city walls and require careful navigation in order to arrive successfully.

✗ **Boghialian Konak Restaurant** ☎ 228 07 00; ⊕ 12.00–15.30 & 19.00–23.00. Housed in a beautiful restored building on Victoria St, just 100m from the Green Line, this splendid restaurant is full of atmosphere & cooks some wonderful traditional kebab-based dishes. Strong contender for best food in the old city & now open lunchtimes as well as evenings. £7

✕ **Califorian Bar & Grill** ☏ 227 07 00. In the new part of town, west of the old city on Mehmet Akif Caddesi. Lefkoşa's trendiest eatery, an American-style diner that's big on quality fast food but also offers Chinese, Italian & Turkish dishes. £7.

✕ **Biyer** ☏ 228 01 43. On the opposite side of the street from the Califorian Bar & Grill, this traditional restaurant serves up good-value Turkish food & kebabs. £6

✕ **El Sabor Latino** ☏ 228 83 22. Making waves with an array of delicious Italian & Spanish dishes that also attract punters from across the divide. With a relaxed ambience, reasonable prices & an unbeatable location in the shadow of Selimiye Camii this is possibly the finest restaurant in the city. £6

🍵 **Sedirhan Restaurant** ☏ 228 1439. A friendly family-run café/restaurant whose short menu provides all that is necessary for light refreshment during a day's sightseeing. Located in the relaxing oasis of the Büyük Han's courtyard. You may even witness al fresco food prep! £6

✕ **Saray Hotel** ☏ 228 31 15. Saray as a rooftop restaurant offering food of modest standard but the best view of Lefkoşa town. £5

✕ **Umutlar** ☏ 227 32 36. Directly next door to Simit Dünyasi, a standard range of kebabs & burgers for those who fancy something a bit more filling. The quality's average but the pleasant al fresco seating area in the alley towards Samanbahçe is a refreshing place to enjoy the cooling breeze. £4

🍵 **Simit Dünyasi** ☏ 229 01 50; ⏱ 06.00–23.30. Convenient location on the main street near the Kyrenia Gate. Haute cuisine it is not, but with a flavoursome array of breads, pastries & cakes it's the ideal place for a quick snack between sightseeing. £5

WHAT TO SEE AND DO

THE CITY WALLS The modern suburbs offer little to the visitor besides good shopping, but as you approach the centre from the north, the one-way system does a wide loop and sweeps round to bring you in through the fine medieval walls at the Girne Gate, which now stands isolated like a traffic island. It looks more like a bewildered little chapel than a major gateway, as cars and trucks whistle past either side of it, through the two breaches in the walls made by the British in the 1930s. An Arabic inscription above the gate reads:

O Muhammad, give these tidings to the Faithful; Victory is from God and triumph is very near. O opener of doors, open for us the best of doors.

In 1878 when the British annexed the island of Cyprus, it was here that the Turkish doorkeeper permitted the British officers to enter the capital. This colourful character, Ali the Cock, as he was known, also made history by living to the age of 121. Today, the gate has found a new purpose as the home of the city's **tourist office**. Maps and directions are given freely and upstairs, past the dead pigeon, there's a few photos of Lefkoşa from yesteryear (⏱ *08.30–16.30 Mon–Fri, 09.00–13.00 Sat–Sun, although this is not a certainty…*).

Just outside the gate, near the **Atatürk statue**, are a couple of huge **iron cannons**, two of several which are to be found displayed here and there in public gardens or on the ramparts. They were British, made in about 1790 at the Woolwich Arsenal, and were used in the Napoleonic wars in Egypt, later finding their way here after being acquired by the Turks.

Lefkoşa has been a walled city since medieval times, but the walls in their current manifestation are the work of the 16th-century Venetians, who were intent on bolstering Cyprus in its role as a major outpost in the Mediterranean to secure their trade routes. The medieval Crusader walls before then had been tall with high towers to defend against catapults and arrows, but with the coming of gunpowder, the priority in wall design was to make maximum use of cannons. Hence the **Venetian walls** are not high, but colossally thick, to allow cannons to be rolled up the ramparts. The population in Venetian times had shrunk, and along with it, the circumference of the Venetian walls shrank from 5km to 3km.

Historical records show that the demolition this entailed meant that many Gothic buildings were razed and some 80 Crusader churches lost.

The wide **moat** area below the walls was never intended for water, but rather as the open space where, unprotected, the enemy soldiers could be fired at as they approached. In times of peace, the town's dung and rubbish was tossed over the walls as natural fertiliser and good yields of corn were obtained. Today these open spaces serve well as football grounds or public parks, or occasionally, alas, as dumping grounds. From the air or using Google Maps they still define the outline of Lefkoşa's walls very clearly . At regular intervals around the circumference of the walls are 11 huge bastions, six of them now in the Turkish sector, five in the Greek. Of the three fortified gates, the Famagusta Gate and the Paphos Gate, now in the southern, Greek sector, were always larger than the northern Girne Gate, reflecting the relative importance of the size of the ports in Venetian times.

The Venetians, belying the beauty and grace of their architecture, were nevertheless unsympathetic rulers. Having built their magnificent fortifications, they proceeded to bleed the islanders of every last drop of revenue, even resorting to such ruses as selling the serfs their own freedom. A Christian abbot at the time spoke for the rueful islanders when he wailed: 'We have escaped from the grasp of the dog [the Lusignan king] to fall into that of the lion [the Venetian lion of St Mark].' The Venetians acquired the island through diplomatic trickery, manoeuvring to have the Lusignan James II marry the daughter of a Venetian patrician, Catherine Comaro. Her husband, and later her son were then poisoned, leaving the hapless queen nominally in charge of the island. In 1489 she was persuaded to retire to Asolo and hand the island over to the Venetian Republic. The Venetian nobles then ruled for the next hundred years, till they lost it to the Turks in 1571.

Unless you are feeling energetic, it is best to drive a quick circuit of the walls on the internal ring road. Forking east (left) on entering the Girne Gate, you can follow the northern perimeter and pass some older-style houses before the road ends at the slogans of the Green Line barricading the street ahead and bisecting the Flatro Bastion. Near the Loredano Bastion on this perimeter street, it is also worth knowing about the patisserie selling cakes and good ice cream, invaluable on hot and dusty afternoons.

THE NICOSIA TRAIL In a city so brutally divided by the Green Line, anyone could be forgiven for thinking that the 'Blue Line' was some kind of bad joke. It's not. Somebody thought it was a good idea to paint an incongruous blue line around the streets of Lefkoşa to direct tourists from one sight to the next. Though the blue paint has flaked off in many places, the 4.5km Nicosia Trail starts and finishes at the Girne Gate and takes one and a half to two hours at a gentle stroll, not allowing for time spent at sights *en route*. Truthfully, the old city isn't big enough to warrant a guided path, and in any case it's often more rewarding to find places for yourself. Having said that, if you should get lost you can always follow the line and eventually you'll arrive at somewhere you recognise. Collect a map from the tourist information centre that shows the route and lists all the attractions.

MARTYR'S MUSEUM (⊕ *08.00–13.00 & 14.00–17.00 daily; £0.80; ask the guards at the entrance for permission to enter, & be prepared to leave some form of ID & any mobile phones/cameras with them*) From the Girne Gate the main road leads you straight on southwards into the heart of the old city. To your left a little way, housed in an army camp built in the shadow of the walls, is the Martyr's Museum, dedicated to the battles of 1974 and the formation of North Cyprus. Though many of the labels have been translated into English, the museum's collection, consisting as it does of rifles and oil paintings, will be of little interest to the average foreigner.

MEVLEVE TEKKE MUSEUM (*summer 07.30–14.00 Tue–Fri, 07.30–14.00 & 15.30–18.00 Mon, 07.30–14.00 Sat; winter 08.00–12.30 & 13.30–17.00 Mon–Fri, 08.00–14.00 Sat; £2.00/£1.00 adults/students*) Returning, and continuing into the heart of the city along the main road, you come to the **Monastery of the Whirling Dervishes** or **Mevleve Tekke Museum**, the mystic order of Islam founded by Mevlana, a Persian-Turkish poet of the 13th century. It is the only monastery of its kind on the island, and your eye will be caught by its low-rise domes immediately to your left after the roundabout just inside the Girne Gate. Street parking outside is supposedly reserved for visitors to the museum.

The early 17th-century building was in use as the dervishes' monastery until the 1920s, when Atatürk banned them along with other monastic orders in his determination to make Turkey a secular state. The Turkish Cypriots followed Atatürk's policy and closed the *tekke*. The remaining dervishes now have their headquarters in Aleppo, Syria. Though much of the original complex was destroyed, the meeting room and part of the shrine were restored in 1963 and reopened as a museum of dervish paraphernalia.

Entering through the arch from Girne Caddesi, you pass through a courtyard flanked by headstones leaning against the whitewashed walls. The ticket booth is straight ahead; opposite is the entrance to the meeting room. The wooden floor is the original one on which the dervishes danced, and at one end stairs lead up to the charming wooden gallery where the long-robed musicians played their eerie trance-inducing music, which is usually playing in the background when you visit, adding some much-needed atmosphere to the display. H V Morton described the scene thus:

> The dancers are dressed in long, high-waisted, pleated gowns that fall to the ground. They wear tall brown felt cones on their heads. Each one, as he begins to turn, stretches his right arm straight up, the palm held upwards to the roof, while the left arm is held stiffly down with the palm towards the earth. The head is slightly inclined to the right shoulder... The dance symbolises the revolution of the spheres, and the hands symbolise the reception of a blessing from above, and its dispensation to the earth below.

On the walls you'll find a useful rundown of the history and beliefs of the order. In one corner is the kitchen and dining area, while leading off from another is the galleried mausoleum of the 16 tombs of the Mevlevi sheikhs, row upon row, as if in mirrors endlessly duplicated. Only six of these tombs have been positively identified. Above them are the domes so conspicuous from the street.

GIRNE CADDESI AND THE SARAY HOTEL Retracing your steps to the main street, immediately on the left is the **Dr Küçük Müsezi** (*⊕ 09.00–12.00 & 14.00–16.30 Mon–Fri, 09.00–12.00 Sat; free*), a small museum dedicated to the memory of Fazıl Küçük, one of the most prominent activists ever to champion the cause of the Turkish Cypriot people. In particular, Dr Küçük stressed the importance of Turkey's association with North Cyprus, without which he proclaimed the island would never be able to live in peace.

For one so revered the museum is disappointingly bland. On display in a shabby room is a hotchpotch collection of medals, photographs, paintings, swords and general artefacts of little significance to the casual observer. Possibly of more interest will be the English information that the friendly curator will happily provide if you ask, which explains in detail the life and times of Dr Küçük. Perhaps most significant of all is his statement which adorns the front of the leaflet: 'Turkish Cypriots! Turkey will never abandon you to foreign hands ... Be sure that you are going to live in this country under your own flag for eternity ...' As the political wrangling over Turkey's accession to the EU continues its tortuous route it will be interesting to see whether the relationship remains so unequivocal.

Continuing south down the bustling main street, down the small street to your left behind the Mevlevi Museum is the **Şehitligi**, the mass grave of the martyrs of Turkish Cyprus. (Actually, most of the bodies have been removed from this site, though according to the sign 160 are still interred here.) The bodies are of those who perished fighting the Greeks in 1963 and 1974. It's a peaceful spot away from the bustle of the main drag, but is of little interest otherwise.

Continuing down Girne Caddesi, 20m further south on the opposite side of the street you can see a small stone water cistern in the heart of the **Samanbahçe district**, down the alley between the Simit Dünyasi and Umultlar cafés. The district is actually one huge social housing project, funded largely by the local mosque.

Eventually, after some 400m you reach the small **Atatürk Square**, recognisable by its solitary grey granite column, probably carried from Salamis. In Venetian times it carried a lion of St Mark, but the Turks overturned it in the conquest of the island. The British replaced the lion with a copper globe, which is still perched on top. Around the square are the pleasant government offices, built by the British colonial rulers from sand-coloured limestone blocks, with elegant arcades and verandas.

Straight on beyond the square you will see the tall **Saray Hotel**, an ugly modern block whose saving grace is its roof terrace on the eighth floor which provides the best vantage point for views all over Lefkoşa. Suitable for either lunch or a drink, it is worth taking the time to go up onto its roof, the closest you will come to a detailed aerial view of the town. An entry fee of about £1.80 applies, to include a soft drink, but during the day no-one seems hugely keen to collect it.

From the rooftop, you will be struck by the situation of Lefkoşa on the flat expanse of the Mesaoria Plain. The only dramatic topography is where the plain collides with the jagged ridge of the Kyrenia Mountains, picturesquely forming the northern backdrop. Somewhat less picturesque is the gouging out by the military of the closest south-facing hillside to write the colossal slogan: *Ne Mutlu Türküm Diyene*, 'How happy is he who can say he is a Turk'. The slogan is said to be an adage of Atatürk, who suggested a true Turk was anyone living within the territory of Turkey, irrespective of ancestry or ethnicity. As such the military are seen to be preserving the memory of Atatürk through such a display of patriotism. However, as with all stories in Cyprus there are two sides to the coin. Over a period of weeks, and in the dead of night, it is claimed that the Turks secretly created the slogan by painting rocks, which they subsequently replaced, face down, before sunrise. Can it be mere coincidence that, on the eve of Greek National Day, scores of troops scaled the hillside to invert the stones and reveal, clear to see for all Greek Cypriots in Nicosia, such a defiant and provocative message?

The next thing to strike you from this aerial vantage point is the difference between the Greek and Turkish sectors. To the south, in the area beyond the old walled town, is a distant sea of high-rise blocks, testifying to the prosperity and development of the Greek sector; new buildings outside the walls in the Turkish sector are much more modest and thinly spread. To the west (right) as you stand with your back to the twin minarets of the Selimiye Camii, is the distinctive long four-storeyed building with white-framed window arches, the famous **Ledra Palace Hotel**, now occupied by UN forces and the main pedestrian crossing point between the Turkish and Greek sectors. Ledra was the name of the original ancient settlement on which Lefkoşa now stands.

Just behind the Saray Hotel is the **Sarayonu Camii**, the most centrally located mosque in Lefkoşa. Dating back to the Byzantine period, the mosque was converted from its original use as a Latin church, and considerably restored in 1902. It is currently used as a wedding hall.

BÜYÜK HAMMAM (⏱ 07.00–22.30; prices vary from £8 (bathing only) to £15 (inc an exuberant massage), or £1.50 if you just want to have a look around) If you walk south from Saray Hotel, you can cross the street to **Rüstem's Bookshop** (Rüstem Kitabevi), once the largest and best-stocked bookshop in North Cyprus, though now rather less fun to browse around since Rüstem's son took over and tidied everything up. If you're in the market for an English-language book, however, it remains your best bet outside of the Green Jacket Bookshop in Girne. Forking left immediately after the bookshop, you walk down a narrow street, on the right-hand side of which, after less than 100m, you will see the **Büyük Hammam** (Great Baths), its entrance sunk well below pavement level. This was the level of the street in the 14th century, and the elaborate entrance portal carved in stone is now all that survives of the church of St George of the Latins, the original incarnation of this building before the Ottomans converted it to a Turkish bath. The sunken level means that the carving on the entrance arch presents itself considerably close for inspection of the intriguing mix of Gothic, Italianate and Muslim elements.

In 1989 these baths were reopened as functioning establishments, the government having rented the premises to private individuals to run, and they can now be used by locals and tourists alike. Both men and women are permitted to use the baths throughout the week and women are able to request a masseuse. The minimum time needed for the whole process of heating up the body and allowing it to sweat freely in the hot room is about an hour. Once this stage has been reached you can either give yourself a self-service wash, using the camel-hair glove provided, or prostrate yourself on a stone slab for massage and the removal of several top layers of dirt and skin by the vigorous glove-rubbing of the masseur or masseuse.

In the large domed room you enter from the street, a huge nail high above floor level marks the height reached by the 1330 flood of the River Pedieos, in which 3,000 people drowned.

KUMARCILAR HAN Continuing past the Büyük Hammam you arrive after some 50m at a little square, on the far side of which is the battered and unkempt Kumarcılar Han, or Gamblers' Inn, built around 1600. Like all caravanserais, the entrance used to lead into an open interior courtyard, where the merchants would gather with their donkeys or camels, having arrived bearing their goods for sale. Inside, all the services they required were on hand: not only accommodation, in the upper rooms of the arcaded courtyard, but also stabling for the animals below, along with food and refreshments and blacksmiths and leatherworkers for repairs. You can still view the courtyard, now overgrown, through the grille in the front door.

BÜYÜK HAN (⏱ 08.00–21.00 Mon, 08.00–24.00 Tue–Fri & 08.00–16.00 Sat) A few steps further down the street, away from the front door of the Kumarcılar Han, is the entrance to the Büyük Han (Great Inn), a khan that has been fully restored and is looking splendid because of it. This, the largest of the caravanserais on the island, was built by the Ottomans in 1572, the year after they seized Cyprus from the Venetians. It was built on the orders of Mustafa Pasha, the first Ottoman governor general of the island. From the outside, the high windows of the downstairs rooms, even though they were only stables, lend a defensive feel to the building, and indeed their role was partly one of protection for the merchants and their goods from brigands and thieves. The British were not slow to see its possibilities, and used it as Lefkoşa's Central Prison in colonial times till 1893.

In the centre of the open courtyard is an octagonal **miniature mosque** with a fountain for pre-prayer ablutions. The other distinctive feature of the khan is the tall **chimneys**, topped with metal pointed cones, as each of the 68 upstairs rooms had an open fire for the merchants to keep warm at night. Lefkoşa, pitilessly hot in summer, exposed as it is to the extremes of the plain, is also fiendishly cold in winter with icy winds. Today the khan has been resurrected as a thriving **arts centre**, a superb collection of galleries, workshops and curios. Where else could you hope to see a traditional show of Turkish Cypriot shadow theatre? With a couple of pleasant courtyard cafés it's the ideal spot to pick up a few souvenirs or just take a break from sightseeing.

THE BEDESTAN Turning right from the entrance of the Büyük Han, follow the narrow street south and then left, to see rising up before you the crumbling façade of the Bedestan, originally a Gothic church of the 14th century. It was originally two churches, and served as the Greek Orthodox cathedral during Venetian times. The Bedestan was converted by the Turks to serve as a grain store and clothes market (*bedestan* means covered market). Its interior is badly damaged, with repaired pillars supporting arches. It is empty save for a few medieval Muslim tombstones, although, at the time of writing, a UN-funded restoration programme is quietly under way and access was prohibited.

The Bedestan's most noteworthy feature is its **entrance portal**, elaborately carved. Especially fine are the gargoyles, their mouths grotesquely shaped to act as spouts for the rain gutters. The gargling noise of the water bubbling through their throats has given us our word 'to gargle'. The British in 1879 put forward a plan to convert the Bedestan into an Anglican church, but the Muslim community rejected this as provocatively close to their mosque. On the street corners just near the Bedestan are a couple of simple kebab restaurants for those in need of nourishment.

SELIMIYE CAMII/ST SOPHIA CATHEDRAL The Bedestan has a certain curiosity value; however, as you approach it from the Büyük Han you'll inevitably find your attention drawn away from the Bedestan to its more complete and magnificent neighbour, the Selimiye Camii, once upon a time the St Sophia Cathedral.

The best place from which to survey the outside of the cathedral is the simple, almost rustic **garden café**, residing in a fine old two-storeyed crenellated building with Gothic windows that was once the **Chapter House**, and reached by walking between the cathedral and the Bedestan. This quiet spot has a superb view of the cathedral's south wall with its flying buttresses, and gives the leisure to appreciate the soft mellow golden stone, harmonising with the background of the green cypress trees and the deep blue sky.

French craftsmen began work on the construction of the cathedral in 1209 and, thanks to the stability of its flying buttresses, it still stands today despite the earthquakes of the 15th, 16th and 18th centuries. The roof is flat, a concession to the geography and climate of the Orient, but a curiosity in a building that in all other respects resembles the great Gothic cathedrals of France.

The cathedral of St Sophia is, architecturally, the most important monument in Lefkoşa (Greek or Turkish), with its superb carving and sculpture in the triple-portalled porch and the colossal high west window. The twin towers were never completed, a fact that made them serve admirably as foundations for the two tall Ottoman minarets added by the Turks after 1571. In appearance these additions, labelled incongruous by purists, have been likened to candles with their snuffers in place.

Today, as it has done for more than the last 400 years, the cathedral serves as Cyprus's principal mosque, and the greatest celebrations of the two major Muslim festivals, Seker Bayramı and Kurban Batramı (equivalents, if you like, of the

Christian Christmas and Easter), are conducted here. Its name-change from Aya Sofya Camii took place only in 1954, when the *mufti*, the religious head of the Muslims of the island, renamed it the Selimiye Camii in honour of Selim II, the sultan in whose reign Cyprus was conquered by the Turks. Since 1959 the *muezzin* has been spared the climb up 170 steps to the minaret gallery every day, five times a day, to summon the faithful to prayer, by the introduction of an automatic recording played through a loudspeaker.

The mosque is open and can be visited anytime, though it is best to avoid the midday prayers on a Friday. During other daily prayer times you can visit but must keep silent. As in all mosques, shoes must be removed at the entrance. No special dress is required, as Turkish Cypriots take a much more relaxed view of bare heads and arms. Inside, the whitewashed interior seems stark, but the beauty of the proportions in the high-pillared nave is if anything enhanced by the absence of decoration.

Colour comes in the form of the carpets, predominantly reds and greens, none older than this century, and all of them orientated towards Mecca. This direction is indicated by the highly colourful *mihrab* or prayer niche in the southern wall. The green wooden structure in the centre of the nave is the prayer platform where the prayer leader or *imam* stands during services, and the closed lattice gallery in the north transept is where the women, the few who come to the mosque, are penned. Unlike churches, where the bulk of the congregation tends to be female, worshippers in mosques are almost always men.

All Christian symbols and decorations were stripped from the cathedral, inside and out, when the Turks conquered Lefkoşa in 1570, save for one or two tombstones hidden underneath the carpets at the far (eastern) end of the cathedral (if you show an interest, a local will help to locate them for you). The Turkish commander, Mustafa Pasha, even had the graves opened and the bones scattered randomly. Paolo Paruta, Venetian historian and statesman, recorded the events thus:

> He destroyed the altars and the images of the saints, and committed other bestial and cruel acts for which he was much blamed even by his own people.

Venetian historians wrote many such accounts, none of which enhanced the Turks' reputation for clemency. The Ottomans had already taken Syria, Egypt, Rhodes and Constantinople before they turned to Cyprus. With a huge fleet and over 100,000 men, they landed at Limassol which they quickly pillaged and burnt, before moving on to Lefkoşa, the capital.

Hearing of the advance, the terrified government gathered the men, women and children within the walls. The Venetian governor at the time was one Nicolo Dandolo, 'a man whose ineptitude was so apparent, his supineness so glaring that it verged on treachery', as one historian wrote. The odds were hopeless. Within the walls were 76,000, of whom only 11,000 were capable of fighting. The strength of the walls was such, however, that the siege lasted 48 days before the city fell. In the marketplace of Lefkoşa a funeral pyre was made of the old, the infirm and any others who were unsuitable as slaves, and the acrid smoke filled the city for days. When the Ottoman ships returned to Constantinople, they were bulging with as many slaves and as much gold and jewels as they had been able to cram aboard. Over 20,000 Turkish soldiers were left behind to settle on the island, and more were subsequently encouraged to emigrate from the mainland.

The Turks retained control of the island for the next three centuries, but despite much mismanagement, along with nature's contributions of famine, drought and plague, there were some important developments. The Greeks were given more autonomy than they had ever enjoyed under any previous ruler. The feudal system imposed under the Lusignans and perpetuated under the Venetians, in which the peasants were forced to work without pay for several days a week, was abolished. The everyday life of Cypriots was also made easier by such foundations as water fountains distributed all over the cities for the first time. The Turks rarely went in for building fancy, self-glorifying edifices like Roman triumphal arches or Egyptian pyramids. Their legacy lay in social welfare buildings, like aqueducts, mosques, *tekkes*, caravanserais, schools, libraries and baths.

No attempt was made to impose Islam on the native population. The Latin Catholic priests were expelled, and the Greek Orthodox Church was restored. The Greeks in fact tore down many Latin Gothic churches and the remainder were turned into mosques or stables. The Turks gave the Orthodox archbishop the responsibility for collecting taxes from both Greek and Turkish elements of the population, and in return, the Church was itself exempt from any tax it collected in excess of the tribute specified. It was from this practice that the habit was established of the archbishop being regarded as the de facto head of the Greek Cypriots, a role which was frequently misused from then until Archbishop Makarios, under whom the Cypriot Church overreached itself for the last time. William Turner, a British diplomat staying on the island in 1815 wrote:

> In short, these Greek priests, everywhere the vilest miscreants in human nature, are worse than usual in Cyprus, from the power they possess. They strip the poor ignorant superstitious peasant of his last *para*, and when he is on his deathbed, make him leave his all to their convent, promising that masses shall be said for his soul.

Skirting round the cathedral from the northern side, you will notice to the right a small fountain set in a pointed arch. Many of these **Ottoman fountains** can be seen on street corners all over old Lefkoşa, and two of them are even still in use. The one on Tanzimat Street is especially fine.

THE SULTAN'S LIBRARY (*at the time of going to press, the library was closed*) Skirting the south wall of the cathedral between it and the Bedestan, past the garden café, you walk under the arch of one of the massive buttresses to reach the Sultan's Library situated at the back of the cathedral. It was named after Sultan Mahmoud, who had it built in the early 19th century.

The guardian opens up the tall doors of the library that lead into the single square room covered from floor to ceiling with bookcases. The gilded ceiling rail under the little domed roof has inscriptions from a poem dedicated to the sultan. From the library, you can study the back end of the cathedral/mosque, with its elaborate doorway, now closed. In the mixture of elements so typical of Lefkoşa, Greek white marble columns flank the doorway, with pictures of green cypress trees either side of Arabic texts from the Koran.

If you are lucky enough to be visiting when the shelves are full, you will find a collection of books in Turkish, Arabic and Persian. Unfortunately, the books seem to be permanently housed elsewhere these days, and you may well wonder whether it was worth paying the entrance fee. A visit to the **Lapidary Museum**, included in the price, will do little to alter this opinion.

LAPIDARY MUSEUM (⊕ *winter 09.00–13.00 & 14.00–16.45 daily; summer 09.00–14.00; £2.00/1.00 adults/students*) Directly behind the Sultan's Library, through a pair of large wooden doors, can be found the Lapidary Museum. The guardian used to open these doors on an ad hoc basis by means of an enormous key that stretched from his wrist to his elbow, but today the museum has more customary scheduled opening times and a regular guardian to take your money. Inside this Venetian nobleman's house, the English colonial rulers, with their love of antiquities, gathered together fragments of stonework from Lefkoşa's ancient palaces and churches.

Unhappily, the place is now little more than a storeroom for all manner of carved stone, covering all eras and styles, from gargoyles to headstones to Corinthian capitals, stacked one on top of the other against every wall. In the open courtyard is the most interesting exhibit, the mildly diverting Gothic **stone tracery window** in 'Gothic Flamboyant' style, flanked with a face on either side, which forms the centrepiece of the back courtyard. This is the last surviving relic of the Lusignan palace that once stood on the site of the government offices beside the Venetian column in Atatürk Square, near the Saray Hotel. The Turks adapted it for their use and called it the serail or palace. A traveller in 1845 described it as 'a poor crumbling lumber chest, with hanging doors, rotten floors, and paper window panes', and so when it fell into total disuse, only the Crusader stonework remained intact. The museum will be of most interest to architecture enthusiasts.

FOLK ARTS INSTITUTE (*summer* ☼ *07.30–14.00 Tue–Fri, 07.30–14.00 & 15.00–18.00 Mon; winter 08.00–12.30 & 13.30–17.00 Mon–Fri*) A worthwhile detour on the way back towards the Selimiye Camii is the Folk Arts Institute, supported by the UN Development Programme to preserve traditional Turkish Cypriot crafts. Inside you'll find a dedicated and talented group of locals turning out a range of high-quality goods. If you want a souvenir of your holiday, their handmade collection of carvings, costumes and basketwork provides a broad selection from which to choose, and you'll also be making a fitting contribution to help conserve local culture.

EAVED HOUSE (SACAKLI EV) (☼ *winter 08.00–13.00 & 14.00–17.00 Mon–Fri; summer 07.30–17.00 Mon & 07.30–14.00 Tue–Fri; extended opening hours, inc w/ends, may apply during exhibitions*) The Eaved House lies just 10m to the south of the Sultan's Library. Its name comes from the large eaves that overhang the courtyard. The house has its origins sometime in the Middle Ages, though you'll have trouble recognising anything from this era in the construction today. Most of it seems to be typically late Ottoman in style, and indeed the '1932' inscription above the door gives a better clue as to the date of much of the building. Fully restored, the house is now a lovely centre for culture and the arts, with gallery space, conference facilities and outdoor seating areas. Regular exhibitions are held here, including some organised by the British Council, and at such times catering facilities might also be provided. The curator, Gürsel Sezgin, is a fount of local knowledge and will happily chat about Lefkoşa's colourful history.

HAYDAR PAŞA CAMII/ST CATHERINE'S CHURCH Returning to the Lapidary Museum you can follow the road that runs to the north along its left-hand wall to bring you, after 100m or so, to the Haydar Paşa Camii, originally St Catherine's Church and instantly recognisable by the Gothic windows and the tall minaret. The stone is the same sandy limestone as that used in all these Gothic buildings, and the distinctive mellow colour helps it to stand out from the later surrounding buildings. After the cathedral, this is the most important of Lefkoşa's mosque/churches, unusual architecturally because of the many tall arcaded windows requiring extra buttresses to strengthen the walls. The style, dating back to the 14th century, is another example of Gothic Flamboyant design. The building has at last undergone internal restoration, UNESCO funding for the project having been withdrawn post-1974, and now serves as an exquisite private art gallery. At one stage it was used as a marriage registration office.

LUSIGNAN HOUSE (☼ *summer 07.30–14.00 Tue–Fri, 07.30–14.00 & 15.30–18.00 Mon; winter 08.00–12.30 & 13.30–17.00 Mon–Fri; £1.20/free adults/students*) Heading north past the western side of St Catherine's, on the corner of a kink in this small but busy road is the restored Lusignan House. Dating back to the 15th century, the house is a typical, if rather grand, dwelling of its time, being a simple two-storey structure, with the second floor reached by a staircase that ascends from a small rectangular courtyard. The (now bricked-up) arches in the back wall suggest the building had an Eastern connection. The rooms themselves have been simply furnished with reproductions of the Lusignan and Ottoman era, including, in one room, a splendid old gramophone from the early years of the 20th century.

YENI CAMII AND ST LUKE'S Those whose appetite for mosques/churches is not yet sated can walk on for a further 20-minute circuit to see the Yeni Camii and St Luke's. Heavily ruined, with only a staircase and one fragmented arch remaining, the **Yeni Camii** was once a 14th-century church. It owes its dilapidated state to one of the more demented Turkish governors, who tore it down in the 18th century in a frantic search for buried treasure. The name means New Mosque, given to it because the temporary mosque built afterwards on its site had to be built almost from scratch.

St Luke's stands in the middle of an open playground area and is now kept locked. Unlike the other churches described, it was never a converted mosque, since it was in fact built under Turkish rule, like many other churches, in the 18th century. In style it is Byzantine, with a bell tower.

TOWARDS THE ARMENIAN CHURCH AND THE GREEN LINE Returning to the Bedestan, a more interesting diversion can be made to see the old quarter in the western area of walled Lefkoşa, where the best examples of Ottoman and British colonial houses are to be found. Retracing your steps up the bustling street west from the Bedestan, instead of forking right to pass the entrance of the Büyük Han, you keep heading west, straight on, passing through a pedestrian precinct shopping area selling jeans and all sorts of other clothes and shoes. This is **Arasta Street**, interesting in itself both for a spot of retail therapy and for its proximity to the Green Line. Just at the end of Arasta Street is the **Turunclu Camii**, the mosque built in 1825 by the governor of Cyprus, Seyit Mehmet Aga.

Keeping on this westward course, passing through an area of engineering workshops and scrapyards, you will come after some 300–400m to a car park, across which, in the distance, behind a fence, rises the bell tower of the lovely **Armenian church**. Held up by scaffolding, it's on the verge of collapse, and perhaps because of its perilous position, nobody seems to be in a hurry to do anything about it.

It was originally a Benedictine convent and the walls conceal an unfinished Gothic cloister. The abbess in the 14th century was involved, so the story goes, in an intrigue to murder the regent, the Prince of Tyre, and was accused of sheltering the assassin. Soldiers broke down the gates and threatened the holy sisters with death and dishonour. The abbess appealed to the papal legate for protection, and she and her nuns were finally spared.

The convent was much altered and repaired over the centuries, and was in use as a salt store when the Turks gave it to the Armenians. The area here around the Paphos Gate had long been the Armenian quarter.

Behind the Armenian church and just on the Greek side of the Green Line is the **Roman Catholic church**, recognisable by its distinctive spire. A walk down this street is to be recommended for the succession of lovely houses it offers. Aptly named **Victoria Street**, the houses were built from the time of the British occupation in 1878, and their distinctive features are the curved ironwork balconies above their huge doorways. No 73 Victoria Street is a good example, built in 1923. Continuing south, you can walk down the street towards the Green Line, where you can peek into no man's land through the bullet-riddled fence. There's also the splendid **Boghialian Konak Restaurant** (see pages 93–4).

The historic Arab Ahmet quarter on the western edge of Lefkoşa's walled city has for years been falling into disrepair. After the 1963 and 1974 peace invasions, the area witnessed an influx of Turkish Cypriot refugees who had been forced out of their villages. Post-1974, however, many of the settlers had the means to return to their former homes, leaving only the elderly and the very poor in this area of Lefkoşa. The resulting physical and socio-economic decline has given rise to considerable concern.

In order to address the severe deterioration of the quarter, the Arab Ahmet conservation project was instigated with the help of the UN. The focus of the project, which is aimed at both the historic quarter and the contemporary city of Lefkoşa, is primarily economic. Balanced development has, with the backing of the whole community, allowed the area to benefit from widespread regeneration and, more importantly, to attract an inward flow of investment. Already a number of families have set up home in some of the new housing units and further projects are under way, providing improved amenities for local residents and hope for the future of the quarter.

Whilst wandering down Victoria Street, your eye may be drawn towards the large blue footprints leading off the main Nicosia Trail. Following these down a side alley will lead to the **Arab Ahmet Art & Culture Centre**, established as part of the regeneration programme and to help boost community relations on both sides of the divide. It's not generally open for public visiting but occasional shows or exhibitions are held so if you're lucky there might be something to see.

More interesting, and tantalisingly just a few steps round the corner, is one of the most surprising sights in Lefkoşa. In a town where life seems to be painted in a series of monotone sandy yellows and browns, artist Farhad Nargol-O'Neill has created an enormous **mural** on the east-facing gable end of the Culture Centre whose vivid colours illuminate the area like the brightest of spotlights. Entitled *Ode to Aphrodite and Hala Sultan*, the fresco reflects the culture of the people of Lefkoşa – two bodies coexisting in the same space. Described as 'cubist symbolism', the piece combines the Hellenistic image of Aphrodite, the goddess of love who was reputed to have emerged from the surf off the shores of Cyprus, with Hala Sultan, aunt of the prophet Muhammad. Nargol-O'Neill was selected from a series of candidates to create the work, and as per a similar commission in Nicosia the painting was completed with the help of youngsters from both north and south.

The Green Line is in fact a somewhat euphemistic description of the barrier of bricks, barbed wire and corrugated iron that divides the old city into two roughly equal halves, abruptly bisecting streets that used to run straight on, rudely separating houses that were once neighbours. In the suburbs of Lefkoşa, it is extended by the Red Line, becoming the Attila Line once out of the city.

DERVISH PASHA MANSION (⊕ *08.00–13.00 & 14.00–16.45 daily; £2.00/1.00 adults/students; inc entrance to the Lusignan House*) Facing out over the car park towards the Armenian church stands the newly renovated Dervish Pasha Mansion, opened in 1988 as an ethnographic museum. Dervish Pasha himself was the editor of a newspaper called *Zaman* (Time), the first Turkish paper in Cyprus, in 1891. The house itself dates back to 1807 and, immaculately presented with whitewashed walls and blue woodwork and rafters, is laid out in a room-by-room re-creation of an early 19th-century mansion. Downstairs are the service rooms: kitchens, stores, with displays of cooking utensils and agricultural implements; while upstairs are the living quarters, furnished with relics of a lavish lifestyle: embroidered bath-towels, exquisitely delicate purses, fine old carpets and sumptuous clothing including some classic platformed mother-of-pearl bath-shoes.

In the open courtyard are the baths and washrooms, and in a corner a prettily laid-out refreshments area offers tea and soft drinks.

ARAB AHMET MOSQUE Forking north (right) up Victoria Street (Salahi Sevket Sokagi) after the Dervish Pasha Mansion, you will arrive at the Arab Ahmet Mosque at the corner of the next major road intersection, set on the left in a lush graveyard. What seem at first glance to be Roman columns in the neat gardens are in fact tall tombstones of various eminent paşas, the fine white marble originally from Beirut. The mosque is a typical example of 19th-century Ottoman, restored in 1955, and the spot is attractive more for its trees and graveyard than for the building itself. Inside are the usual whitewashed walls with medallions near the dome bearing the names in Arabic of Abu Bakr, Umar, Uthman, Ali, Hussein and Hassan, the first caliphs of Islam. The pulpit is, as so often, painted green, the colour of Islam, and beside it is the *mihrab*, the prayer niche that indicates the direction of Mecca, so that the faithful can orientate themselves correctly during prayer. The crass modern carpets conceal the tombstones of some Frankish knights, reused in the floor paving as conveniently large slabs. The mosque guardian will pull back the carpets if you ask to see. If at this point you should need a rest, you could do a lot worse than sit in the immaculately tended garden courtyard and marvel at the absence of North Cyprus's otherwise ubiquitous litter.

LEDRA PALACE Heading northwest from the Arab Ahmet area it is but a short stroll to one of the city's newest tourist attractions, the Ledra Palace border crossing. Formerly one of the grandest hotels on the island, Ledra Palace has for many years served as the UN's Wolsley Barracks and the strain shows all too clearly. Pock-marked walls, overgrown gardens and abandoned properties mark this as the only section of no man's land through which civilians are free to walk.

There's nothing special about being checked in and out by the border police (just turn up with your passport), but for many this is the closest they'll ever get to a disputed military area and there's an eerie fascination with the whole process. Of course, for the locals this is all part of the routine and their casual approach helps lend an air of normality to the whole affair. Today most visitors will wander outside Lefkoşa's walls to see this decrepit old relic, and to take in the vitriolic Greek Cypriot propaganda on the other side of the line. At this point, having reached the other side, if you have no real business in Nicosia you'll probably wonder why you bothered crossing in the first place.

It's worth noting that at peak hours queues can be considerable and that Ledra Palace provides a particular fascination for German tourists, who since the fall of the Berlin Wall are captivated by the world's only remaining divided capital city. If you plan to go just for the experience, stick to early morning or later in the evening and you'll be mercifully left to your own devices.

EXIT FROM THE WALLED CITY By car, the one-way system encourages you to leave from the Saray Hotel area in a westerly direction towards the walls and then north along Tanzimat Street, where many older-style private houses can be seen. Some of these, exposed as they are to the Ledra Palace Hotel directly across from the Venetian ramparts, were targets for the EOKA terrorists, and many of the houses still bear the bullet holes. Also on this street, the old women, enjoying the chance to meet neighbours and gossip, still collect water from the old octagonal Ottoman fountain with its fine brass taps set in elaborate panels.

Heading north inside the walls, the Mula Bastion is now a disused military area, and at the Qurini Bastion, the large white building is the president's residence. Before partition, it was designated the Vice-President's Palace, and Mehmet Ali Talat still has his official residence here.

THE SUBURBS As you enter Lefkoşa from the north, the main road crosses a bridge over a riverbed, almost invariably dry. No river in Cyprus flows all the year round, and the watercourses are highly seasonal, full and rushing after a heavy downpour, dwindling to a trickle shortly after. When Nicosia was founded in the 4th century BC, it lay on the banks of the Kanli (Greek Pedios) River, and the plain all around was thickly forested.

After the river bridge, a fork can be taken to the right at the traffic lights, to follow a road that runs more or less parallel to the main street. Now Mehmet Akif Caddesi, this was called Shakespeare Avenue and is still commonly referred to as such by the foreign community.

ACROSS THE MESAORIA PLAIN

East from Lefkoşa, the character of the landscape changes as you enter the vast expanse of the Mesaoria Plain. It is not an area worth visiting in itself, but simply has to be crossed on the way to what in most cases will be Gazimağusa or Salamis. Some background is provided here to help relieve the monotony of the journey. Fertile but now near treeless, the Mesaoria was once thickly forested. Hunting wild animals was the great sport of the early rulers, and whole retinues of nobles, barons and princes would go into the forest for anything up to a month at a time, living in tents. One account written in 1336 described how the party took with it 24 leopards and 300 hawks to aid in the sport. By the 16th century, many species verged on extinction. The huge forests were gradually cut down for domestic fuel, but also for smelting in the copper furnaces throughout the ages. The abundance and ease of obtaining this fuel enabled Cypriot craftsmen to attain a high standard of metallurgy, and Alexander the Great is said to have had a Cypriot sword. Great expanses were also cleared for crop growing. The plain owed its fertility to the alluvial deposit brought down from the mountains in heavy winter rains, like the fertility bestowed on the banks of the Nile in flood. As the climate changed over the centuries, less and less rainfall occurred and the area around Nicosia became a semi-desert-like plain.

TOURING THE MESAORIA PLAIN A more interesting route to Gazimağusa than by the main highway is via Ercan, a former military airport (previously called Tymbou). It was constructed by the British in World War II, and has now been transformed into a small but quite slick passenger terminal for all non-military flights that connect to the Turkish mainland.

Eight kilometres west of Ercan, at Gaziköy, is the only antiquity along this route, an **Ottoman aqueduct**. It runs close beside the left of the road, quite well preserved for a long stretch, beginning about 1km before Gaziköy. One of the major legacies of the Ottomans was the transformed water distribution on the island via several such aqueducts. The water was sent, not just to wealthy rulers' houses, as had been the case under previous occupations, but also to public fountains in the cities and towns, introducing a higher standard of hygiene and cleanliness than had been possible before.

The villages you pass along this route have interesting old rural-style houses, and lifestyles here have remained largely unchanged since the 18th and 19th centuries. The streets also have more than their fair share of mud. After rain, the whole area is very liable to flooding, with roads and fields becoming indistinguishable in sheets of water. Rain in Cyprus can often be violent, and it is not unusual, anytime from mid-October to mid-March, for two or three inches to fall in a day. It is mercifully brief, though, and the day after is quite likely to be bright and sunny.

Further east, **Paşaköy** is, like so many villages in the vicinity of the Attila Line, a bit like a military garrison. Though the forest of military barriers is a little daunting at first, you are in fact never stopped as a tourist vehicle. South of Paşaköy near the village of Erdenli (Greek Tremetousha), you may feel tempted to visit **Ayios Spiridon**, the monastery marked on some old maps. It is however heavily guarded, due to its proximity to the Attila Line, and no attempt should be made to approach it. One of the oldest and largest monasteries on the island, Ayios Spiridon was also the place where icons were sent for restoration from all over the island. As a result, it has the largest collection of valuable icons in northern Cyprus. Though these are not on view to visitors, independent archaeological authorities have been allowed in to see them since 1975 and have confirmed they are all safe and neatly catalogued.

The road on to Gazimağusa forks north through Turunçlu. If you are continuing to Salamis rather than Gazimağusa, be careful not to miss the fork left near Mutluyaka to save yourself the unnecessary and unsightly detour through the industrial outskirts of Gazimağusa. The traffic along this road is, by northern Cypriot standards, very busy, with many lorries and goods vehicles heading for the commercial freeport of Gazimağusa.

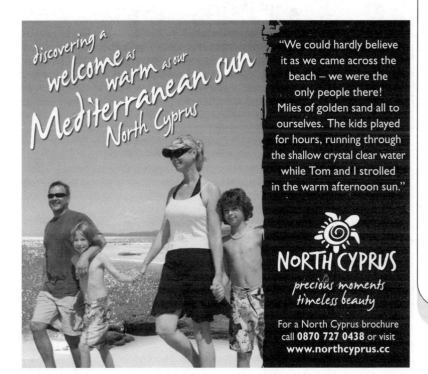

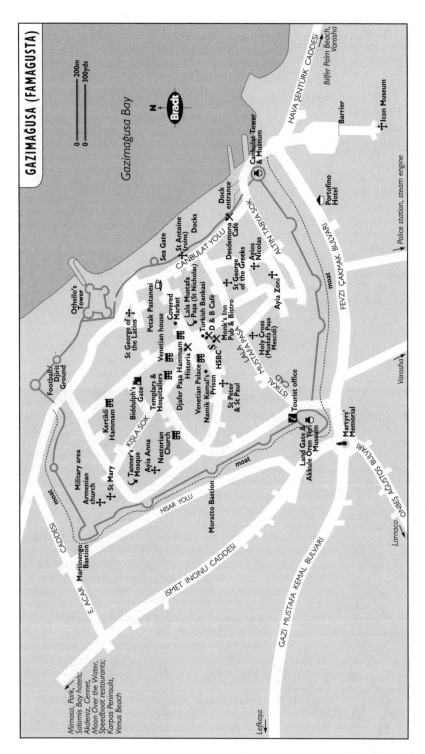

GAZIMAĞUSA (FAMAGUSTA)

Gazimağusa Bay

0 — 200m
0 — 300yds

Bradt

Mimosa, Park,
Salamis Bay hotels;
Akdeniz, Cennet,
Moon Over the Water;
Speedboat restaurants;
Karpas Peninsula,
Venus Beach

E. ACAR   CADDESI

Martinengo Bastion

moat

Military area

Football/
Djirit Ground

Othello's
Tower

Armenian church

St Mary

Kertikli Hammam

Tanner's Mosque

Ayia Anna

Nestorian Church

Biddulph's Gate

Templars & Hospitallers

St George of the Latins

Petak Pastanesi

Venetian house

Covered Market

Djafer Pasa Hammam

Historia

Venetian Palace

Namik Kemal's Prison

St Peter & St Paul

KIŞLA SOK

HISAR YOLU

Moratto Bastion

İSMET İNONU CADDESI

GAZI MUSTAFA KEMAL BULVARI

Lefkoşa

Larnaca

Varosha

Tourist office

Land Gate &
Akkule Oren Yeri
Museum

Martyrs' Memorial

ONBEŞ AĞUSTOS BULVARI

FEVZI ÇAKMAK BULVARI

moat

İSTİKAL CAD

LALA MUSTAFA PAŞA

HSBC

Lala Mustafa Pasa (St Nicholas)

Turkish Bankasi

D & B Café

Monk's Inn Pub & Bistro

Holy Cross (Mustafa Pasa Mescidi)

St George of the Greeks

Ayios Nicolas

Ayia Zoni

Desdemona Café

ALTIN TABYA SOK

CANBULAT YOLU

Sea Gate

St Antoine (ruins)

Docks

Dock entrance

Canbulat Tower & Museum

HAVA SENTÜRK CADDESİ

Bilfer Palm Beach, Varosha

Barrier

Icon Museum

Portofino Hotel

Police station, steam engine

5

Gazimağusa (Famagusta)

If beaches are your priority, then the Gazimağusa region is for you. The immense sweep of Gazimağusa Bay is one of the finest stretches of sand anywhere in the Mediterranean. The hotels of the region are almost entirely along this bay and have excellent beaches and watersports facilities. For sightseeing, the major Classical site of the island, Salamis, is on your doorstep, Kantara Castle is close by and you are well placed to explore the Karpas Peninsula.

As a base for a holiday on the island, the Gazimağusa region is more limited than Girne. Most meals will probably be taken in the hotel, since eating elsewhere becomes an excursion in itself, unless you are staying in Boğaz. Shopping is a lot less sophisticated. Visits to the major sights of the Girne area, such as Bellapais and St Hilarion, become quite lengthy trips, and visits even further west to places like Vouni and Soli become impracticable. The flat landscapes inland from the bay can also become a bit monotonous.

GETTING THERE AND AROUND

From Gazimağusa the drive to Girne takes about one hour and ten minutes, and to Lefkoşşa about 50 minutes. Ercan Airport is 40 minutes away. From the walled town of old Gazimağusa it takes 10–15 minutes to drive to Salamis.

🏠 WHERE TO STAY

🏠 **Palm Beach** (216 rooms) ☎ 366 20 00; f 366 20 02; e info@northernpalmbeach.com; www.northernpalmbeach.com. The only hotel still accessible on the top edge of Varosha, close to old Gazimağusa. Slightly surreal location, lovely sandy beach, neat beach umbrellas & sunbeds all set against an '80s Beirut-style cityscape of empty & collapsing high-rise hotels in the prohited zone. If this ambience intrigues, be aware that hotel staff advise that taking pictures is prohibited. Has its own sandy beach, swimming pool, restaurants, bars, Turkish bath, tennis courts, health club, casino, disco & bicycle hire. AC rooms with balconies, the more expensive of which look out over the sea. $$$$
🏠 **Salamis Bay** (404 rooms) ☎ 378 82 00; f 378 82 09; e info@salamisbay-conti.com; www.salamisbay-conti.com. Cavernous complex 11km north of Gazimağusa, well located on its own private beach & a 45min walk from the ruins of Salamis.

The hotel is associated with a large empty annex, at the time of writing undergoing some cosmetic building works. How long this will take is unclear. Facilities include restaurants, bars, outdoor & indoor pools, shopping centre, Turkish bath, massage, tennis, fitness centre, watersports, enormous casino & crèche (mini-club). $$$$
🏠 **Venus Beach Residence & Hotel** (94 rooms) ☎ 378 90 30; f 378 90 13; e info@ venusbeach.cc; www.venusbeach.cc. The newest property on this stretch of coast, a little further along from the Salamis Bay. Located right on the beach & offering rooms & apts, some with butler service. For a large modern hotel it seems to maintain a friendly & personal feel. $$$
🏠 **Mimoza Hotel** (51 rooms) ☎ 378 82 19; f 378 90 77; e mimoza1@north-cyprus.net; www.mimozabeachhotel.com. Standing right on the beach, guests at this hotel have use of the facilities

at the nearby Salamis Bay Hotel. Restaurant, bar & beach service. All rooms are en suite & have AC & minibar. There are 2 restaurants, one by the pool & the other by the beach under the trees. The hotel also runs a free bus service into town every day except Sun. $$

🏠 **Park Hotel** (93 rooms) ☎ 378 95 71; f 378 91 11. Bavarian-style hotel set on the beach 10km north of Gazimağusa. Some 20mins' walk from Salamis ruins. Closed for refurbishment at the time

of inspection but now fully open. Watersports, large pool, tennis courts & restaurant. $$

🏠 **Portofino Hotel** (53 rooms) ☎ 366 43 92; f 366 29 49; e reservation@portofino-cyprus.com; www.portofino-cyprus.com. Excellent budget option next to the walls of the old town, family run & offering rooms with AC, TV, balcony & minibar. Swimming pool & restaurant. Doesn't have a beach location but it's a reasonable choice for anyone who needs a bed for a couple of nights. $$

✗ WHERE TO EAT

In and around the old walls of Gazimağusa there is a selection of kebab houses and cafés. The central square dominated by St Nicholas Cathedral is a relaxing place to sit and eat.

✗ **Monk's Inn Pub & Bistro** ☎ 366 97 44. Near the Turkish bank, a new place run by a South African/Cypriot couple. Sandwiches, salads & fresh home-cooked main course that changes every day. £5

✗ **Historia** ☎ 367 01 53. Friendly service & a central location, simple but tasty Turkish food with a couple of European dishes. Delicious fresh orange & lemon drinks. £4.50

✗ **D & B Café** ☎ 366 66 10. Gazimağusa's trendiest & best-located eatery, next to the Turkish Bank & directly opposite the cathedral/mosque. Popular with

the local youth, the café offers free wireless internet access for customers. Prices remain reasonable, & the pizzas are particularly fine. Good ice cream too. £4

☕ **Petek Pastanesi** ☎ 366 7104. Something of an institution, this café on Yeşil Deniz Sokagi, is part of a successful chain that made its name selling wonderful sticky pastries & sweets, though they also do reasonable sandwiches & other snacks. On a hot day the downstairs water feature is a welcome dining companion. £5

Outside the walls there are a few good restaurants. The road towards Boğaz has a number of bistro-type establishments with Boğaz itself offering some superb fish restaurants, whilst several options exist on the road to Salamis:

✗ **Speedboat** ☎ 371 26 40. Still Boğaz's finest fish restaurant, despite some stiff competition, situated right on the coast. Menu depends on the day's catch, of course, but dishes are of a uniformly & reliably high standard. £10

✗ **Moon Over the Water** ☎ 371 32 97. A friendly well-established English-run bar & bistro serving European-style food. On the road into Boğaz with views out to sea. Also operates a thriving foreign-language book exchange. £7.50

✗ **Cennet** ☎ 378 82 34. Between the old town & the Salamis Bay Hotel, this is another Turkish Cypriot place serving hearty down-to-earth fare set against an expansive backdrop of local artefacts. Oven kebab with salad & yoghurt is a lunch special. £6.50

✗ **Akdeniz** ☎ 378 82 27. Anyone out near Salamis could do worse than pull over to the side of the road & enjoy a variety of deliciously prepared local dishes on a beautifully shady terrace. £5

WHAT TO SEE AND DO

The old town of Gazimağusa boasts some of the most superb medieval architecture in the Middle East, and no less a figure than Leonardo da Vinci is thought to have been involved in the design of its colossal Venetian fortifications. Within the town walls an intriguing range of monuments, mainly churches, can still be visited.

Gazimağusa today is a fascinating hotchpotch, perpetually startling in its incongruities and juxtapositions. Here a Leeds steam locomotive stands in front of the Turkish police station against the backdrop of skyscraper shells in decaying Greek Varosha. There a Crusader church appears in the garb of a cultural centre, while another serves as a café. One tower built by Venetians holds a museum to Ottoman military might, and another holds the ghost of Shakespeare's Othello. In the main square, the French Gothic cathedral, topped with a misshapen minaret, faces out at the façade of a Venetian palace supported by Greek marble columns from Salamis. Next door, the Faisal Islamic Bank, once an Ottoman school, looks across at a Turkish bath, now converted to a trendy bar and restaurant. Today's Turkish inhabitants have blended the city's relics so casually with their own daily needs, that the preservation of these monuments is almost synonymous with the routine maintenance of their public buildings and offices.

The expanse of the modern town entails an extensive industrial sprawl that belongs to a bustling port. Elsewhere, the surrounding landscape is flat and featureless, and the busy commercial port means that traffic can be heavy, with many noisy goods vehicles. However, for the visitor the quiet streets of the old medieval walled town possess an understated wealth of interest.

It has been said Gazimağusa has little of the sophistication of Girne or Lefkoşa. However, a deal of reconstruction and restoration, some UN-funded such as the covered market project, has combined to lift the ambience of the central old town. More smart cafes and bars are in evidence of late, though whether there's the trade to support them remains to be seen. Most tourist accommodation lies further north near Salamis leaving the five-star Palm Beach and the budget Portofino Hotel as the best options near to the old town. It's true that good restaurants are limited inside the walls, but frankly how many do you need? Pick a quiet day and it's enough to sit quietly in a public space and take in the city's remarkable architectural testament One full day should ideally be devoted to Gazimağusa, to give yourself time to stroll in the streets of the old walled town seeking out the early churches and Venetian buildings, and to explore the walls and bastions fully. These are really Gazimağusa's most remarkable features today, and if you are limited to just a couple of hours, the essentials could be reduced to a drive round the walls from the outside, noting especially the Land Gate with its drawbridge, and the Martinengo Bastion; a walk round Othello's Tower; and a stroll round the St Nicholas Cathedral/Lala Mustafa Paşa Mosque in the main square. The ghost town of Varosha, the modern Greek suburb which is now a sealed-off no man's land, also holds an eerie fascination and is worth a quick look from the car.

Conveniently located at the Land Gate is Gazimağusa's excellent **tourist office** (⏰ *07.30–14.00 & 15.30–18.00 Mon, 07.30–14.00 Tue–Fri, 09.00–18.00 Sat–Sun*), where the staff are extremely helpful. If you're driving this makes the Land Gate the most sensible way to enter the old city, and, on passing through the walls, there are parking areas clearly signposted both to the left and right. Mercifully, traffic within the walls remains light and there's no problem in finding alternative parking in other areas.

THE WALLS OF OLD GAZIMAĞUSA Any visit today would best begin with a tour of the walls. Originally Lusignan Crusader, these walls were redesigned and strengthened by the Venetians, making the square towers round and generally adapting them for cannon warfare rather than for the outmoded bow and arrow. The result was to make Famagusta one of the most impressive walled cities in the Middle East. To appreciate the walls properly it is best to drive around the moat gully, viewing them from directly below.

As you enter the bustle of modern Famagusta (now named Gazimağusa) from the direction of Salamis, you arrive at a roundabout with a sign to Geçithavaalani.

At the roundabout, you take the left exit, west towards the sea, and this road will bring you over a little hump to the northern edge of the walls at the mighty **Martinengo Bastion**. Squat and muscly rather than tall and towering, these Venetian ramparts are not visible from the modern town until you are nearly upon them. Their height, some 15m, is less than twice their thickness, often 8m. At the turn of the 20th century, before industrial development had burgeoned, the imposing outline of the cathedral within the walls could be seen from a great distance as you approached. The soft brown limestone that was quarried to create the moat was then used to construct the walls, an immense task, which must have taken decades. Fifty years is the usual estimate. Leonardo da Vinci is recorded as visiting Cyprus in 1481, and is thought to have advised his fellow countrymen on the design.

A slow drive around the moat takes just ten minutes, and you can get onto the track either at the point where the road enters the walls from the north, or from beside the **Canbulat (Djamboulat) Tower** on the south. The circuit can of course also be done on foot, and in the winter months makes a pleasant stroll of about an hour. North of the Land Gate, the moat is invariably deserted. In summer, when the heat is trapped in the airless gully, all but the most hardy would be best advised to save their energy for the walk within the walls, in itself more than sufficiently sapping. In many places around the moat, especially between the Land Gate and the Canbulat Tower, you can still find old cannonballs and other bits of metalwork left over from the Turkish bombardment. Iron was expensive, and whenever possible, the bravest soldiers would sneak into the moat at night to retrieve the cannonballs for reuse. If you choose to drive the moat, look out for carelessly discarded glass bottles on the track. Anyone suffering a puncture down here would no doubt believe that the experience of viewing the walls from below wasn't quite worth the trouble of having to change a tyre.

As for the ramparts themselves, you can still – sometimes – walk along the top of them with ease between the Canbulat Tower and the Land Gate. In the 1930s, the British colonialists, ever amused by games, engineered a nine-hole golf course on top of the ramparts, on which 'the accuracy of direction' more than made up for 'the comparative shortness of the holes'. If you are prepared to be agile, you can also walk a little way from the Land Gate towards the Martinengo Bastion, though you will certainly be stopped soon after the Moratto Bastion as the area becomes military. A large chunk of northern walled Gazimağusa is now a military zone, which for a long time rendered inaccessible four of the city's remaining 15 churches. Relaxation of these boundaries means that today's visitors can view all of the remains up close, together with the fine craftsmanship of the Martinengo Bastion, the most powerfully built of Gazimağusa's 15 strongholds.

The **Land Gate** is certainly the most impressive of the bastions, with its arched stone 19th-century bridge spanning the moat. Today it also houses the tourist office, and beside it is a colossal ramp leading up onto the walls, used for rolling up the cannon. The gate has also been converted into the **Akkule Ören Yeri tourist attraction** (⊕ *07.30–14.00 & 15.30–18.00 Mon, 07.30–14.00 Tue–Fri; £0.80*), and it takes a full 15 minutes to explore its labyrinth of rooms, dungeons, steps, ramps and arches. Here and there in the ceiling, chimney holes can be seen, essential to let out the smoke that billowed up every time the cannons were fired. The cannons used by both the Venetians and the Turks during the siege of Famagusta in 1571 were more powerful than any ever used before in any other country.

It was the sheer power of Gazimağusa's walls that enabled it to hold out for ten months against the Ottoman Turks. Nicosia had fallen in 48 days, Kyrenia surrendered without a fight, as did the rest of the island, but Famagusta resisted to a degree that has become famous. The Turks, with an immense force of 100,000, approached along tunnels and trenches so deep that a man on horseback could not be seen, and so extensive that their entire army could disappear inside them. Using mines and artillery, the Turks commenced their firing, lobbing more than 150,000 cannonballs into the city. Inside, a force of a little over 5,000 men, Venetians, Cypriots and Albanian mercenaries, waited in terror behind the walls. Using clever tactics, making lots of brief sorties, the Venetian commander managed to trick the Ottomans into thinking that his troops were far more numerous, and the siege lasted an incredible ten months before the city fell, with the besieged, weak with plague and famine, reduced to eating cats, dogs and rodents. The Turks lost over 50,000 of their men in these ten months, and their rage on final victory was expressed in the most appalling form. Surging through the gates, they overran the entire place, randomly killing men, women and children, desecrating churches and plundering houses. The Venetian commander Bragadino surrendered and was promised safe passage, only for the Turks to renege on the promise and murder him most horrifically. He was flayed alive in public, having first had his nose and ears cut off, then his body was stuffed with straw to be sent to Constantinople dangling from the prow of a ship. The Turk, when roused, may justify his epithet 'terrible'.

THE CANBULAT (DJAMBOULAT) TOWER Emerging from the outer wall circuit beside the Canbulat Tower, you can now turn left to enter the walls. The tower is named after one of the Turkish commanders of the siege. Here, the Venetians had erected a huge revolving wheel spiked with knives, onto which Turks were tossed as they scaled the walls, until the gully below was choked with dismembered bodies. Canbulat rushed at the wheel, and deliberately impaled himself and his horse, thereby putting it out of action. His fellow soldiers were thus able to breach the defences.

Today the tower holds his tomb and has been converted to a small **museum** (⊕ *approx 08.30–17.00 daily; £0.80/0.40 adults/students*). As a place of pilgrimage for Turks, this tower ranks second in Cyprus only to the shrine of Hala Sultan Tekke on the lake at Larnaca. The vaulted interior, with its huge long hall leading to the tower at the end, is in some ways more interesting than the exhibits. These include displays of guns, 17th-century Turkish tiles and bowls, and a couple of pretty but unexceptional 15th-century Venetian plates. The attendant should be able to give you the keys that enable you to climb the steps and get onto the roof, though there is no access to the ramparts. If the attendant is unable to produce these keys, by heading in the direction of the Land Gate it's possible to ascend the stone steps and reach the top of the wall at this southeast extremity of the fortifications, which is as good as emerging from within the tower itself.

OTHELLO'S TOWER (⊕ *10.00–17.00 daily; £2.80/1.00 adults/students*) From the Canbulat Tower you now continue along the dockside, passing the Sea Gate on the way to Othello's Tower. The **Sea Gate** was, along with the Land Gate, one of the two original gates of the walled city, and was built by the Venetians in 1496. The side that faces the harbour has a magnificent archway surmounted by a Venetian lion in a white marble gabled plaque. Since the gate is now closed, this is only visible from within the harbour itself or by craning one's head over the walls.

It's worth climbing the steps here for a view over the wall to the docks or back towards Lala Mustafa Paşa Mosque in the heart of the old town. Those who are tempted to walk along the top of the wall towards Othello's Tower may do so, but the process is ultimately futile as there's no way down at the other end. Inside the Sea Gate the huge, rusting portcullis is well and truly lowered and whilst the impressively domed ceiling is worth a look most visits will be limited to the length of time the explorer can hold his or her breath against the somewhat overpowering stench.

The emotively named **Othello's Tower** is not just a tower. It would be more aptly called Othello's Castle, for it was built as a fort within a fort, a citadel to defend the entrance to the harbour. Its sea-side now looks directly onto the quayside of the modern port, out of bounds to all but port traffic. In the pre-1974 days, when cruise ships and passenger ferries called at Famagusta, this citadel was the first thing that would have confronted visitors as the ship docked. Today, the ferries come only from Turkey.

The entrance to the tower today is from just inside the walls, through the gateway crowned by the white marble Venetian lion. The moat was drained of water on British instructions in 1900, because of the risk of malaria. Beside the gate is a simple **restaurant**, attractively set in green gardens with a playground. Opposite is the heavily ruined shell of **St George of the Latins**, a fortified 13th-century church, the earliest church in the town. A little to the north, just inside the walls, is a football field marked on old maps of the 1960s as the Turkish polo field, Djirit.

The tower has an entry fee (see above for details) and it takes a good 20 minutes to have a proper look round inside; longer, if you enjoy the fun of re-enacting Shakespeare. You may even be able to tread the boards, as staging is often in place for contemporary theatrical or musical events now held inside the tower. Scattered about in the open courtyard are **old Turkish cannons**, recognisable by the heavy iron rings round their barrel. In several places, the iron cannonballs can be seen, along with some stone balls that were tossed by the giant catapults.

Flanking the fine courtyard are the rooms of the citadel, regal in their proportions, especially the **Great Hall** or **Refectory**, used in 1915 by Syrian refugees fleeing from the Ottoman Turks.

Although Shakespeare had never visited Cyprus, probably indeed never left England's shores, he had evidently read or at least heard of Sir Cristoforo Moro, who was sent by Venice to be governor of their colony of Cyprus in the early 1500s, and whose wife, to whom he was newly wed, died on her way from Cyprus. Othello, the Moor of Venice, was likewise sent by his masters:

> Duke: The Turk with a most mighty preparation makes for Cyprus. – Othello, the fortitude of the place is best known to you; … you must, therefore, be content to slubber the gloss of your new fortunes with this more stubborn and boisterous expedition.
>
> Othello, *Act I, scene iii*

From Act II onwards, the setting is 'A seaport in Cyprus'. Scene 3 of Act II takes place in 'a hall in the castle', which must be the Great Hall or Refectory, where much revelry and drinking was ordered by Othello's herald. The tower was named Othello's Tower by the British during the colonial period.

THE WALLED TOWN Old Gazimağusa maintains a surprisingly quiet and unhurried feel, despite more shops and cafés springing up to meet perceived increasing tourist demands. The flat dusty streets, the neglect and the randomly sprouting palm trees give the place a more Middle Eastern feel than any other Cypriot town. Its population has grown to in excess of 5,000, all of whom have been Turkish Cypriots ever since the 16th-century siege of Gazimağusa, when a number of Turks stayed behind to colonise the island. The bombardments of the siege, however, along with the destruction wrought when the place was finally overrun, were permanent scars, and in the 18th century travellers described it as miserable and deserted, 'a confused mass of ruins and filth', with scarcely 300 inhabitants. The Ottomans also used Gazimağusa as a quarry: its ruined churches were exported as stone blocks to Egypt, prompting the retort that Alexandria is virtually Gazimağusa rebuilt in Egypt.

The state of the town and its churches cannot be wholly laid at the door of the Turks however. In the 15th century, Venetian troops were quartered in disused churches and private houses and, later on, earthquakes also played their role. Today, an air of dereliction continues to pervade the place, as the husks of churches still tower above the modest low-rise houses, and bombed-out open areas have never filled up again.

Gazimağusa's name, from the Greek *ammochostos*, means 'buried in the sand', and its history was, until medieval times, as undistinguished as that implies. (The Turkish name Gazimağusa is more impressive sounding, for in Turkish the prefix *gazi* means 'victorious warrior'.) However, when Acre, the last Crusader toehold in the Holy Land, fell to Saladin in 1291, Gazimağusa received an influx of new blood and burgeoned into sudden life. As the largest natural harbour on the island and also the closest to the Holy Land, it was the natural choice: Cyprus is the only foreign landmass visible from the hills of Palestine. Protected from storms by the natural calm of the bay, Gazimağusa became virtually the only safe deep harbour left to Christendom in all the Levant. Suddenly the European kings and merchants were all concentrated here, and Gazimağusa quickly grew rich from its new role as middleman between the East and West, import/export centre of the Mediterranean, trading in perfumes, spices and ivory from the East and selling the island's produce of sugar cane, wine and silk. On the crest of the wave of wealth came the inevitable wave of immorality, and the city's prostitutes were said to be as wealthy – and as numerous – as the merchants.

Lala Mustafa Paşa Mosque/St Nicholas Cathedral (⊕ *summer 09.00–19.00; winter 09.00–17.00; £0.80*) Set in the main square in the heart of old Gazimağusa, the twin towers of the cathedral are visible from most parts of the old city. Making them even more distinctive is the incongruous minaret that tops one of them. There is usually somewhere to park near the main square (though the square itself is pedestrianised), and this is the best place to begin your walking tour within the walls.

The imposing western façade of the cathedral has been likened to Rheims Cathedral in France, and it dominates the main square. Its towers were badly hit in the Turkish bombardment of the 16th century, and further damaged by earthquakes. Nevertheless, the cathedral is an undeniably beautiful building, its Gothic grace and elegance far exceeding that of its sister cathedral in Lefkoşa. It was built 100 years later than St Sophia, in the early 14th century, and its more delicate tracery work and ornate design reflect the more luxurious lifestyle and tastes of the ostentatious merchants of the port. The architects were themselves brought from France, and the cathedral may well have taken 100 years to complete. A tradition tells that the architects were a master and his pupil, and the master, on seeing the pupil's genius in the work, was consumed with jealousy. He invented a technical error he claimed to have noticed in the top of the towers, and having led the pupil up there to point out the error in detail, pushed him headlong over the edge – the first of much blood spilt at St Nicholas. The cathedral is built from the same familiar soft brown limestone that is used in the ramparts and walls. All the Crusader and Venetian buildings are from this stone and you need only walk round the town looking out for this colour to identify immediately all the older buildings.

The atmosphere of the square is conducive to reflection and despite the proximity of modern buildings, nothing can detract from the overwhelming presence of the cathedral/mosque. To the left of the façade the small domed building was once an Ottoman *madrasa*, built around 1700. Next to it is a small shrine.

Foreign visitors to St Nicholas today must buy a ticket, the only one of the churches where this is the case. Inside, the whitewashed walls almost serve to emphasise the superb proportions and height of the nave. The stained glass was all blown out in the bombardment and blasting of the siege, save for the high rose window in the front façade. Today, the remaining colour is supplied by the mosque accessories, painted the usual reds and greens – the raised platform for the Koran-recitation classes, the wooden pulpit or *minbar*, and the *mihrab* niche, indicating the direction of Mecca and around which all the decorative effort is concentrated, as in all mosques. If you're lucky, the keeper will take you to the northern corner of the building where, behind the green screens and hidden under the carpet, lies a stone slab etched with a medieval depiction of St Nicholas.

Your imagination has to work hard to recreate the splendid coronation ceremonies that took place here under the Lusignans. The custom had developed that each ruler was first crowned King of Cyprus in St Sophia in Nicosia, and then, after an elaborate and exhausting procession on horseback, was crowned King of Jerusalem here in St Nicholas, Gazimağusa being symbolically that bit closer to the Holy Land.

The huge **old tree** that looms to your right as you come out of the cathedral/mosque main door is thought to have been planted around 1250, shortly before construction of the cathedral began. It is a type of tropical fig, originally from east Africa, and it keeps its foliage all year round except in February. The **old Venetian loggia** (open-sided arcade) facing the tree now serves as the mosque ablutions area. Beneath one of its two circular windows is a section of frieze with barely discernable animals and garlands, taken from the cornice of a Roman temple, probably in Salamis.

The Venetian Palace Opposite the cathedral, on the far side of the square, is the triple-arched façade of the 15th-century Venetian Palace, supported by four granite columns that the Venetians brought from Salamis. This fragmentary relic is all that now remains of the once magnificent palace where the Venetian governor Bragadino lived. Its courtyard behind the arches was the stage for the excruciating death of the unfortunate Bragadino, a scene difficult to reconjure here in this peaceful spot filled with cafés. The building was badly damaged in the Turkish bombardment, and when the Turks took over the city, they did little to repair it. The section that still stood, on the west side, was turned into a police barracks, and it still serves this function today.

Beside the Venetian façade, just to the right, also facing into the main square, notice the little **Ottoman fountain** for distribution of drinking water. The basin is an adaptation of a Roman sarcophagus taken from Salamis.

Those legions of Turkish poetry aficionados can visit **Namik Kemal's prison** (⊕ *07.30–14.00 & 15.30–18.00 Mon, 07.30–14.00 Tue–Sun*) in the courtyard of the Venetian Palace. In a move that has some modern analogues, the writer and poet was locked up here for over three years for criticising the sultan in Istanbul. Inside, there is nothing but four bare walls and an earth floor, while in the upstairs room are simply photos of Namik Kemal (1840–88) and his contemporaries. His writings were political and patriotic, and he wrote articles, novels, plays and essays as well as poetry, reviling the stifling lifestyle under the last sultans, loathing the legacy of 600 years of stagnant cultural values.

Namik Kemal's bronze bust stands by the cathedral/mosque, facing the square.

THE CHURCHES It has often been said that Gazimağusa had 365 churches, each one paid for by a man or woman intent on buying their place in heaven. The number of churches is indeed high, and can be partially explained by the plethora of sects that coexisted in the city. Here we have Latin and Greek, Maronite, Armenian, Coptic, Georgian, Carmelite, Nestorian, Jacobite, Abyssinian and Jewish.

Of the 17 churches still standing today, only two are in use: the Nestorian church, now well restored, has undergone a recent reincarnation as the Cultural Centre of the Eastern Mediterranean University of Gazimağusa; and the cathedral church of St Nicholas, in service since the 16th century as Gazimağusa's main mosque, and now called Lala Mustafa Paşa, after the Ottoman commander-in-chief during the siege. A third church, the church of St Peter and St Paul, has been recently used as a theatre venue, though it has been unused and locked up for a while now.

To visit all the churches described in the following itinerary will take you three and a half to four hours on foot, but if you have only an hour, then just visit the central cluster round the main square, the church of St Peter and St Paul, and the huge haunting shell of St George of the Greeks, once the Greek Orthodox cathedral.

Church of St Peter and St Paul Following the road away from the main square, leaving the Venetian Palace on your right, you soon reach the large tall church of St Peter and St Paul, unmistakable with its heavy flying buttresses, essential props for the high walls. It was built around 1360 and is still in a reasonable state of preservation because the Turks always found a use for it. It was at one time a mosque as evidenced by the ruined minaret, missing its cone, built onto the southwest corner. Under the British it was a grain and potato store. In 1964 it was restored and used as the town hall for a while, and it then served as Gazimağusa's municipal library, with a wonderfully pious atmosphere. Schoolchildren used to come here to do their homework in the peace and quiet that is difficult to find at home. Although it has since become a venue for plays and recitals, it has been locked up for a while now, and its future remains uncertain.

The Nestorian church Walking on further, leaving the mosque on your left, you can now follow the road as it swings round gradually to the north (right) towards the cluster of five churches that lie near the western edge of the walls, and continue in a huge lap round the town before returning to the main square.

The first church you notice, down a side street opposite the Moratto Bastion on Necip Tozu Sokagi, is the small pretty Nestorian church, neat and well looked after in its new role as the **Cultural Centre of Gazimağusa's Eastern Mediterranean University**, the major university of North Cyprus. Earlier, it was used as a camel stable, though as recently as 1963 it still served as a church. Its style is different from the other churches, with its unusual but attractive bell tower and small rose window. It was built for the Syrian community of Gazimağusa by a wealthy businessman, as many Nestorians were rich financiers. Inside, it was decorated with frescoes by Italian and Syrian painters of the 14th and 15th centuries. Traces of these frescoes survive on the back wall opposite what is today the stage. Originally it was called St George the Foreigner to distinguish it from St George of the Greeks and St George of the Latins.

Martinengo Bastion and surrounding churches Following the path of the wall towards the Martinengo Bastion, four churches previously inaccessible now present themselves for closer inspection. The military zone that occupies a large chunk of the northwest of the city still exists, but concessions have been made to allow the right of access for visitors to both the churches and the Bastion itself. Yet confusion over the exact status of the areas still exists; there are none of the usual yellow information signs, and some locals report being randomly escorted back to the public road by the military, seemingly without explanation. There's no danger though, and whilst some will feel self-conscious at the thought of possibly trespassing in a restricted area, if you are asked to leave it will almost certainly be with the military's usual dignity.

Ayia Anna, known locally as the **church of the Maronites**, is the first of these churches, with a sturdy belfry and a few frescoes inside. It is tiny but perfectly formed. Unfortunately the military have sealed off the doorways which means the view from the road is almost as good as walking around the inside of the fence. Next, on the corner and sharing the same fenced-off compound is the **Tanner's Mosque**, originally a 16th-century church. Today, as you peer into the gloom through the stark, grey iron gate, it's difficult to discern anything other than the overpowering aroma of pigeon droppings.

On the other side of the road is the tall **Carmelite Church of St Mary**, originally part of a monastery, now disappeared, for the mendicant friars. It was richly adorned with frescoes by Italian artists of the 14th and 15th centuries, and some traces remain, although the ravages of neglect have ensured that the images are indistinct to the point of near invisibility. Behind it stands the tiny 14th-century **Armenian church**, the most forlorn of the group. Now predominantly serving as a pigeon loft, a solitary discarded refrigerator hints at the recent use of this beautifully proportioned relic. Sadly, the interior of the church is now almost totally derelict, with just a few smoke-blackened frescoes still visible towards the top of the walls. In what was presumably one of the Turkish army's occasional acts of preservation the lower parts of the walls have been whitewashed, making it impossible to assess whether or not anything of worth remains beneath.

Many of these churches suffered severe damage in the 1960s and 1970s, when Turkish Cypriots came here as refugees, having been turfed out of their villages by the Greeks. Shortage of accommodation meant that some had to camp inside the churches along with their possessions and animals. Cooking fires caused blackening and damage to frescoes, while children larked about trying to prise off pieces of decoration with penknives or to dislodge higher mosaics with catapults.

Behind the Armenian church the large ramps that sweep underground lead the visitor down to the bowels of the **Martinengo Bastion**, named after a Venetian commander who was sent to Cyprus to relieve the Turkish siege, but who died at sea before arriving. This was to be his final resting place. From close up the sheer imposing power of the architecture looms large, but as in so many other areas medieval history sits uneasily with incongruous modern adaptation. Thus are the various chambers of the bastion divided by ugly breeze-block and concrete walls, which together with the ubiquitous pigeons do little to enhance the ambience. The hope is that in the near future the walls will be removed and free access between the vaults restored, but until such times all but the enthusiast would do well to save their energy for the more visitor-friendly Land Gate.

Some 300m beyond the Tanner's Mosque you now fork back south towards the main square to complete your circuit. On your right you can glance at the ruined **Kertikli Hammam**, a Turkish bath with its six domes still intact.

Further on you pass on your right, just after a street junction, the structure known as **Biddulph's Gate**, an archway built from the old brown stone with three steps leading up into what was once the house of a wealthy merchant, but is now a small piece of open scruffy wasteland. Sir Robert Biddulph was the British High Commissioner in Cyprus in 1879 who stopped the gate being destroyed.

Beyond the next junction on the right is one of the very few relics of a private as opposed to a public building, the shell of a **Venetian house**. The Venetians were in Gazimağusa for only 82 years and the bulk of their building effort went into the fortifications. The house's exterior is elegant and pleasing like all Venetian architecture in the style of the Italian Renaissance. By peering through the keyhole you can see into the courtyard wilderness inside. Both doors are locked and the roof has collapsed. It used to be called the Queen's House.

Up a side street to the right, just before the Venetian house, you will come to the twin churches of the **Templars and the Hospitallers**, both orders of the Latin Church formed at the time of the Crusades in 1350, yet often at loggerheads despite their apparent embrace. The left one has been converted to a private art gallery.

Just before the main square you pass the renovated **Djafer Pasha Hammam**, a Turkish bath built in 1605 and now operating as a trendy café bar. Thick glass pieces set into the roof allowed the sun in by day, and the starlight by night.

From the main square you can now head off south to see the remaining four churches in a small loop. This route can also be driven, by taking the only permitted exit from the main square to the south, a narrow road which winds round to the right and takes you through a picturesque Ottoman archway like a gatehouse with rooms above.

Southern churches By far the most impressive of these four southern churches is the huge shell of **St George of the Greeks**, standing alone in an area of wasteland. Its roof was blown off in the Turkish bombardment in 1571, and the most damaged part is visibly the side that faces the Canbulat Tower, the direction from which the Turkish artillery was firing. The pockmarking in the walls tallies with the size of the cannonballs. Many of these can still be seen lying about in the waste ground in and around the churches of this area. Some can be seen put to such ingenious uses as marking the edges of flower beds in manicured gardens.

You can enter the church from the southern side, through a hole in the railings. It was built as the rival cathedral for Gazimağusa's Orthodox community. Its three apses once held frescoes showing the life of Christ, and some small fragments survive in the eastern apse. In what remains of the roof, you can see the bottoms of pottery jars embedded. Their function is mysterious, but one clever suggestion is that they may have been used to improve the acoustics. Abutting the church to the south is the much smaller Ayios Simeon.

Some 200m further to the south, also standing in open waste ground, is the small, 15th-century church of **Ayios Nicolas**, still with its roof but no frescoes inside, and further away, tucked behind it, the little dome of **Ayia Zoni**, a church in typical rustic Cypriot style. It is now kept locked to protect the fragmentary frescoes of the Archangel Michael, and you can just glimpse them if you peer in through cracks in the door.

The final church, further to the north on Mustafa Paşa Sokak, is the barrel-vaulted church of the **Holy Cross or Stavros**, long used as a store, and later as a mosque. It now has the sign 'Mustafa Paşa Mescidi' out front.

TOWARDS VAROSHA Opposite the Land Gate outside the walls is a large modern roundabout. In the centre of the roundabout stands a rather gory colossal bronze **Martyrs' Memorial**, depicting the suffering of the Turks. Driving south from here, just by the old tourist office, a wide road, previously known as Independence Avenue, leads off towards Varosha. Some 300m down this wide avenue on the left-hand side, your eye may be caught by the little **steam locomotive** that stands just behind a wire fence. A plaque announces it was the first locomotive to be imported into Cyprus, in 1904. The little railway line on which it ran was the only one in Cyprus, built by the British, running from Gazimağusa via Nicosia to Morphou. There were passenger services, but very few Cypriots took advantage of them, being either too poor to afford a ticket, or content to travel more slowly by donkey or cart. The railway's primary function was to transport the copper and chrome from the Skouriotissa mines to the port at Gazimağusa, from where they were then exported. The coal on which it ran was brought all the way from England by boat. By 1945 the railway began to fall into disrepair, and diesel trucks were found to be more economical for transporting the copper ore. The last train ran in 1951.

Following the road further south you soon come to the edge of **Varosha**, lying about 1km south of old Gazimağusa. Once the affluent Greek suburb (*varoş* is Turkish for suburb), Varosha, the 'Monte Carlo of the Middle East', grew in the 1960s to be far larger than the old walled town. While the Turkish walled town decayed, this fashionable resort of Greek Cypriots and expatriates mushroomed with hotels and holiday flats along the 6km beach of Glossa, said to be the best beach in the eastern Mediterranean. By the early 1970s it had a population of 35,000, overwhelmingly Greeks. In March the annual Gazimağusa Orange Festival used to take place here, in which visitors were showered with as many oranges as they could eat. Varosha was famous for its orange groves and fertile gardens, and the district had so many windmills it was sometimes called the Town of the Windmills.

Now fenced off and forlorn, it was evacuated in 1974 when the Turks captured it for use as a bargaining card in any future negotiations. There was no military necessity for its capture since no Turkish Cypriots lived there. On paper it is now in the hands of the UN, but in practice the Turkish army uses one hotel as a barracks, another two as student hostels and a further one as an officers' club. Furniture looting still goes on, despite the fence, and as you peer inside you can spot many houses where boarded-up doors have been forced, window frames ripped out, and weeds are growing up through the floor. It is difficult to see how this or any other property formerly Greek could be returned. Here in Varosha, most of the houses would need total renovation and in some cases even demolition before starting again. Where Greek houses have been used and inhabited in other parts of the north, many have been sold on to foreigners who have since spent much money on restoration. After 1974 the Turkish Cypriots were given Greek houses under a government scheme in compensation for property and land they lost in the south. They were issued with a paper which gave them title to it and they were then at liberty to sell it. In some cases there have been several sales of the same house since 1974 and to unravel all these transactions now would be a mighty task.

You can drive south all the way along the edge of the fenced-off area, until you see the check-point barrier blocking your path: the Attila Line is just a kilometre or two beyond. You can return a slightly different way by forking off towards the sea whenever you can, hugging the Varosha fence throughout.

Emerging near a sea lagoon, you will see another cluster of simpler restaurants facing out onto the modest yacht marina. On the headland beyond it is the **Palm Beach Hotel**. Originally Greek-run and called the Constantia, the Palm Beach has been renovated and is the only high-standard hotel that remains accessible in this part of Varosha, albeit in far from scenic surroundings. The other once-famous hotels, like the Grecian, the Florida and the King George, are all within the fence. The Greek Cypriots, ever mindful of a commercial opportunity, run cruises from Ayia Napa for tourists to stand off and peer at the ghost city. They also organise minibus or taxi trips to a viewing platform at the village of Dherinia, from where Varosha can be discerned through telescopes and binoculars.

The one official sight that tourists can visit in Varosha is the **Icon Museum** (⊕ *09.00–13.30 Mon–Fri; £0.80*). To reach here, from the Canbulat Gate drive southeast and continue straight on past the northern end of Fevzi Cakmak, ignoring the turn-off left towards the Palm Beach Hotel. Parking your car in the square next to the guard post, you can walk through the barrier to the museum, housed in a fairly modern Orthodox church of Maras. The icons are nothing special – most date from the last 50 years, with the oldest less than 300 years old – though the acoustics are impressive, particularly noticeable if one of the resident pigeons flies under the dome; that, and the feeling that you are penetrating into the heart of the militarised zone, make this short detour worthwhile.

SALAMIS

(⊕ *07.30–19.00 daily. £3.60/2.00*) Ancient Salamis, the first city of Cyprus in classical Greek times, boasts some of the most impressive monuments to be found on the island. The pleasantly overgrown ruins lie among fragrant eucalyptus and acacia trees, alongside one of the island's finest beaches, with excellent and safe swimming. Situated some 9km north of Gazimağusa, it makes an easy visit and is readily accessible.

The area covered by the site is huge, so huge that although archaeologists first began work here in 1890 and have continued intermittently throughout the last century, the site is still only partially excavated. Networks of roads run across it, none signposted, and it can be fairly easy to lose your way, and difficult to get an overview as the site is so flat. A few minutes studying the map will help. Cars have recently been banned from driving through the site, so be prepared for some lengthy walking under a blisteringly hot sun. Bring comfortable shoes, suntan lotion and a sunhat; the flat landscape offers precious little shade. Go well equipped with liquid refreshments, too, or else you may find yourself hallucinating that the marble basins in the gymnasium are still sparkling with cool water. If you don't fancy walking much, don't be put off: the main sites (the gymnasium and theatre) are right next to the entrance and car park where you leave the car.

The only **entrance** into the site now is the northern side entrance on the coast; the former main entrance, opposite the turn-off for St Barnabas (see pages 128–9) is no longer open. It takes about two to three hours to visit the major parts of the site, but you could easily spend a whole day here if you wanted to explore the site exhaustively – much of it spent walking between different excavated areas. If you are coming from the Girne area and only have a day to devote to Gazimağusa and its environs, you could spend the morning in old Gazimağusa, then drive on to Salamis for lunch at the pleasant seaside restaurant beside the entrance – though you'll probably have time only for the gymnasium and theatre areas of Salamis before you have to return. Those based in the Gazimağusa area will probably make separate visits to Salamis and the other sites close by. Recommended times for visits would be three to four hours for Salamis, two hours for the Tombs of the Kings and St Barnabas Monastery, and one hour for Enkomi.

TOURING SALAMIS Heading north out of Gazimağusa towards Salamis, you pass, near the outskirts of town, a busy area with lots of cafés and pizza restaurants full of young people. Directly opposite is the reason – the Eastern Mediterranean University, North Cyprus's major university, offering degree courses in sciences, engineering, management and economics. The medium of instruction is English.

The road continues north past a most ridiculously ostentatious new nightclub, adorned with leaping lions and bugling cherubs (you can't miss it!), reaching

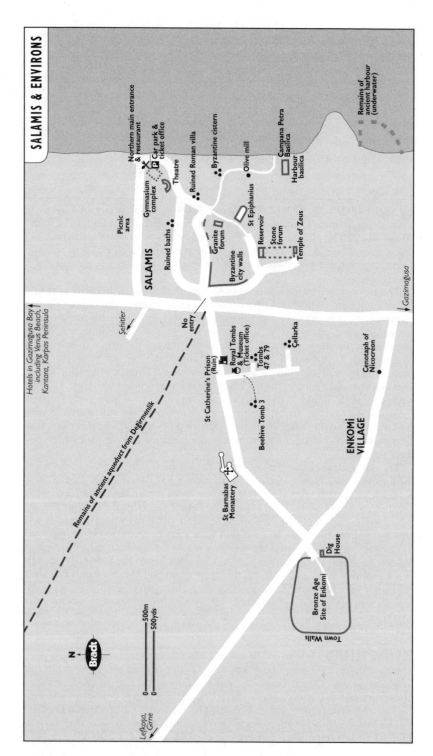

SALAMIS & ENVIRONS

Lefkoşa, Girne

0 500m
0 500yds

Bradt
N

Remains of ancient aqueduct from Değirmenlik

Hotels in Gazimağusa Bay,
including Venus Beach,
Kantara, Karpas Peninsula

Şehitler

No entry

St Catherine's Prison (Ruin)

St Barnabas Monastery

Royal Tombs & Museum (Ticket office)

Beehive Tomb 3

Tombs 47 & 79

Çellarka

ENKOMİ VILLAGE

Cenotaph of Nicocreon

Bronze Age Site of Enkomi

Dig House

Town Walls

SALAMIS

Picnic area

Ruined baths

Gymnasium complex

Theatre

Ruined Roman villa

Byzantine cistern

Northern main entrance

Car park & ticket office

Granite forum

Byzantine city walls

St Epiphanius

Olive mill

Reservoir

Stone forum

Temple of Zeus

Campana Petra Basilica

Harbour basilica

Remains of ancient harbour (underwater)

Gazimağusa

Salamis after about 5km. Driving past the previous main entrance on your right, take the signposted road running along the northern edge of the site, which brings you out at the beach by the pleasant restaurant raised up overlooking the bay. Its spacious shady terrace makes a cool haven in summer, and in winter the indoor seating area is warm and cosy. Simple fare is on offer, like curry, kebabs and steak, and, for the non-drivers, can be washed down with beer or wine.

Climbing back into the car, you then drive between the restaurant and the shore to the ticket office just a few metres along. Having bought your ticket, park at the car park by the office, right next to the **baths/gymnasium complex**. The theatre is just 100m further on.

These two areas together form the most spectacular part of Salamis, the part you should explore most thoroughly. They have also received the bulk of the excavators' attention. Suspiciously headless statues have been re-erected in the gymnasium and the theatre has been renovated. Though discovered in 1882 and dug erratically since then, the site was not excavated systematically until 1952. From then, work was in progress every season until 1974, when the University of Lyons excavators left. In 1998 regular work began again under the auspices of Ankara University and Gazimağusa's Eastern Mediterranean University. New structures have been revealed and abandoned digs reopened. However, walking round the site today vast tracts of the city remain untouched, and without a very much greater resource, progress will inevitably continue slowly. The task is undoubtedly a daunting one, for Salamis was the victim of two severe earthquakes in the 4th century within ten years of each other. Tidal waves combed across the city bringing in sand and debris. Later that century, the Byzantine emperor Constantine II rebuilt it, but on a smaller scale, and renamed it Constantia in honour of himself. It suffered badly again in the Arab raids of the 7th century, and most of the population that survived the massacres moved to Gazimağusa, then called Arsinoe. Abandoned, its collapsed buildings were used as a quarry for medieval Famagusta, and the sand and vegetation reclaimed the city.

The gymnasium and baths The gymnasium is the pearl of Salamis and the glimpse of lifestyle afforded here helps convey more than any other monument yet exposed the magnificence and wealth the city must have enjoyed in Hellenistic and Roman times. As you first enter along the marble pavements, you feel the elegant colonnaded courtyard must have been the forum, the market place and heart of the city, rather than simply an outbuilding devoted to education and the culture of the body, the ancient Greek version of a school and health centre. It is now thought there were originally three gymnasia, two for boys and one for girls. The open forecourt (*palaestra*) was where the boy athletes would exercise and train. Afterwards they would plunge in the cool water of the two pools, watched by the naked white marble statues of their gymnasiarchs or headmasters. These were wealthy citizens who were elected for a one-year term to help with the school's finances, and also provided the expensive olive oil for body massage for those boys who had won free attendance by scholarship. Today these gymnasiarch statues have been replaced by women draped in robes, headless to a woman, decapitated it is thought by early Christian zealots, who took the statues to be relics of the pagan religion. Nudity offended them, and all bare statues were broken up or tossed into drains. Clothed statues were just tolerable if their faces were removed. Today the most striking statue is the handless and faceless black marble Persephone.

The columns of the porticoes were re-erected in the 1950s by the excavators, and on close examination, the apparent harmony of the whole reveals its mixed origins, for it was destroyed and re-erected many times in its history. In the east portico, for example, the Corinthian capitals are too small for their columns, which are taller and larger than this on the other three sides, presumably brought from somewhere else in the city by the later Byzantine builders.

The Hellenistic and Roman latrines are situated in the southwest corner of the *palaestra*, and are the largest on the island. Arranged in a semicircle, with open-plan seating for 44, they strike us today, with our prudishly solitary cubicles, as most improper. The puritanical Christians of the 4th century, too, considered them indecent, and had them walled up.

Beside the gymnasium are the colossal Byzantine baths, an impressive complex of tall chambers with marble and mosaic flooring and underfloor heating so deeply buried in sand they were only discovered in 1926. In two of the vaulted arches traces of Roman mosaics can still be seen, mainly in reds and browns. In the largest mosaic, the central figure is thought to be Apollo with a lyre and quiver below.

The walls throughout are of immense thickness, often 3m or more. Columns and capitals lie scattered about, but much of the more elaborate marble carving was taken away and is now on display in the Cyprus Museum in Greek Nicosia. Some of the finds used also to be on display at the Museum of Gazimağusa within the suburb of Varosha. Now they are doubtless heavily cobwebbed. The intricate water system, here and in the gymnasium, is a perpetual source of amazement. A 56km aqueduct brought water from the abundant spring at Kythrea (now Değirmenlik) to a large tank which can still be seen in the undergrowth. Scholars have estimated that this water system could supply the needs of 120,000 people.

The theatre The theatre was not discovered until 1959 and archaeologists have now rebuilt it to under half its original height, 18 of the 50 rows of seats. Of these, only the first eight rows are original, and the division is clear where their white limestone casing gives way to the brown limestone used in the reconstruction. Badly damaged in the earthquakes of the 4th century, many of its original stones and decorative blocks were carted off for reuse in other buildings. The marble tiles of its orchestra for example were taken off to renovate the nearby baths after an earthquake. The channel in the middle of the orchestra was the drainage for blood from animals sacrificed to Dionysus before each performance. With an original seating capacity of between 15,000 and 20,000 it is far and away the largest theatre in Cyprus, reflecting the fact that Salamis was the foremost city on the island for much of its history. Eschewing blood-letting, these days the theatre again hosts crowds for regular music and theatre performances.

Most of the extant ruins date from the Roman and Byzantine times, but Salamis was in fact said to be founded in the 12th century BC by a hero of the Trojan War. Brother to Ajax, his name was Teucer, and he named the new Greek colony in Cyprus after the small island of Salamis (near Piraeus) which had been his homeland. All over the island, other heroes of the Trojan War also founded their own cities, such as Paphos, Soli, Lapithos, Kyrenia, Marion (Polis), and each was independent, ruled by its own king. At one time there were ten such tiny kingdoms on the island. Salamis was generally the most powerful, and by virtue of its excellent harbour, became the greatest commercial centre, trading with the Levant, Greece and Rome. It was the first city in Cyprus to mint its own coinage.

The forums, basilicas and other ruins Although the theatre and gymnasium together form the most impressive part of Salamis, there are plenty of other ruins in the area that are worth visiting. A circular tour of the other major sites can be made if you have the time (a minimum of about an hour and a half to two hours) and energy (to walk the 5km or so). Taking a left at every junction should ensure you cover most of Salamis.

After the gymnasium and theatre area, the next most impressive section of ruins at Salamis is to be found beside the **old Roman harbour**. To reach them, you head south from the theatre and fork left at the first junction of tarmac roads. Passing the sorry remains of a **Roman villa**, take the next left. Some 100m or so after this junction on the left of the road is an **underground Byzantine cistern** with paintings on the walls, but now kept locked. The key is held by the Gazimağusa Department of Antiquities, beside the Namik Kemal prison. The cistern consists of three interconnecting chambers, in one of which are faded water scenes of fish and sea plants with a bearded Christ above. Access involves descending a ladder with torches (supplied).

Beyond the cistern and past an old olive mill on the right, as the road heads towards the sea you will see rising up on your right the columns of the recently excavated but already overgrown basilica identified as **Campana Petra**, standing just above the sandy beach. This large attractive building has been dated to the 4th century and has elegant columns and many beautiful geometric floor designs. The bulk of the stone is white marble and in summer the impression is of dazzling brightness as the sun glints off the sea and the gleaming stone. The most elaborate floor patterning of all is to be found in the lowest section of the basilica near the sea, where the diamond-shaped stones are set in very modern-looking swirls of colour.

After exploring the basilica, you can go onto the beach for a swim or to seek out the remains of the Roman harbour. In the clear shallow water are thousands of fragments of Roman sherds, and beyond, the harbour wall is still only at waist height. The main harbour of ancient Salamis in fact lies a little further south, and you can explore it by strolling along the beach and rounding the first headland.

The Stone Forum, St Epiphanius and the Granite Forum Returning to the junction near the olive mill, take a right to return to the theatre and car park, or a left to explore the rest of Salamis. Though these last ruins are unexcavated, they remain impressive and for those with the time it is pleasant to stroll around the ancient city to find them, enjoying the gentle breeze which blows in the fragrant eucalyptus trees. In spring and early summer, the walk across the gentle rise and fall of the land, alive with the yellow blossom of acacia mimosa, is especially lovely.

Most memorable, perhaps, is the **Agora or Stone Forum**, thought to be the largest forum or marketplace in the entire Roman Empire, with origins going back to the Hellenistic period. On the way to the forum you will come, on your right, to the foundations of **St Epiphanius**, the largest basilica in Cyprus. It was built in AD345, just after the earthquakes, by Epiphanius, the Bishop of Constantia. Utterly devastated as it is, the church still conveys its vastness. Salamis has an important place in the early history of Christianity, and St Barnabas himself was born here. Barnabas accompanied Paul on his first missionary journey from Antioch:

> For the jews require a sign, and the Greeks seek after wisdom: But we preach Christ crucified, unto the Jews a stumbling-block, and unto the Greeks foolishness.
>
> I Corinthians I: 22–23

Later Barnabas split from Paul and came to Cyprus again with his nephew, the young John Mark. He became, according to Church tradition, the first bishop of the Church of Cyprus, and was martyred by the Jews of his native Salamis in AD75. On the site where he is buried, the St Barnabas Monastery now stands, described on pages 128–9.

Close to the basilica, just a little further north on the opposite side of the road, look out for the huge tumbled **granite columns** of another, smaller forum. These hefty 50-tonne, 6m-long columns are in the unmistakable pinkish colour of Aswan granite from Egypt.

Measuring 230m by 55m, the Agora or Stone Forum is best viewed from the temple end (ie: not from the trackside but from the far side of the ruins; see map on page 122), though this involves a long walk, taking a left where the path forks near the Gazimağusa–Boğaz highway. Don't try to pick your way through the forum ruins, for they are heavily overgrown and somewhat dangerous. (If you can't be bothered to traipse all the way to the temple, the view from the end of the forum nearest the path is almost as good. Lying between the forum and the path is a deep, pillared reservoir that supplied the city.) The little temple, whose well-crafted marble steps are still visible, is known to have been dedicated to Zeus (Jupiter), who was also the protector of the island of Salamis, the city's namesake. Having reached the temple, you must pick your way across to the temple podium, slightly raised, from where you can then look out over the forum. The column stumps lining the sides are still visible and a solitary capital remains on its full-height column to help evoke the scale of the whole. These columns would have formed part of the forum's twin arcades, protecting shoppers from the fierce heat. The central courtyard would have been filled with temples, statues and fountains.

To return to the entrance, follow the path as it loops round alongside the **Byzantine city's walls**. All around are more buildings, covered in sand and undergrowth, awaiting excavation. Sections of town wall belonging to the smaller Byzantine town of Constantia can be glimpsed here and there. Of the earlier Greek city wall, nothing remains except earth banks. Just opposite the former entrance to Salamis, next to the highway, you can still see in the scrubland a fragment of the aqueduct that brought water down from Kythrea. At the beginning of the century, parts of it were still in use.

THE ROYAL TOMBS AND THE NECROPOLIS OF SALAMIS

(*The gates to the tomb enclosures are usually open, but the adjacent little museum adheres to office-like hours: ⊕ 08.00–16.00 weekdays; £2.00/1.00 adults/students*) To the west of Salamis sprawls a huge necropolis covering some 7km². Some of the tombs that have been uncovered have been of great importance archaeologically, helping us to understand more about the beliefs and rituals of the early islanders. Chief among these finds is an unusual collection of tombs, unique on the island, interesting for their strange Homeric associations. They are less than 1km from the main site of Salamis.

TOURING THE ROYAL TOMBS Leaving Salamis, take a left and then a right opposite Salamis's former entrance. The road continues inland and takes you to the Necropolis of Salamis after just 500m or so on your left, with the St Barnabas Monastery 1km further inland on the same road.

Drive up to the Royal Tombs' ticket office (follow the yellow signposts as usual) and leave your car here. Next to the ticket office is a very useful **museum**, providing you with the necessary background information to the tombs. Both the office and museum are closed at weekends, but you can usually still gain access to the tombs themselves as their gates are not generally locked. If the museum is shut, you can peer in through the windows to see the reconstructions of the bronze horse chariots and drawings showing the course of excavations, and how the tombs were found. The discovery of these tombs and their accompanying chariots has yielded some evidence that would seem to confirm Salamis's origins as a Trojan foundation, and Homer's *Iliad* describes precisely such funeral pyres as were found here, piled high with jars of honey and oil, and then the four horses on top.

There are six major royal tombs and a visit to all would take at least an hour. It is not actually known if these tombs belonged to royalty or not, but the quality and

THE CENOTAPH OF NICOCREON

Of all the tombs in the vast, sprawling necropolis that lies on the plain to the west of Salamis and Gazimağusa, **Tomb No 77** stands out for a number of reasons. For one thing it is not actually a tomb at all, there being no bodies buried there (hence its official description as a cenotaph, or memorial). For another, it lies some distance apart from the main tomb complex, in the village of Tuzla (Engomi), just a couple of kilometres to the west of Gazimağusa.

Furthermore, the story behind the cenotaph is rather unusual too. In 311BC, Nicocreon, King of Salamis, sided with Antignon against Ptolemy I. This quite naturally upset Ptolemy who besieged the city with a huge army. Nicocreon, realising that his own forces stood no chance against the might of Ptolemy, decided to commit suicide. When his wife, Queen Axiothea, heard this, she chose to kill their daughters – and persuaded the wives of Nicocreon's brothers to do the same – to prevent them from being raped by Ptolemy's soldiers. In a final act, Axiothea then burnt the palace with herself and the remains of her extended family inside.

To commemorate what they saw as a highly virtuous act – choosing death over the perceived disgrace of being violated by the soldiers – somebody (presumably the Salamians, though nobody is exactly sure) constructed this curious cenotaph. The site consists of a platform, 52m in diameter, with a ramp on one side and steps on the other three. In the centre a pyre was built, where clay statues (thought to represent the members of the royal family), rosettes and other offerings were burnt in their honour. The whole lot was then covered in earth to a depth of over 10m.

The cenotaph was finally excavated in 1965–66. Unfortunately, little remains of the site today, which sits behind the church in Tuzla and is usually locked (though you can look over the fence). The Royal Tombs Museum, however, has a reconstruction of the cenotaph, along with various statues and offerings found at the site.

value of the objects buried with the deceased to accompany them to the next life suggest that they were at the least very important and wealthy people.

If you are short of time you might confine yourself to three: St Catherine's Prison and tombs No 47 and No 79. These last two sit directly behind the museum and are generally reckoned to be the most interesting. On their wide sloping entrance passages are the skeletons of the horses that had pulled the deceased's hearse to the grave. The skeletons are now preserved under glass cases like confectionery. The king's body was cremated and the horses were then sacrificed, still yoked together. Their death agony is evident in their contorted positions, their necks broken and twisted in panic.

The tomb known as **St Catherine's Prison** is unmistakable, with its stone vaulted hump clearly visible to the right of the road as you drive up from Salamis. It is unique in appearance because the Romans built a chapel above the original tomb, using these huge stone blocks, and dedicated it to St Catherine. Inside, pieces of church furniture like lecterns and tables still lie in alcoves. Another alcove, to judge from the smell, is used as a latrine.

St Catherine, the early Christian martyr of Alexandria, was born in Salamis, daughter to one of the island's puppet kings under Roman administration. She refused to marry unless her parents found her a groom as fair and learned and wise and rich as her. Her parents considered this impossible and sent her to a holy hermit, who told her the only man she could marry with these attributes was Jesus Christ. Her father was later exiled to Alexandria and the Christians on the island severely tortured. Catherine proclaimed herself of the faith and was thrown in prison, and later sent to Alexandria herself, to be martyred on a gruesome, spiked wheel, cited as the origin for the name given to today's pyrotechnic Catherine Wheel. When the site was excavated in 1965, her tomb was shown to be of the same type as the others in the necropolis, dated to the 7th century BC. Like them, it has the skeletons of a pair of royal horses yoked together in the entrance passage, sent to the afterlife with their mistress.

On the opposite side of the road, the huge anthill mound with a modern gabled roof of asbestos is prominent. This was imaginatively christened **Tomb No 3** by the archaeologists working the site in the 1960s. Inside, you simply clamber down to the empty grave chamber. The remaining tombs lie behind the beehive No 3, in fenced-in areas. They are in a sorry state, overgrown and vandalised, the glass skeleton cases smashed, scarcely warranting the extra walk for the non-specialist.

THE ÇELLARKA More interesting in many ways to those who have the time, is the short detour to visit the additional group of tombs known as the Çellarka. This is an area some 15m by 100m dug out in a maze of interlinking underground tombs, at least 50 in all. Some are approached by rock cut steps down to the grave chamber, and one of the tomb doorways has simple decoration with what looks like a fish carved into the rock.

To reach the Çellarka you simply continue along the track past the museum for 300m or so, then fork left up an equally rough track lined with oleander bushes. You arrive at a fenced-in area with a gate (usually unlocked). Don't go round these tombs after a beer too many at lunchtime, lest you slip and entomb yourself.

ST BARNABAS MONASTERY

St Barnabas Monastery (Ayios Varnavas), along with Ayias Mamas in Güzelyurt and Apostolos Andreas on the Karpas tip, is a complete monastery preserved as it was pre-1974 and open for viewing as an **icon museum** (⊕ *summer 08.00–19.00 daily; rest of year 08.00–17.00; £2.80/1.00 adults/students*). Its atmosphere is relaxed and pleasant, and it lies less than 2km from Salamis.

A visit takes at least 40 minutes. There are toilets here and a pleasant café in the gardens.

TOURING ST BARNABAS MONASTERY Set on the road between Enkomi and the tombs of the kings, a signpost announces the monastery and you drive up to the door opposite the attractively carved **water fountain**.

The monastery was functioning until 1976, having been lived in since 1917 by three monks, all brothers, said to be indistinguishable from one another. The youngest, a mere 79, was a painter, prolific in the production of necessarily mediocre icons, sold to visitors in order to finance monastery repairs. The other brothers, despite their age, then effected these repairs, adding the new bell tower and finishing the rooms and cells around the courtyard. The attractive garden and cloister courtyard contain quantities of carved blocks and capitals brought from nearby Salamis. Many of the rooms around the courtyard are bursting with pottery from the Enkomi site, much of it in fantastic condition. The courtyard garden is still well tended, with jasmine and hibiscus flame trees, huge pink flowering cacti and citrus trees, one of which is a chimera, producing oranges, lemons and mandarins from different parts of the same tree. Refreshments are on offer here.

The monastery church itself has also changed since the monks left. The pulpits and wooden lecterns are still in place, though the pews have been removed and the place has now been converted to a gallery for the church's collection of icons. The newer, crasser ones are the work of the pragmatic painter brother. A series of four depict the story of how the Cypriot archbishop went to Constantinople to request and be granted independence for the Church of Cyprus by the Emperor Zeno. This story is especially pertinent to the monastery, as it was thanks to Barnabas that this came about. As the Apostle who, with Paul, brought Christianity to Cyprus, Barnabas is revered as the real founder of the Cypriot Church. Born in Salamis, Barnabas returned here later with Paul and died in his native town, martyred by Jews. A number of his followers who witnessed his murder and watched as his body was dumped in marshland are said to have taken his corpse before his murderers could dispose of it properly, and brought it to this spot. Here it lay undisturbed and forgotten for centuries until its location was revealed to Anthemios in a dream in AD477.

Its rediscovery prompted the archbishop to set off to Constantinople and ask that the Cypriot Church be granted its independence. The Byzantine emperor agreed, persuaded by the gift of the original Gospel of St Matthew, in Barnabas's own handwriting, allegedly found clasped in the dead saint's arms. Zeno even donated the funds for this, the first monastery on Cyprus. Today, the self-governing Church of Cyprus ranks fifth in the world of Greek Orthodoxy – after the patriarchates of Constantinople, Alexandria, Antioch and Jerusalem, but before the patriarchates of Russia, Greece, Serbia, Romania, etc.

The monastery as it stands now dates largely to the 18th century, as the original 5th-century building was destroyed in the Arab raids. Of the icons in the church, one, portraying two men and now hanging from the iconostasis, is said to be 1,000 years old. Carved capitals from Salamis peep out from the whitewashed walls, and the blackened pillar inside the painted apse is also from Salamis. Near the altar is the wax effigy of a leg, from a family whose child had an illness in this limb, hung here for the saint to cure.

Perhaps more impressive than the church is the monastery's **museum**, housed in the rooms surrounding the courtyard. Among the collection are some wonderfully complete pottery pieces from various eras, some equally complete Roman glassware and some gold jewellery.

Outside, opposite the entrance, new excavations have revealed several deep rock tombs and the tree-lined road straight ahead from the monastery door leads to Barnabas's tomb. The plain domed mausoleum was erected in the 1950s above an old rock tomb, and you can still clamber down the steps to see where the bones of Barnabas and his Gospel of St Matthew are said to have been found. These days there's a small shrine with a few lighted candles and the smell of incense to venerate the spot.

ENKOMI: BRONZE AGE CAPITAL OF CYPRUS

(£2.00/1.00 adults/students. Don't worry if the ticket office is closed as the entrance is not locked anyway) Enkomi, the first ancient capital of the island, dated to 2000BC, is a much underrated site. Even though at first glance it looks uninspiring, the longer you stay down inside the site, the more you notice the details that gradually bring it alive. Allow anything from 30 minutes to an hour.

TOURING ENKOMI To reach the site you drive inland (west) from the St Barnabas Monastery. The site, clearly signposted, sits just to the right of the first major junction you come to, opposite a water tower. At the entrance, the cluster of derelict buildings on the left were originally the French excavators' headquarters for the digs that went on here under Professor Schaeffer (excavator of Ugarit/Ras Shamra in Syria) from the 1930s until the 1960s. The site was in fact first excavated in 1896 by the British, who found quantities of treasure and Mycenaean pottery, now in the British Museum.

5

Since the late 1960s Enkomi has been neglected, though today this process has been at least arrested if not reversed. The entrance fee includes a map and brief history of the site. However, it's quite likely that apart from solemn accompaniment by the ticket collector's two dogs you'll have the island's former capital to yourself. Watch out for hidden wells and snakes.

The whole site is remarkably large, about 1km², as befits the ancient capital of Cyprus or Alassia as it was called then. Although first settled around the beginning of the second millennium BC, the town came to prominence around two hundred yeas later, when, according to clay tablets found at various sites around the Levant, Alassia traded with many of the region's great powers. Its main trade was in copper ingots, notably with the pharaohs of Egypt and the Hittites of Asia Minor, and Professor Schaeffer also found much evidence of Enkomi's role as a staging post between the Mycenaean towns of the Aegean and the towns of the Syrian coast. The merchants grew wealthy on this trade, and the prosperity is visible in the strikingly grand and well-built houses for this early period of history.

The town never really recovered, however, from an invasion in around 1200BC by the enigmatic 'Sea peoples', a group who feature prominently in the history of the Near East at this time, but whose real identity has never been satisfactorily discovered. With the silting of its inland harbour by the Pedios River, Enkomi fell into permanent decline, and an earthquake in 1075BC finished the town off for good. There is a story that the last inhabitants went off to found a new settlement by the coast. That settlement was Salamis.

The town is encircled by a **defensive wall**, which closely followed the line of the modern fences that ring the site today, and was built to a loose grid pattern, with perpendicular streets bisecting each other at right angles. Signs tell you not to walk on the ruins themselves, and if you do stray from the main path be very careful: there are tombs and wells everywhere, with new ones opening every year.

Follow the old path down into the site and walk first along the main street, looking out for the **houses** built of large and well-crafted blocks. The whole town is littered with fragments of sherds and greeny-black pieces of stone lying about on the tops of the walls. Abandoned by human visitors, the site is alive with lizards and birdlife. All around, you will come across wells, grinding stones, cisterns and tombs. One well, some 20m deep, still has water, and all around there's evidence of a remarkably sophisticated **water system**. Especially impressive are the huge door lintel blocks, and the vast door openings, sometimes 3m wide, notably into the so-called House of the Pillar, to the left of the main street.

Also to the right of the path, look out for the large stone block in the shape of a bull's horns, highly reminiscent of the Minoan fertility symbol. The building in which it stands is known as the **Sanctuary of the Horned God**, and it was here, in the corner of the building, that the little bronze horned statue of a god was found, often seen on pictures and now in the Cyprus Museum.

In another large house known as the **House of the Bronzes** to the left of the main street, many finely wrought bronze objects were unearthed by the French in the 1930s, now also in the Cyprus Museum. At the extremities of the site, particularly in the north and south, large sections of the town wall can still be seen, with the foundations of fortified city gate-towers.

CHURCHES ON THE MESAORIA PLAIN

Scattered about in the countryside or in the villages of the Mesaoria Plain are a few other churches which enthusiasts may care to visit. They can be seen in a two-hour circuit from a starting point of Boğaz or Salamis, and the drive also affords the chance to see the deeply rural communities of the plain whose lifestyle is so far removed from that of the towns and cities close by.

Starting inland from Gazimağusa towards İskele (Greek Trikomo, birthplace of George Cirivas Dighenis 1878–1973, the EOKA leader), you come in the very heart of this pretty little rural town to the tiny Dominican **chapel of St James**, nearly bisected by crossroads, like a sort of traffic island. Its tiny floor area and relatively high dome give it a distinctly Armenian look. It is now kept locked to protect the 15th-century interior and the porcelain plates set in its vaulted ceiling. Unfortunately, these defences have not been enough to stop the local pigeons moving in, and the floor is now ankle deep in their droppings.

Heading out west from İskele, you will come to the 12th-century domed **church of Panayia Theotokos**, now converted to an **icon museum** (⊕ *09.00–19.00 daily; £1.00/0.50 adults/students*). Inside, it also has traces of 12th- and 15th-century wall paintings.

Continuing westwards and turning right at the main road, Sınırüstü (Greek Syngrasis) is the next village you come to, strikingly set under a small escarpment with the occasional palm tree peeping out of the fertile greenery. Here you turn left (south) and, as you leave the village outskirts, you will notice on your left a wonderfully pretty domed church surrounded by a cluster of cypress trees, approached by a derelict tarmac lane. This is the 13th-century **Ayios Prokopius**. Open and empty but for a few wooden pulpits and pews, the interior has two large frescoes of *St George and the Dragon* on a deep blue background, and opposite is an older fresco of a saint on a horse. Unfortunately, the pigeons have once again moved in, and the place stinks to, appropriately enough I suppose, high heaven.

Returning to the Sınırüstü junction you now continue west towards Geçitkale, a large town of the plain. Its recently opened airport tends to be used only when Ercan is closed for repairs. Just before the village of Akova (Greek Gypsos), you will pass a desecrated **Greek cemetery** on the left of the road. Beside it is a new Turkish cemetery with the first graves dated 1987.

Turn left (south) at Akova and at the next village, Yildirim (Greek Milea), turn left again to head back towards the coast. Leaving the outskirts of the village, the medieval church of **Ayios Yeoryios** is to be found to the right of the road.

Also on the right some 3km further on, set a good 500m off the road and not visible from it, is the 17th-century **Panayia Avgasida Monastery**, 1km northeast of Şehitler (Greek Sandlaris), with a double-aisled domed church. The striking thing with all these churches is how numerous they are: the tiniest village usually boasts a church and it is quite common for larger villages to have two or three. The reason for this lies in Cyprus's history, where the church long represented political power as much as religious devotion. During the 20th century the church bells were used by Greek Cypriot EOKA zealots as summons or as danger signals. All the churches are now derelict, or if their location lends itself, they are turned into barns or stables. Mosques, on the other hand, are few and far between: recent surveys have confirmed that Turkish Cypriots are among the least zealous Muslims in the world.

Driving through Şehitler, which has a **mass grave** and, nearby, a **memorial** to the victims of the fighting of 1974, you eventually reach the coast in about ten minutes, arriving almost opposite the entrance to Salamis.

5

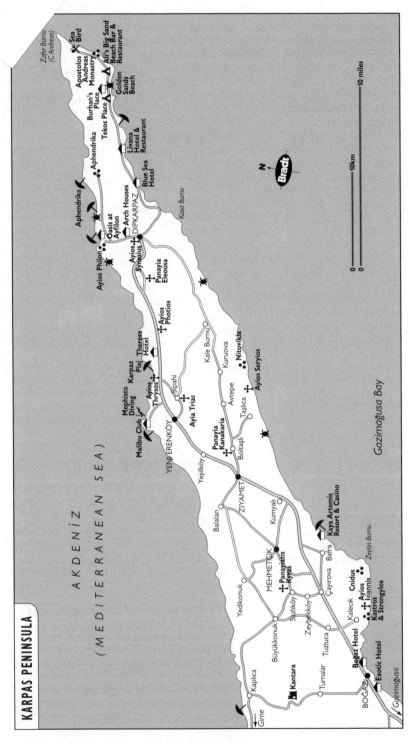

KARPAS PENINSULA

AKDENIZ
(MEDITERRANEAN SEA)

Zafer Burnu
(C Andreas)

Sea Bird

Apostolos Andreas Monastr

Alli's Big Sand Beach Bar & Restaurant

Burhan's Place

Golden Sands Beach

Tekos Place

Aphendrika

Livana Hotel & Restaurant

Aphendrika

Blue Sea Hotel

Aphendrika

Kaso Burnu

Oasis at Ayfilon

Arch Houses

DIPKARPAZ

Ayios Philon

Ayios Synesius

Panayia Eleousa

Ayios Photios

Kale Burnu

Kuruova

Theresa Hotel

Karpaz Plaj

Nitovikla

Ayios Seryios

Mephisto Diving

Ayios Thrysos

Sipahi

Avtepe

Malibu Club

YENİ ERENKÖY

Ayia Trias

Panayia Kanakaria

Taşlıca

Yeşilköy

Boltaşlı

N

Bradt

10km

10 miles

0

0

Gazimağusa Bay

Balalan

ZIYAMET

Kumyalı

Kaya Artemis Resort & Casino

Zeytin Burnu

Yedikonuk

MEHMETÇIK

Panayiatis Kypas

Bafra

Cnidus

Büyükkonuk

Sazlıköy

Zeybekköy

Çayırova

Kaleçik

Ayios Ioannis

Kastros & Strongylos

Kaplıca

Tuzluca

Boğaz Hotel

Kantara

Turnalar

Exotic Hotel

Girne

BOĞAZ

Gazimağusa

132

6

The Karpas Peninsula

The Karpas has been called the nature reserve of Cyprus, with abundant wildlife and flowers, as yet still relatively untouched by encroaching development. Remote and isolated by virtue of its geographical position, it holds itself aloof from the rest of the island, and almost feels like a different country. The peninsula was predominantly Greek pre-1974, and boasts some exquisite early churches which should not be missed. A few are still in use, as the Karpas retains a small community of Greeks, some 600 strong, who chose to stay behind after 1974, and they continue to live in and around Dipkarpaz (Greek Rizokarpaso). Driving across the sparsely populated rural landscapes, it's possible to imagine that you are heading out to the end of the earth. The corollary of its isolation is that accommodation and restaurants are relatively few and far between in the Karpas, so it is best to go well equipped and self-sufficient, or plan ahead to build your itinerary round the available facilities. However, though the island's indigenous population of donkeys continue to lollop across the tarmac in a timeless and oblivious manner, the Karpas is opening up to tourism.

That said, while there are no luxury hotels, over the past few years some characterful places have sprung up, and if you have the time, at least one night on the peninsula is highly recommended. Restaurants, too, are beginning to grow in number, and in Boğaz, in the very west of the peninsula, a number of quality fish restaurants can now be found. Petrol stations used to be sparse in North Cyprus, especially in the Karpas, but now as the country's embrace of capitalism tightens you're unlikely to drive far without seeing a shiny new row of pumps, although who they are designed to serve remains unclear.

It takes at least two days to explore the Karpas properly, especially if you are coming from Girne. The drive from Girne to Dipkarpaz takes about three hours, whereas from Salamis it takes less than two, and from Boğaz, one and a half. These timings are based on a gentle pace suited to the narrow winding roads. An early start is essential.

🏠 WHERE TO STAY AND EAT

Accommodation along the Karpas Peninsula has expanded somewhat in the last few years, with more opportunities now to spend a few nights on this most unspoilt part of the north. Although facilities are mainly basic, there are hotels, motels, bungalows and campsites, offering some of the most beautiful deserted beaches and a very friendly welcome. Places to eat are really limited to the restaurants, bars and catering provided by the hotels, lodgings and campsites detailed below. This section takes you to the tip of the peninsula along the main road, from Boğaz and then via Ziyamet, Yeni Erenköy and Dipkarpaz.

BAFRA AND İSKELE

🏠 **Kaya Artemis Resort & Casino** (726 rooms) 📞 630 60 00; **f** 630 60 60; **e** info@ kayaartemis.com; www.kayaartemis.com. Las Vegas comes to the Karpas, or at least it's on the way there, with the largest & currently newest resort hotel in North Cyprus. Given the scale of this brash development, its own grandiose allusions & the emphasis placed on the size of its casino it's hard to understand the context of this development. However, all the trappings of 5-star luxury are here, from fancy restaurants & spas, fitness & sports facilities to multi-media-equipped conference facilities. As with casino resorts worldwide, prices are mitigated by the high rollers, so as long as you don't lose your shirt at the tables, the resort offers remarkable value for money. $$$

BOĞAZ AND SURROUNDING AREA

Boğaz itself offers rooms in two hotels which makes good bases for exploring both the Karpas Peninsula and Gazimağusa town, 25km away.

🏠 **Boğaz Hotel** (43 rooms) 📞 371 25 59; **f** 371 25 57; **e** bogazhotel@superonline.com; www.bogazhotel.com. This hotel has an attractive outdoor terrace shaded by jacaranda trees; it has a beach across the road & a restaurant serving fish & other seafood. $$

🏠 **Exotic Hotel** (22 rooms) 📞 371 28 81; **f** 371 32 20; **e** exoticmirillo@superonline.com; www.cyprusexotic.com. Despite its large size, this is a personable place that caters wonderfully for children with a swimming pool with big waterslides. $$

YENI ERENKÖY AND SURROUNDING AREA

🏠 **Club Malibu Hotel** (40 rooms & 5 bungalows) 📞 374 42 64; **f** 374 43 99; **e** info@ clubmalibucy.com; www.clubmalibucy.com. 3km beyond Yeni Erenköy. It is a pleasant spot to stop for a rest, the beach is small but inviting, & it's also home to the PADI-registered Mephisto Diving School (**m** 0533 858 29 35; www.mephisto-diving.com). There's a small harbour here too, where local fishermen dock & sell their catch to the Malibu's restaurant. $$

🏠 **Theresa Hotel** (25 rooms) 📞 374 42 66; **m** 0533 863 2787; **f** 374 40 09; **e** theresahotel@hotmail.com; www.theresahotel.com. 4km past Malibu Motel is a wonderfully friendly hotel & restaurant with a small beach. With all rooms the same price regardless of the view, try to secure one on the 1st floor with a balcony & sea view. A bargain. $

DIPKARPAZ AND BEYOND

🏠 **Oasis at Ayfilon** (6 rooms) **m** 0533 868 55 91; **e** info@oasishotelkarpas.com; www.oasishotelkarpas.com. Standing in glorious isolation in one of the most stunning locations on the island — the ancient ruins & crystal waters combine to form an intoxicating brew. Originally the brainchild of ecotourism pioneer Michael de Glanville, Oasis now provides simple but clean accommodation for those seeking sustainable tourism. A refreshing counterblast to kitsch casinos & resort hotels, there can be nowhere else with such a '5-star' location. $$

🏠 **View Hotel** (13 rooms) 📞 372 22 34; **m** 0533 864 10 50; **f** 372 22 90. Just before the monastery this large white building on the right-hand side is otherwise known as Dipkarpaz Belediyesi Turistik Tesisleri. If this doesn't put you off then maybe its institutional hospital-like reception area will. However, for those who don't want to sleep on the beach it's the closest hotel bed you'll find to Cape Andreas. $$

🏠 **Ali's Big Sand Beach Bar & Restaurant** (5 bungalows) **m** 0533 844 13 22. Further along this splendid stretch of beach, 3km from Apostolas Andreas, Ali's Big Sand offers new bungalows & basic camping facilities. The restaurant & bar are excellent, set high above the beach, offering a magnificent breezy panoramic of the coastline. $

🏠 **Arch Houses** (12 rooms) 📞 372 20 09; **f** 372 20 07; **e** www.karpazarchhouses.com. Delightful honey-coloured farm buildings, the oldest dating back to 1911, that have been lovingly restored & converted into tourist accommodation. Spacious rooms that come with their own kitchen (inc a hotplate) for those who don't want to take advantage of the excellent Manolyam restaurant across the road. $

🏠 **Burhan's Place** (6 bungalows) **m** 0542 854 29 88; **e** burhankalin2002@yahoo.co.uk; www.burhansgoldenbeach.com. Next door to Turtle Beach & looking a deal more shipshape, Burhan's is

just above Golden Sands Beach. There's a shady restaurant & bar &, as well as bungalows, travellers can rent tents or pitch their own. $
🏠 **Blue Sea Hotel** (11 rooms) ☎ 372 23 93; **f** 372 22 55; **m** 0533 862 1177; **e** info@blueseahotel.org; www.blueseahotel.org. A few kilometres outside of town, this splendid hotel is a long-time favourite with tourists. Family-run & solar powered, the hotel has some lovely rooms, all with a sea view (at least of sorts) & balcony, with many overlooking the nearby harbour. $
🏠 **Livana Hotel Restaurant & Bungalows** (26 rooms) ☎ 372 23 96; **m** 0533 846 09 34; **e** livanahotel@hotmail.com. Equally charming though much more rustic, Livana offers rooms in its main building or 'tree-houses' (really just huts on stilts with a separate shed for the toilet down below) set on the beach for the same price. Though they are primitive in the extreme (with a bed the only furniture), the chance to drift off to sleep to the sound of the sea is one not to be missed. Livana also has a little restaurant. $
🏠 **Sea Bird Restaurant** (4 bungalows) **m** 0533 875 63 36. Past the monastery, Sea Bird offers a few bungalows to rent, a restaurant & pretty curving beach & forms the last building you see before heading off, dust clouds behind you, to the end of the island. $

🏠 **Tekos Place** (4 bungalows) **m** 0533 863 73 65; **e** info@tekosplace.com; www.tekosplace.com. Also on the monastery road, just off Golden Sand Beach, Tekos Place has bungalows & camping places & offers a simple restaurant & bar — what more do you need? $
🏠 **Turtle Beach Restaurant, Bungalows & Camping (Hasan's Turtle Beach)** (6 bungalows) **m** 0533 864 1063; **f** 372 20 07; **e** hasan.turtlebeach@yahoo.com.tr. Hasan Korkmaz has run this laid-back site, located amongst the dunes of Golden Sands Beach, just before you reach Apostolos Andreas Monastery, for years & with business being depressed of late, its bohemian ambience may have crossed the line to Mad Max chic. Mixed reports have been received by the Bradt offices of late — you'll have to judge for yourself. However, there are bungalows & a number of tents available, as well as plenty of room to pitch your own. Hasan prepares & cooks all the food to order, serving up *köfte*, kebabs, fish & other delights. The sand stretches, clean & golden, for near on a mile & the sea is crystal clear. Though the beach here was once favoured by nesting turtles, it appears that through increased human traffic most have been displaced. Whether you encounter turtles or not, it's still a beautiful location. $

TOURING THE KARPAS PENINSULA

The Turks, ever since Sultan Selim first took a fancy to 'the rock called Cyprus', have regarded the island as an extension of Anatolia. The long tapering peninsula that reached up to the northeast was described by Churchill as 'the dagger which points at the soft underbelly of Turkey'. If you choose to see in the landmass of Cyprus the shape of an oblong frying pan, you could choose to see in the Karpas the shape of the panhandle. Viewed this way rather than as a dagger, the handle is conveniently turned towards Turkey, the master who can seize it and take control.

The peninsula falls into three distinct sections: first, from the fishing village of Boğaz to Ziyamet, the least interesting section, forming a kind of transitional zone from the mainland (for details of Kantara see pages 89–90); next, from Ziyamet to Dipkarpaz, scenically much prettier with smaller roads and more contours, this section also has the much publicised Kanakaria Church and the early Ayia Trias basilica with its mosaic floor; and finally there is the section beyond Dipkarpaz, definitely the most rewarding stretch, with the northern fork to Ayios Philon and Aphendrika, and the southern fork to the Apostolos Andreas Monastery and Kastros at the very tip. In an ideal world, this section would warrant an entire day in itself, with time to enjoy one of the many deserted beaches, something that is best achieved by spending the night at one of the hotels along here.

Those who can devote only a day to the Karpas should head out beyond Dipkarpaz to Ayios Philon and Aphendrika, then drive on for lunch at the Blue Sea Hotel and take a quick look at the Apostolos Andreas Monastery. On the way back, call in at Ayia Trias in the Greek village of Sipahi. Kanakaria Church is kept locked, and the key has to be extracted from the village *muhtar* or headman, so that is best left for an occasion with plenty of time. There are many other minor churches and sites, and the more leisured visitor can take his/her pick from the following itinerary.

TO ZIYAMET The first section of the Karpas, before Ziyamet, has the largest number of sites to visit, albeit minor, and for those with the time and inclination to explore fully, there are three possible detours from the main road.

Starting at Boğaz, the first is at the turn-off right (south) towards Kalecik. There is no signpost but the landmark is the group of oil storage tanks visible some kilometres away on the coast. Kalecik means 'little castle' and by the sea near the tanker terminal are the heavily ruined 12th-century twin Templar castles of **Kastros** and **Strongylos**. A few foundations and cisterns are all that remain today. Nearby is the ruined **chapel of Ayios Ioannis**. In the village itself, the school is a former Byzantine church. Kalecik is the second port of North Cyprus after Gazimağusa and before Girne, used for exporting quantities of cargo, especially the tobacco grown in the Karpas, and for importing oil. It has no passenger traffic.

At Tuzluca, the village on the crossroads to the north, the curious can seek out the large stone to be found in the old churchyard. The stone has a hole in the middle and local tradition held that every Easter Monday, if the married men of the village clambered through the hole, they could check that their wives had remained faithful. Any that had been cuckolded got stuck because of their 'horns' and having extricated themselves, rushed off to beat their wicked spouses and begin divorce proceedings. Records show that the last such event occurred in 1935. With scarcely 600 inhabitants one would have thought the opportunities for infidelity were limited, and the chances of keeping it quiet even more so, but perhaps that betrays a lack of familiarity with village life.

At Çayırova (Greek Ayios Theodhoros), the next village on the way to Ziyamet, an 8km dirt track forks south to the headland of Zeytin Burnu, Olive Cape (Greek Cape Elea). Here, to the right of the track, close to the sea, are the ruins of ancient **Phoenician Cnidus** set in a natural harbour. Today they are scarcely visible among the ploughed fields, but the town was inhabited from the 5th century BC until the 2nd century AD.

From Çayırova you can take the fork to the north to the village of Zeybekköy, then to the right again to the hamlet of Sazliköy (Greek Livadhia). At the foot of the hill behind this village, alone in a bucolic setting, you will see the pretty little church of **Panayiatis Kyras**, thought to be 7th century. It can be approached from a track to the left that starts directly opposite the mosque, but most of the last section has to be done on foot, about five minutes across the fields. Empty and desecrated, it has a little arched side entrance with a charming sitting area. Inside there was a mosaic of the Virgin, now largely disappeared as a result of the local superstition that a cube of the mosaic would, if kept in a pocket, banish pimples and spots.

A fork south from Çayırova leads to the village of Bafra, and beyond to a sandy bay where an uncompleted holiday village stands awaiting its fate. Further north at Kumyalı a fork off to the harbour leads to a sandy beach. In the village itself, raised up on a hillock, is a small **15th-century church** built above an ancient tomb, and all around are vestiges of a classical necropolis.

BEYOND ZIYAMET At Ziyamet (Greek Leonarisso) the character of the Karpas changes, becoming much more rural and hilly. Just beyond Ziyamet, a small town inhabited largely by mainland Turks, is a crossroads, where a fork right to Gelincik will take you, after just a couple of kilometres, to the monastery church of Kanakaria. This fork continues all the way to Kale Burnu, but the track marked on most maps between Kuruova and Sipahi is terrible and any ideas you may have of a shortcut to Sipahi should be abandoned. Even with a Jeep, the going is so slow that it is quicker to return to Ziyamet and double back on the tarmac.

The large Byzantine monastery church of **Panayia Kanakaria** stands on the left of the road soon after entering the village of Boltaşli (Greek Lythrangomi). The monastery outbuildings are gradually decaying and in the graveyard round the back, three desecrated graves of the last monks peep out above the weeds. In the semicircular ceiling above the main entrance is a well-preserved fresco of the Virgin dated 1779. The original 11th- to 12th-century church was restored at that time, giving the church stone a (comparatively) newish look.

The door is kept locked but you can go into the village to ask the *muhtar* or headman for the key if you are really keen. Inside, a fragment of a mosaic of the *Virgin and Child* in the central apse was all that survived of the earliest 5th- or 6th-century church, making this the earliest Byzantine mosaic on the island. This is the fragment that was stolen on the instructions of black-market art dealers. Four sections, each measuring 61cm square, were chipped away. They depicted the Christ Child, an angel and the saints James and Andrew. On the black market for antiquities they found their way to Indianapolis, to an art dealer who paid US$1.1 million for them. She in turn tried to sell them to the J Paul Getty Museum in California for US$20 million, but Getty's curator notified the Cypriot authorities, leading to an international court case. By standing on piles of stones outside the apse windows, you can just about peer inside to glimpse the badly damaged interior. Traces of fresco can still be made out on the walls, but the pigeons have taken over wholesale.

The drive further along this little road towards Kale Burnu is interesting for its scenery, rather than the sites along it, which are essentially minor. The stretch between Derince and Avtepe is most unusual, with a dramatic drop down into a huge valley and bare rolling hills all around. A track leads along this river valley to the sea, some 4km away, where a ruined 14th-century domed chapel, **Ayios Seryios**, can still be seen, to the right of the river mouth. Northeast of Avtepe there is also an unusual cave tomb of unknown date cut into a bare cliffside at a height of some 200m, and visible as you approach from afar. The climb up to it is very tricky and should be attempted only by those who relish heights and unsure footholds. Inside are many deep corridors leading to grave chambers, cut some 26m deep into the hillside. Be sure to take a good torch. At the very back is a well shaft of immense depth, which village tradition has it, leads either to hell or to paradise, depending on which is more deserved.

At Kuruova a bumpy track to the right heads for the coast, winding 4km across the riverbed and ploughed fields. Always bearing right when there is a choice, you will eventually reach the sea where the stones of the Middle Cypriot (c1800BC) fortress of **Nitovikla** stand a few courses high. It was excavated back in 1929. After wet weather the track is impassable for cars, as tractors gouge out great ruts which fill with water.

At the curious semi-troglodyte village of **Kale Burnu** (Greek Galinoporni), the tarmac stops. On the slope around it are many rock tombs, thought to have been originally Phoenician. On the outskirts, near the ruined church of Ayia Anna, is an extraordinary **cave tomb** 21m long.

Returning to Ziyamet, you now continue on the main road to **Yeni Erenköy** (Greek Yialousa), the second-largest town of the Karpas, with 2,500 inhabitants, the resettled Turkish Cypriots from the enclave of Erenköy (Greek Kokkina) to the west. The Karpas Peninsula **tourist office** (☉ *summer 08.00–17.00 daily*) is ably run by the helpful Meryem Gürler, an expat from Essex. The owner of the pastry shop at the lower end of the main street is also a mine of information (in English).

Beyond the pleasant rambling town, the road heads towards the north coast, and some 2km from the edge of town a track to the left leads down to the Halk Plaj or **public beach**, a sandy bay with swings, changing cabins and, in the season, a barbecuing area offering snacks and kebabs.

One kilometre further on is the **Karpaz Plaj**, where a simple but wholesome place offers fish and kebabs and a good sandy beach. The beach could be kept cleaner, as a certain amount of rubbish and eel grass gets washed up.

After another 2–3km, a typical yellow signpost points the way to the Greek village of Sipahi and the ruined church of **Ayia Trias**. Situated on the right of the road on the edge of town, the ruined column stumps of this large early 5th-century basilica are visible from the road. When staffed, the site has an entrance fee of £1.20/0.40, though frequently the place is deserted and the gates left unlocked. The setting is wonderfully pastoral, not to say overgrown, in the middle of orchards and fields, and sheep are frequently to be found grazing in the aisles. The site was excavated in the 1960s to reveal a large three-aisled structure. Few of the columns stand higher than head height, and the walls are rarely above waist height, but the memorable feature of the basilica is its mosaic floor paving. Open to the sky, its colours, mainly reds, blues and whites, are faded, but the intricate geometric designs are striking, mixed in with patterns of foliage and the occasional Christian symbol. The north aisle shows two curious pairs of sandals facing in opposite directions. The font can still be seen, and its cruciform shape is unique on the island.

The village of **Sipahi** (Greek Ayia Trias, Holy Trinity) still has 100 to 200 Greeks who chose to stay behind despite partition, and as you walk about in the village you will still see old men dressed in traditional rural baggy black trousers, and only Greek is spoken. Even in the times of mixed villages, Greeks and Turks always had separate schools and there was no official intermarriage between the communities. Today the non-Greek inhabitants are Turks from Trabzon and Samsun on the Black Sea. Some 600 or so Greek Cypriots still live on the Karpas, the bulk of them in Dipkarpaz. Every Wednesday, the UN Peace Keeping Force in Cyprus, the 'Blue Berets', bring in about ten tonnes of food and mail for them from Greek Nicosia. Relatives from the Greek side are allowed to visit, though problems sometimes occur. On one such visit, a Greek girl met and married a local Turk. The Greek Cypriots of Nicosia were outraged, convinced she had been abducted, and a band of friends marched on the Green Line in protest, demanding her return. A few months later, the girl returned to visit her parents in Nicosia, and stayed there. Her husband followed her, and was promptly deported by the Greek Cypriots. The numbers of this Greek community are, not surprisingly, slowly declining.

Some 8km east of Ayia Trias, back on the main Dipkarpaz road, you pass the derelict **Ayias Thrysos Church** on the left, with the Deks Restaurant almost immediately opposite on the right. A simple lunch can be taken here, and it is possible, though not ideal, to swim from the rocky bay below. The restaurant also has ten simple but adequate rooms in a separate annexe. The 15th-century church is whitewashed, with no frescoes, and empty except for a few wooden pews and the shell of the iconostasis. Lower down, close to the shore, is a smaller ruined medieval chapel, and beside it to the right is an even smaller cave church, probably Byzantine.

Some 3km further on, the observant may spot the isolated church of **Ayios Photios** uphill to the right, approached by a bad but driveable track. Thought to be 10th century, the church has no door, and inside there are traces of frescoes showing figures on horseback and a saint with a halo. Goat droppings form the major floor embellishment and the ceiling is adorned with swallows' nests.

Another 5km further east on the main road, an easily driveable dirt track leads inland just by a bridge over a dry stream-bed. This brings you after 2km to an open clearing in the thick prickly scrubland. Here, abandoned, stands the monastery of **Panayia Eleousa**. The small 16th-century whitewashed church has a decorated doorway, but inside the frescoes are covered in whitewash. Turks and Christians alike share the unfortunate habit of covering everything in whitewash. Swallows and wasps have also moved in. The monks' cells, looking of fairly recent build, stand in a row a little apart from the church. From here a tarmac road continues round in a loop to rejoin the main road a few kilometres further on.

The main road now begins a steep ascent up a fertile valley to reach Dipkarpaz, set on a hilltop. A lot of tobacco is grown in the area, and the soil's fertility is due to the abundance of wells, for the Karpas is rich in underground water reservoirs.

FROM DIPKARPAZ TO THE TIP OF THE PENINSULA

The town of **Dipkarpaz** (Greek Rizokarpaso) has little to delay the visitor today, except perhaps the petrol station and a line of grocery stores selling ice creams, bread and picnic fodder. A few 18th-century houses remain, and the restored Arch Houses, now a hotel, are worth a quick nose around, but on the whole the modern buildings are unmemorable. Set up on the hill to the left is the plain whitewashed church of **Ayios Synesius**, still used by the Greek community. The church stands on the site of the Orthodox cathedral which was built here in the 13th century when the Greek Orthodox bishop was banished from Famagusta to Rizokarpaso by the Catholic Crusaders. The town has always been predominantly Greek, and you will notice a prevalence of blue or green eyes in the locals. Travellers of earlier centuries imagined the place filled with exotic beauties, but most modern visitors will search in vain.

Ayios Philon

Beyond Dipkarpaz, to reach the northern coastline, you must turn left uphill from the centre of town, passing the long white school building on your left near the brow of the hill, and follow the arrows to Ayios Philon. Soon you'll join the tarmac road to begin the long descent to the coast, 4km away.

As you make the descent you can already see in the distance the church of Ayios Philon, standing alone on the shoreline. This was the site of the ancient city of Karpasia, founded by the legendary King Pygmalion of Cyprus. It was a flourishing Christian community until the Arab raiders burnt and sacked it in 802. Its inhabitants fled inland at that time and Rizokarpaso grew up. Today Ayios Philon is the spectacular location for **Oasis at Ayfilon**, the sustainable ecotourism venture spearheaded by Michael de Glanville, offering simple fresh food and several rooms by the beach (see *Sustainable tourism* box, pages 36–7).

The spot is beautifully remote, with only the sound of the sea against the rocks and the twittering of the birds. The church is set on the cliffs above a rocky bay with six solitary palm trees breaking the skyline. Traces of the old harbour wall can still be seen where you swim, the large stone blocks still extending some 100m, while the remainder of the town lies hidden under the sand dunes away to the west. Philon was the name of the 5th-century bishop who converted the inhabitants of the Karpas to Christianity. The well-preserved church complete with roof is 10th century, but beside it, open to the elements, the red, white and grey mosaic pavement and column remnants belong to a 5th-century basilica, the original church of Bishop Philon. Nearby are a few heavily vandalised Greek houses of this century.

Aphendrika Beyond Ayios Philon an old dead-end tarmac road leads to Aphendrika in just ten more minutes. There is no habitation at all on this stretch of coastline, and the tarmac turns into dirt track some 400m short of the mined Christian settlement of Aphendrika, where the shells of three churches clustered together can still be easily explored. Silent except for the birdsong and the buzzing of flies echoing in the ruined church, the spot is utterly deserted.

In 200BC, Strabo the Greek historian tells us, Aphendrika was one of the six great cities of Cyprus, and the site is deceptively extensive. Apart from the three **churches** – Panaghia Chrysiotissa, St George and Asomatos – which date from the 12th and 14th centuries, you should also search for the **citadel**, set up on the hill east (inland), with many of its rooms cut into the bedrock.

Walking towards the west, you will stumble on the **necropolis**, a whole area scattered with rock tombs, and the site of a temple beyond it. To the north, a 2km walk across the fields, lies the silted-up **harbour** of the ancient city, with a lonely sandy beach. The city has never been properly excavated.

From Aphendrika, the furthermost point of road on the north coast, it is 104km back to Kyrenia.

Apostolos Andreas Monastery Returning to Dipkarpaz you now look out for the sign saying Zafer Burnu Manastirsi (Zafer Burnu being the name of the headland at the very tip of the island) opposite the shops which points to the left (south) from the centre of town.

Scenically this stretch of isolated road along to the tip is the most magnificent on the island. There are no villages at all, and the only life you are likely to see is the occasional shepherd with his sheep and goats. Still dressed in the 19th-century fashion of baggy trousers, he is often spinning wool as he minds the flock. The bucolic landscape has an old-world charm, and the gentle hills occasionally give way to magnificent vistas over huge sweeping bays. Scattered about all over the fields are fine buildings made from beautifully crafted stone. They look sufficiently grand to have been the residences of local mayors, but in fact they are simply storage barns and stables built by the former Greek inhabitants. Sometimes they even have crosses carved above the door.

As the road winds down through the hills from Dipkarpaz towards the sea, the landscape is covered in thick scrub. At certain seasons, the roadside is thick with vehicles disgorging men wearing camouflage gear, with rifles and a glint in their eyes. This is not, however, some relic of intercommunal strife, but the hunting season for birds. The hunters are legion, and as they quiver in the bushes, the chances of shooting each other must be quite high. The prey is mainly partridge and francolin, and the season, only on Sundays from November to January, is strictly controlled by the police. The sport is so popular that hunters travel all the way from Güzelyurt at the other end of the island for what is reckoned to be the best shooting. The catch is then taken home for eating. Cyprus is used by millions of birds as a stepping stone on their migrations between Europe and the Nile Delta. The best birdwatching spot for these migrants is at the Gönyeli reservoir on the northern edge of Lefkoşa.

Just where the road leaves the hunters in the hills and swoops round to the coast, you come to the **Blue Sea Hotel and Restaurant**, opened in 1989, in a lovely spot on a promontory a little above a beach and harbour. The proud owner, an ex-captain in the army, bought the building which had been left unfinished by his Greek predecessor. He has furnished it to a surprisingly high standard and his willing service makes a stop here very relaxing, either just for a meal or overnight.

The spot is known as **Khelones**, from the Greek for turtle, probably because turtles have always come here to lay their eggs in the sand. Behind the hotel is a ruined carob store and customs house, a relic of the days when carobs were exported from here, and the old harbour still remains below.

The road from here onwards stays more or less within sight of the coast, every corner bringing new panoramas over endless deserted bays. Most spectacular of all is one stretch some 4km before the monastery with an immense sandy beach and wild red sprawling dunes, reminiscent of the Gower coast in Wales.

The road emerges suddenly at the **Apostolos Andreas Monastery**, arriving at a large open courtyard with one-roomed cells round the edge for pilgrims' accommodation. The current buildings date from 1867, though you could be forgiven for thinking them older as they have been crumbling steadily for years. The monastery is also a police post and a pair of friendly policemen are based here, along with dozens of cats that hang around the car park. North Cyprus's very own indigenous donkeys can usually be seen grazing in the scrubland on the other side of the road. Incidentally, there is no longer any need to register with the police here. It comes as something of a surprise to find several tour buses already at the monastery, such is the scene likely to be at the busiest times of year. Showing that capitalism knows no bounds, you'll also find an army of locals peddling all sorts of generic junk. Heaven only knows how they got their stalls here.

The monastery has traditionally been the Lourdes of Cyprus, with pilgrims coming from afar seeking cures for their afflictions. St Andrew was the great miracle worker and protector of travellers. Brother of Peter, and a fisherman like him, Andrew preached his mission in Greece and Turkey. On one such trip, the ship in which he was sailing ran out of drinking water, as they were passing Cyprus, so he told the one-eyed captain to put ashore here on the rocky headland. The sailors returned with water, and Andrew restored the captain's full sight. The captain and crew were converted and baptised by Andrew, and on his return trip the captain placed an icon of Andrew beside the wells. Hence the sanctity of the spot grew up. Andrew eventually settled in Patras on the Greek mainland, where he was crucified aged 80.

The modern church beneath the bell tower is bare and unexciting, housing an icon of the saint, hosts of wax effigies of adults, children, limbs and even a cow, all seeking cures for long-term illnesses. Below the church, closer to the sea, is the rock grotto (the chapel was a 15th-century addition) where you can still see the tiny spring of freshwater that Andrew is said to have endowed with special healing powers. Enough stories of cure exist to encourage the shrine to keep its reputation. A recent one tells of a paralysed girl whose parents reluctantly brought her here for the saint to effect a cure. They were both highly sceptical, but the girl insisted. It was late evening and she persuaded one of the monks to carry her into the rock chapel and leave her there. Two hours passed and the monk was suddenly startled by a cry. He turned to see the girl coming up the path on all fours at first, but then staggering weakly on her thin legs.

On Assumption Day, 15 August, and St Andrew's Day, 30 November, many pilgrims still come, Muslims and Christians alike, bringing offerings. Pre-1974 they would come on Sundays in their hundreds from Famagusta for family outings, and the priests were asked to perform so many baptisms that the font was fitted out with hot and cold taps. Numbers have dwindled somewhat since then. An old woman speaking Greek is often still to be found holding the key to the church and the grotto. She'll open the doors, pull back the curtains to show icons of the saint, and expect you to kiss them.

Zafer Burnu (Cape Andreas)

Having come all this way, if you still have a spare half-hour you will probably want to complete your pilgrimage by driving the remaining 5km to the very tip of the island. The track is stony and bumpy but quite driveable in a saloon car, ending at the abandoned meteorological customs hut. It takes 15 to 20 minutes one way from the monastery but, though the landscape is fairly flat, you cannot see the sea on both sides until the final 200m when the track approaches the bulbous rocky outcrop. Scramble up to the summit of this rock (where immense Turkish and KKTC flags are flying) for the best views of all.

A **Neolithic fort**, the oldest yet found on Cyprus along with Petra Tou Limniti and Khirokhitia (c6000BC) was excavated on this summit in 1971–73, but only a few shapeless walls and foundations remain to the layman's eye.

Perched on the top, there is almost a climatic change, and the rock gives way to grass and lovely white flowers, alive with butterflies and gentle wafts of breeze. A temple of Aphrodite once stood here to protect sailors from the treacherous rocks or to lure them in, according to her whim. It's a wonderful spot for a picnic, here, at the end of the earth, lolling on the grass, flags flying overhead, gazing out at the string of little islands opposite, the Klides, the Keys of Cyprus, home only to the rare Audouin's Gull.

Aphendrika

Appendix I

LANGUAGE

Turkish is a fiendishly difficult language for foreigners to become proficient in but, fortunately, English and German are widely understood. Its grammatical structure is unrelated to Indo-European and Romance languages and the major stumbling block to forming a sentence is the word order, which almost requires you to think 'backwards'. A sentence for example like 'The cake which I bought for you is on the table' retains the same shape in French, German, Spanish, Greek and even Arabic. In Turkish it becomes 'You-for buy-in-the-past-pertaining-to-me cake, table's surface-thereof-at is'. Not only is the order reversed, but the 11 English words become six in Turkish because of the Turkish habit of what is graphically called 'agglutinating', that is sticking on extra words to the base word.

For those who would just like to have the bare minimum of vocabulary and expressions, see the following list.

PRONUNCIATION AND ALPHABET Vowels and consonants are pronounced as in English and German except for:

- the dotless i (ı) which is peculiar to Turkish and is pronounced like the initial 'a' in 'away'. (Note that the upper case letters are respectively written İ for i and I for ı.)
- Turkish 'c', pronounced as English 'j', so cami meaning mosque = jami, and Ercan Airport = Erjan Airport
- Turkish 'ç', pronounced as English 'ch', so Akçiçek = Akchichek
- Turkish 'ş', pronounced as English 'sh', so Lefkoşa = Lefkosha
- Turkish 'ğ', unpronounced at the end of a word, or in the middle of a word, so Gazimağusa = Gazima'usa

Everyday situations

hello	*merhaba*	how much is it?	*ne kadar?*
good morning/ afternoon	*günaydın/iyi günler*	cheap	*ucuz*
		expensive	*pahalı*
good evening	*iyi akşamlar*	money	*para*
goodbye (by person staying)	*güle güle*	I have no money	*para yok*
		new	*yeni*
goodbye (by person leaving)	*allaha ısmarladık or iyi günler* (lit 'good day')	old	*yıldız*
		at what time?	*saat kaçta?*
yes	*evet* or *var*	shop	*dukkan*
no	*hayır* or *yok*	open	*açık*
please	*lütfen*	closed	*kapalı*
thank you	*teşekkür ederim*	bank	*banka*
very nice, beautiful	*çok güzel*	post office	*postane*
how are you?	*nasılsınız?*	chemist/pharmacy	*eczane*

hospital	*hastahane*	gents (men's room)	*baylar*
police	*polis*	ladies	*bayanlar*
toilet	*tuvalet*	room	*oda*
towel	*havlu*	petrol	*benzin*
soap	*sabun*		(fill it up *doldur*)

Food and drink

breakfast	*kahvaltı*	chicken	*piliç* or *tavuk*
eggs	*yumurta*	chips (french fries)	*patates*
tea	*çay*	fruit	*mayva*
more tea	*daha çay*	ice cream	*dondurma*
coffee	*kahve*	cake	*pasta*
milk	*süt*	water	*su*
sugar	*şeker*	mineral water	*maden suyu*
bread	*ekmek*	beer	*bira*
butter	*tereyağ*	wine	*şarap*
jam	*reçel*	red wine	*kırmızı şarap*
honey	*bal*	white wine	*beyaz şarap*
cheese	*peynir*	dry	*sek*
soup	*corba*	sweet	*tatlı*
salad	*salata*	the bill, please	*hesab, lütfen*
fish	*balık*		

Numbers

1	*bir*	20	*yirmi*
2	*iki*	30	*otuz*
3	*üç*	40	*kırk*
4	*dört*	50	*elli*
5	*beş*	60	*altmiş*
6	*altı*	70	*yetmiş*
7	*yedi*	80	*seksen*
8	*sekiz*	90	*doksan*
9	*dokuz*	100	*yüz*
10	*on*	1,000	*bin*
half	*yarim*		

Days of the week

day	*gün*	Tuesday	*Salı*
morning	*sabah*	Wednesday	*Çarşamba*
afternoon	*öğle*	Thursday	*Perşembe*
Sunday	*Pazar*	Friday	*Cuma*
Monday	*Pazartesi*	Saturday	*Cumartesi*

Signs and notices The following words may often be seen on notices or street signs:

askeri bölge	military area	*satılık*	for sale
çöp	rubbish, waste	*yasak*	forbidden
dikkat	warning, watch out	*yasak bölge*	forbidden zone
dur	stop	*yavaş*	slow
kiralık	to let/hire	*yol kapalı*	road closed
orman	forest		

Appendix 2

PLACE NAMES

TURKISH	GREEK	TURKISH	GREEK
Akçiçek	Sisklipos	Karaağaç	Kharcha
Akdeniz	Ayia Irini	Karakum	Karakoumi
Akova	Gypsos	Karaoğlanoğlu	Ayios Yeoryios
Alevkaya	Halevga	Karaman	Karmi
Alsancak	Karavas	Karşıyaka	Vasilia
Ardahan	Ardhana	Kayalar	Orga
Avtepe	Ayios Symeon	Kaynakköy	Sykhari
Bafra	Vokolidha	Kırpasa	Karpas
Bahceli	Kalogrea	Koruçam	Kormakitis
Bellabayıs	Bellapais	Kuruova	Korovia
Beşparmak	Pentadaktylos	Lapta	Lapithos
Boğaz	Boghaz	Lefke	Lefka
Boğaztepe	Monarga	Lefkoşa	Nicosia
Boltaşlı	Lythrangomi	Malatya	Paleosophos
Çamlıbel	Myrtou	Maraş	Varosha
Çatalköy	Ayios Epiktitos	Mutluyaka	Styllos
Çayırova	Ayios Theodhoros	Ozanköy	Kazaphani
Değirmenlik	Kythrea	Paşaköy	Asha
Derince	Vathylakkas	Sazlıköy	Lavidhia
Dikmen	Dhikomo	Şehitler	Sandlaris
Dipkarpaz	Rizokarpaso	Sınırüstü	Syngrasis
Edremit	Trimithi	Sipahi	Ayia Trias
Ercan	Tymbou	Şirinevler	Ayios Ermolaos
Erenköy	Kokkina	Taşkent	Vouno
Erdenli	Tremetousha	Tatlısu	Akanthou
Esentepe	Ayios Amvrosios	Tepebası	Dhiorios
Gaziköy	Aphania	Tirmen	Trypimeni
Gazimağusa	Famagusta	Turnalar	Yerani
Geçitkale	Lefkoniko	Turunçlu	Strongylos
Gemikonağı	Karavostasi	Tuzla	Engomi
Girne	Kyrenia	Yedidalga	Potamos tou
Güngor	Koutsovendis		Kambou
Gürpinar	Ayia Mani	Yeni Erenköy	Yialousa
Güzelyurt	Morphou	Yıldırım	Milea
İlgaz	Phterykha	Yılmazköy	Skylloura
İskele	Trikomo	Zafer Burnu	Cape Apostolos
Kaleburnu	Galinoporni		Andreas
Kalecık	Gastria	Zeydn Burnu	Cape Elea
Kaplıca	Dhavlos	Ziyamet	Leonarisso

Appendix 3

FURTHER INFORMATION
BOOKS
Background and history
Dodd, Clement H *The Cyprus Issue: A Current Perspective* Eothen Press, 1994.

Dodd, Clement H *The Political, Social and Economic Development of Northern Cyprus* Eothen Press, 1993.

Durrell, Lawrence *Bitter Lemons* Faber and Faber, 1957. Entertaining and moving account of Durrell's years at Bellapais from 1953 to 1956. The title is taken from an evocative poem he wrote about the island's political turmoil.

Gunnis, Rupert *Historic Cyprus* Methuen, 1936, republished Lefkoşa 1973. Architectural description of all the churches and monuments on the island.

Halliday, Sonia and Lushington, Lara *High above Kibris* Angus Hudson Ltd, 1985. Coffee-table book with many splendid photos.

Hitchens, Christopher *Hostage to History: Cyprus from the Ottomans to Kissinger* Verso, 1997. Absorbing study examining how the world's powers helped to turn a local dispute between the Greeks and Turks on Cyprus into a full-scale war. In a new afterword, Hitchens examines Cyprus's application for EU membership and its likely outcome. Riveting.

Home, Gordon *Cyprus Then and Now* J M Dent & Sons, 1960. Good for historical background before partition.

Luke, Sir Harry *Cyprus under the Turks 1571–1878* Hurst, 1971. Interesting historical account based on British consular archives.

Oberling, Pierre *The Road to Bellapais* Columbia University Press, 1982. Account of intercommunal strife and events leading up to partition.

Reddaway, John *Burdened with Cyprus – the British Connection* Weidenfeld & Nicolson, 1987. Readable account of Britain's involvement with Cyprus from 1878 onwards. Reddaway was Administrative Secretary in the British Embassy in Nicosia during the EOKA period.

Thubron, Colin *Journey into Cyprus* Heinemann, 1975. Fascinating description of his 600-mile walk through the island in 1972.

Volcan, Vamik D and Itzkowitz, Norman *Turks and Greeks: Neighbours in Conflict* Eothen Press, 1995.

Guidebooks
Flora, fauna and walks The following reference material will be of particular interest:

Flint, P and Stewart, P *The Birds of Cyprus: An Annotated Checklist* British Ornithologists Union (BOU), 1992.

Halliday, Sonia and Lushington, Lara *Flowers of North Cyprus* Angus Hudson Ltd, 1988.

Makris, C *Butterflies of Cyprus* Bank of Cyprus Cultural Foundation, 2003.

Meikie, R D *The Flora of Cyprus* Bentham-Moxon Trust, 1985. Two volumes.

Oddie, B and Moore, D *A Birdwatcher's Guide to the Birds of Cyprus* Suffolk Wildlife Trust, 1993 (out of print).

Pantelas, V, Papachristophorou, T and Christododoulou, P *Cyprus Flora in Colour: The Endemics* MAM, 1993.
Took, J M E *Birds of Cyprus* Char J Phillipides, 1992.

Language
Eat Smart in Turkey Gingko Press Inc, 2005.
Just Enough Turkish McGraw-Hill, 1990.
The Rough Guide to Turkish Rough Guides, 2000.
Turkish Compact Dictonary Berlitz, 2006.
Turkish Phrasebook Chambers, 2006.

WEBSITES North Cyprus has now built a whole range of web pages and sites. Listed below are a few which may help as starting points in arranging a holiday or in simply reading about what the country has to offer:

www.brstrnc.com Website of the British Residents Society of North Cyprus. Useful information, especially for those thinking about buying property in North Cyprus.
www.cypnet.com Comprehensive site on North Cyprus tourism.
www.cypyp.com North Cyprus *Yellow Pages*, a very handy resource for all kinds of services.
www.cyprusive.com Excellent information website – the best to be found.
www.cyprus44.com General travel resource with details of property for sale.
www.emu.edu.tr Website of the Eastern Mediterranean University.
www.gau.edu.tr Website of Girne American University.
www.grayling.dircon.co.uk/index.html Exhaustive exploration of the butterflies of Cyprus. Provides accurate species lists and hundreds of photographs.
www.kitsab.org Official website of Cyprus Turkish Tourism and Travel Agencies Association. Aimed more at those in the industry, but a useful resource for hotel, restaurant and local tour operator listings, country maps and general information.
www.kyreniaanimalrescue.org Charity set up by expats to look after strays and wild animals on the island.
www.mc-med.org Website of the Management Centre in Lefkoşa, involved in the development of sustainable tourism options in North Cyprus.
www.northcyprus.cc Official website of the North Cyprus Tourism Centre in London. Recently thoroughly updated, good city maps and general information.
www.northcyprusonline.com General tourism website.
www.northcyprus.net Northern Cyprus Hoteliers Association website.
www.north-cyprus.com General tourism site on northern Cyprus.
www.turkishcyprus.com Large business-orientated and tourism website on the country.
www.walksnorchidsnorthcyprus.com Website of the Hutchinsons who run flower walks in North Cyprus (see page 34).

Bradt Travel Guides

www.bradtguides.com

Africa

Africa Overland	£15.99
Algeria	£15.99
Benin	£14.99
Botswana: Okavango, Chobe, Northern Kalahari	£15.99
Burkina Faso	£14.99
Cape Verde Islands	£13.99
Canary Islands	£13.95
Cameroon	£13.95
Congo	£14.99
Eritrea	£15.99
Ethiopia	£15.99
Gabon, São Tomé, Príncipe	£13.95
Gambia, The	£13.99
Ghana	£15.99
Johannesburg	£6.99
Kenya	£14.95
Madagascar	£15.99
Malawi	£13.99
Mali	£13.95
Mauritius, Rodrigues & Réunion	£13.99
Mozambique	£13.99
Namibia	£15.99
Niger	£14.99
Nigeria	£15.99
Rwanda	£14.99
São Tomé & Principe	£14.99
Seychelles	£14.99
Sudan	£13.95
Tanzania, Northern	£13.99
Tanzania	£16.99
Uganda	£15.99
Zambia	£17.99
Zanzibar	£12.99

Britain and Europe

Albania	£13.99
Armenia, Nagorno Karabagh	£14.99
Azores	£12.99
Baltic Capitals: Tallinn, Riga, Vilnius, Kaliningrad	£12.99
Belarus	£14.99
Belgrade	£6.99
Bosnia & Herzegovina	£13.99
Bratislava	£6.99
Budapest	£8.99
Bulgaria	£13.99
Cork	£6.99
Croatia	£13.99

Cyprus see North Cyprus	
Czech Republic	£13.99
Dresden	£7.99
Dubrovnik	£6.99
Estonia	£13.99
Faroe Islands	£13.95
Georgia	£14.99
Helsinki	£7.99
Hungary	£14.99
Iceland	£14.99
Kiev	£7.95
Kosovo	£14.99
Krakow	£7.99
Lapland	£13.99
Latvia	£13.99
Lille	£6.99
Lithuania	£13.99
Ljubljana	£7.99
Macedonia	£14.99
Montenegro	£13.99
North Cyprus	£12.99
Paris, Lille & Brussels	£11.95
Riga	£6.99
River Thames, In the Footsteps of the Famous	£10.95
Serbia	£14.99
Slovakia	£14.99
Slovenia	£12.99
Spitsbergen	£14.99
Switzerland: Rail, Road, Lake	£13.99
Tallinn	£6.99
Ukraine	£14.99
Vilnius	£6.99
Zagreb	£6.99

Middle East, Asia and Australasia

China: Yunnan Province	£13.99
Great Wall of China	£13.99
Iran	£14.99
Iraq	£14.95
Iraq: Then & Now	£15.99
Kyrgyzstan	£15.99
Maldives	£13.99
Mongolia	£14.95
North Korea	£13.95
Oman	£13.99
Sri Lanka	£13.99
Syria	£14.99
Tibet	£13.99
Turkmenistan	£14.99
Yemen	£14.99

The Americas and the Caribbean

Amazon, The	£14.99
Argentina	£15.99
Bolivia	£14.99
Cayman Islands	£14.99
Colombia	£15.99
Costa Rica	£13.99
Chile	£16.95
Dominica	£14.99
Falkland Islands	£13.95
Guyana	£14.99
Panama	£13.95
Peru & Bolivia: The Bradt Trekking Guide	£12.95
St Helena	£14.99
USA by Rail	£13.99

Wildlife

100 Animals to See Before They Die	£16.99
Antarctica: Guide to the Wildlife	£14.95
Arctic: Guide to the Wildlife	£15.99
Central & Eastern European Wildlife	£15.99
Chinese Wildlife	£16.99
East African Wildlife	£19.99
Galápagos Wildlife	£15.99
Madagascar Wildlife	£15.99
North Atlantic Wildlife	£16.99
Peruvian Wildlife	£15.99
Southern African Wildlife	£18.95
Sri Lankan Wildlife	£15.99

Eccentric Guides

Eccentric America	£13.95
Eccentric Australia	£12.99
Eccentric Britain	£13.99
Eccentric California	£13.99
Eccentric Cambridge	£6.99
Eccentric Edinburgh	£5.95
Eccentric France	£12.95
Eccentric London	£13.99
Eccentric Oxford	£5.95

Others

Your Child Abroad: A Travel Health Guide	£10.95
Something Different for the Weekend	£9.99

Index

Page numbers in **bold** indicate major entries; those in *italic* indicate maps